Collins
Spanish
Grammar
& Practice

HarperCollins Publishers
Westerhill Road
Bishopbriggs
Glasgow
G64 2QT
Great Britain

First Edition 2011

Reprint 10 9 8 7 6 5 4 3 2 1

© HarperCollins Publishers 2011

ISBN 978-0-00-739140-0

Collins® is a registered trademark of
HarperCollins Publishers Limited

www.collinslanguage.com

A catalogue record for this book is available
from the British Library

HarperCollins Publishers
10 East 53rd Street
New York, NY 10022

COLLINS BEGINNER'S SPANISH GRAMMAR
AND PRACTICE.
First US Edition 2012

ISBN 978-0-06-219174-8

www.harpercollins.com

HarperCollins books may be purchased for
educational, business, or sales
promotional use. For information, please
write to:
Special Markets Department
HarperCollins Publishers
10 East 53rd Street, New York, NY 10022.

Typeset by Davidson Publishing Solutions,
Glasgow

Printed in Italy by LEGO Spa, Lavis (Trento)

Acknowledgements
We would like to thank those authors and
publishers who kindly gave permission
for copyright material to be used in the
Collins Word Web. We would also like to
thank Times Newspapers Ltd for providing
valuable data.

SERIES EDITOR
Rob Scriven

MANAGING EDITORS
Gaëlle Amiot-Cadey
Ruth O'Donovan

EDITOR
Susanne Reichert

CONTRIBUTORS
Sinda López Fuentes
Cordelia Lilly

Contents

Foreword for language teachers

The *Easy Learning Spanish Grammar & Practice* is designed to be used with both young and adult learners, as a group revision and practice book to complement your course book during classes, or as a recommended text for self-study and homework/coursework.

The text specifically targets learners from *ab initio* to intermediate or GCSE level, and therefore its structural content and vocabulary have been matched to the relevant specifications up to and including Higher GCSE.

The approach aims to develop knowledge and understanding of grammar and to improve the ability of learners to apply it by:

- defining parts of speech at the start of each major section, with examples in English to clarify concepts
- minimizing the use of grammar terminology and providing clear explanations of terms both within the text and in the **Glossary**
- illustrating all points with examples (and their translations) based on topics and contexts which are relevant to beginner and intermediate course content
- providing exercises which allow learners to practice grammar points

The text helps you develop positive attitudes to grammar learning in your classes by:

- giving clear, easy-to-follow explanations
- highlighting useful **Tips** to deal with common difficulties
- summarizing **Key points** at the end of sections to consolidate learning
- illustrating **Key points** with practice examples

In addition to fostering success and building a thorough foundation in Spanish grammar, the optional **Grammar Extra** sections will encourage and challenge your learners to further their studies to higher and advanced levels.

Introduction for students

Whether you are starting to learn Spanish for the very first time, brushing up on topics you have studied in class, or revising for your GCSE exams, the *Easy Learning Spanish Grammar & Practice* is here to help. This easy-to-use revision and practice guide takes you through all the basics you will need to speak and understand modern, everyday Spanish.

Newcomers can sometimes struggle with the technical terms they come across when they start to explore the grammar of a new language. The *Easy Learning Spanish Grammar & Practice* explains how to get to grips with all the parts of speech you will need to know, using simple language and cutting out jargon.

The text is divided into sections, each dealing with a particular area of grammar. Each section can be studied individually, as numerous cross-references in the text guide you to relevant points in other sections of the book for further information.

Every major section begins with an explanation of the area of grammar covered on the following pages. For quick reference, these definitions are also collected together on pages viii–xii in a glossary of essential grammar terms.

What is a verb?

A **verb** is a 'doing' word which describes what someone or something does, what someone or something is, or what happens to them, for example, *be, sing, live*.

Each grammar point in the text is followed by simple examples of real Spanish, complete with English translations, helping you understand the rules. Underlining has been used in examples throughout the text to highlight the grammatical point being explained.

➤ In orders and instructions telling someone <u>TO DO</u> something, the pronoun joins onto the end of the verb to form one word.

Ayúda<u>me</u>.	Help me.
Acompáña<u>nos</u>.	Come with us.

In Spanish, as with any foreign language, there are certain pitfalls which have to be avoided. **Tips** and **Information** notes throughout the text are useful reminders of the things that often trip learners up.

Tip

Don't forget to use personal **a** before indefinite pronouns referring to people when they are the object of a verb.

¿Viste <u>a</u> alguien?	Did you see anybody?
No vi <u>a</u> nadie.	I didn't see anybody.

Key points sum up all the important facts about a particular area of grammar, to save you time when you are revising and help you focus on the main grammatical points.

> ### KEY POINTS
> ✔ Like other adjectives, Spanish indefinite adjectives (such as **otro** and **todo**), must agree with what they describe.
> ✔ They go before the noun to which they relate.

After each Key point you can find a number of exercises to help you practice all the important grammatical points. You can find the answer to each exercise on pages 277-294.

If you think you would like to continue with your Spanish studies to a higher level, check out the **Grammar Extra** sections. These are intended for advanced students who are interested in knowing a little more about the structures they will come across beyond GCSE.

Grammar Extra!
por is often combined with other Spanish prepositions and words, usually to show movement.

Saltó <u>por encima</u> de la mesa.	She jumped over the table.
Nadamos <u>por debajo del</u> puente.	We swam under the bridge.
Pasaron <u>por delante de</u> Correos.	They went past the post office.

Finally, the supplement at the end of the book contains **Verb Tables**, where 7 important Spanish verbs (both regular and irregular) are conjugated in full. Examples show you how to use these verbs in your own work.

We hope that you will enjoy using the *Easy Learning Spanish Grammar & Practice* and find it useful in the course of your studies.

Glossary of Grammar Terms

ABSTRACT NOUN a word used to refer to a quality, idea, feeling or experience, rather than a physical object, for example, *size, reason, happiness*. Compare with **concrete noun**.

ACTIVE a form of the verb that is used when the subject of the verb is the person or thing doing the action, for example, *I wrote a letter*. Compare with **passive**.

ADJECTIVE a 'describing' word that tells you more about a person or thing, such as their appearance, colour, size or other qualities, for example, *pretty, blue, big*.

ADVERB a word usually used with verbs, adjectives or other adverbs that gives more information about when, where, how or in what circumstances something happens or to what degree something is true, for example, *quickly, happily, now, extremely, very*.

AGREE (to) in the case of adjectives and pronouns, to have the correct word ending or form according to whether what is referred to is masculine, feminine, singular or plural; in the case of verbs, to have the form which goes with the person or thing carrying out the action.

APOSTROPHE S an ending ('s) added to a noun to show who or what someone or something belongs to, for example, *Danielle's dog, the doctor's wife, the book's cover*.

ARTICLE a word like *the, a* and *an*, which is used in front of a noun. See also **definite article, indefinite article**.

AUXILIARY VERB a verb such as *be, have* or *do* used with a main verb to form tenses and questions.

BASE FORM the form of the verb without any endings added to it, for example, *walk, have, be, go*.

CARDINAL NUMBER a number used in counting, for example, *one, seven, ninety*. Compare with **ordinal number**.

CLAUSE a group of words containing a verb.

COMPARATIVE an adjective or adverb with *-er* on the end of it or *more* or *less* in front of it that is used to compare people, things or actions, for example, *slower, less important, more carefully*.

COMPOUND NOUN a word for a living being, thing or idea, which is made up of two or more words, for example, *tin-opener, railway station*.

CONCRETE NOUN a word that refers to an object you can touch with your hand, rather than to a quality or idea, for example, *ball, map, apples*. Compare with **abstract noun**.

CONDITIONAL a verb form used to talk about things that would happen or would be true under certain conditions, for example, *I <u>would help</u> you if I could*. It is also used to say what you would like or need, for example, *<u>Could</u> you <u>give</u> me the bill?*

CONJUGATE (to) to give a verb different endings according to whether you are referring to *I, you, they* and so on, and according to whether you are referring to the present, past or future, for example, *I have, she had, they will have*.

CONJUGATION a group of verbs which have the same endings as each other or change according to the same pattern.

CONJUNCTION a word such as *and, because* or *but* that links two words or phrases of a similar type or two parts of a sentence, for example, *Diane <u>and</u> I have been friends for years; I left <u>because</u> I was bored*.

CONSONANT a letter that isn't a vowel, for example, *b, f, m, s, v*. Compare with **vowel**.

CONTINUOUS TENSE a verb tense formed using *to be* and the *-ing* form of the main verb, for example, *They're swimming* (present continuous); *He was eating* (past continuous).

DEFINITE ARTICLE the word *the*. Compare with **indefinite article**.

DEMONSTRATIVE ADJECTIVE one of the words *this*, *that*, *these* and *those* used with a noun to refer to particular peope or things, for example, <u>*this*</u> *woman*, <u>*that*</u> *dog*.

DEMONSTRATIVE PRONOUN one of the words *this*, *that*, *these* and *those* used instead of a noun to point out people or things, for example, <u>*That*</u> *looks fun*.

DIRECT OBJECT a noun or pronoun used with verbs to show who or what is acted on by the verb. For example, in *He wrote a letter* and *He wrote me a letter*, *letter* is the direct object. Compare **indirect object**.

DIRECT OBJECT PRONOUN a word such as *me*, *him*, *us* and *them* which is used instead of a noun to stand in for the person or thing directly affected by the action expressed by the verb. Compare with **indirect object pronoun**.

ENDING a form added to a verb, for example, *go —> goes*, and to adjectives, nouns and pronouns depending on whether they refer to masculine, feminine, singular or plural things or persons.

EXCLAMATION a word, phrase or sentence that you use to show you are surprised, shocked, angry and so on, for example, *Wow!; How dare you!; What a surprise!*

FEMININE a form of noun, pronoun or adjective that is used to refer to a living being, thing or idea that is not classed as masculine.

FUTURE a verb tense used to talk about something that will happen or will be true.

GENDER whether a noun, pronoun or adjective is feminine or masculine.

GERUND a verb form in English ending in *-ing*, for example, *eating*, *sleeping*.

IMPERATIVE the form of a verb used when giving orders and instructions, for example, *Shut the door!; Sit down!; Don't go!; Let's eat*.

IMPERFECT one of the verb tenses used to talk about the past, especially in descriptions, and to say what was happening or used to happen, for example, *It was sunny at the weekend; We were living in Spain at the time; I used to walk to school*. Compare to **preterite**.

IMPERSONAL VERB a verb whose subject is *it*, but where the *it* does not refer to any specific thing, for example, *It's raining; It's 10 o'clock*.

INDEFINITE ADJECTIVE one of a small group of adjectives used to talk about people or things in a general way, without saying who or what they are, for example, *several, all, every*.

INDEFINITE ARTICLE the words *a* and *an*. Compare with **definite article**.

INDICATIVE ordinary verb forms that aren't subjunctive, such as the present, preterite or future. Compare with **subjunctive**.

INDEFINITE PRONOUN a small group of pronouns such as *everything*, *nobody* and *something*, which are used to refer to people or things in a general way, without saying exactly who or what they are.

INDIRECT OBJECT a noun or pronoun used with verbs to show who benefits or is harmed by an action. For example, in *I gave the carrot to the rabbit*, *the rabbit* is the indirect object and *the carrot* is the direct object. Compare with **direct object**.

INDIRECT OBJECT PRONOUN a pronoun used with verbs to show who benefits or is harmed by an action. For example, in *I gave him the carrot* and *I gave it to him*, *him* is the indirect object and the *carrot* and *it* are the direct objects. Compare with **direct object pronoun**.

INDIRECT QUESTION a question that is embedded in another question or instruction such as *Can you tell me <u>what time it is</u>?; Tell me <u>why you did it</u>*. Also used for reported speech such as *He asked me <u>why I did it</u>*.

INDIRECT SPEECH the words you use to report what someone has said when you aren't using their actual words, for example, *He said that he was going out*. Also called **reported speech**.

INFINITIVE a form of the verb that hasn't any endings added to it and doesn't relate to any particular tense. In English the infinitive is usually shown with *to*, as in *to speak, to eat*.

INTERROGATIVE ADJECTIVE a question word used with a noun, for example, *<u>What</u> instruments do you play?; <u>Which</u> shoes do you like?*

INTERROGATIVE PRONOUN one of the words *who, whose, whom, what* and *which* when they are used instead of a noun to ask questions, for example, *<u>What's</u> that?; <u>Who's</u> coming?*

INTRANSITIVE VERB a type of verb that does not take a direct object, for example, *to sleep, to rise, to swim*. Compare with **transitive verb**.

INVARIABLE used to describe a form which does not change.

IRREGULAR VERB a verb whose forms do not follow a general pattern. Compare with **regular verb**.

MASCULINE a form of noun, pronoun or adjective that is used to refer to a living being, thing or idea that is not classed as feminine.

NEGATIVE a question or statement which contains a word such as *not, never* or *nothing*, and is used to say that something is not happening, is not true or is absent, for example, *I <u>never</u> eat meat; <u>Don't</u> you love me?* Compare with **positive**.

NOUN a 'naming' word for a living being, thing or idea, for example, *woman, desk, happiness, Andrew*.

NOUN GROUP, NOUN PHRASE a word or group of words that acts as the subject or object of a verb, or as the object of a preposition, for example, *my older sister; the man next door; that big house on the corner*.

NUMBER used to say how many things you are referring to or where something comes in a sequence. See also **ordinal number** and **cardinal number**. Also the condition of being singular or plural.

OBJECT a noun or pronoun which refers to a person or thing that is affected by the action described by the verb. Compare with **direct object**, **indirect object** and **subject**.

OBJECT PRONOUN one of the set of pronouns including *me, him* and *them*, which are used instead of the noun as the object of a verb or preposition. Compare with **subject pronoun**.

ORDINAL NUMBER a number used to indicate where something comes in an <u>order</u> or sequence, for example, *first, fifth, sixteenth*. Compare with **cardinal number**.

PART OF SPEECH a word class, for example, *noun, verb, adjective, preposition, pronoun*.

PASSIVE a form of the verb that is used when the subject of the verb is the person or thing that is affected by the action, for example, *we were told*.

PAST PARTICIPLE a verb form which is used to form perfect and pluperfect tenses and passives, for example, *watched, swum*. Some past participles are also used as adjectives, for example, *a <u>broken</u> watch*.

PAST PERFECT see **pluperfect**.

PERFECT a verb form used to talk about what has or hasn't happened, for example, *I've broken my glasses; We haven't spoken about it*.

PERSON one of the three classes: the first person (*I, we*), the second person (*you* singular and *you* plural), and the third person (*he, she, it* and *they*).

PERSONAL PRONOUN one of the group of words including *I, you* and *they* which are used to refer to you, the people you are talking to, or the people or things you are talking about.

PLUPERFECT one of the verb tenses used to describe something that <u>had</u> happened or <u>had</u> been true at a point in the past, for example, *I <u>had forgotten</u> to finish my homework*. Also called **past perfect**.

PLURAL the form of a word which is used to refer to more than one person or thing. Compare with **singular**.

POSITIVE a positive sentence or instruction is one that does not contain a negative word such as *not*. Compare with **negative**.

POSSESSIVE ADJECTIVE one of the words *my, your, his, her, its, our* or *their*, used with a noun to show who it belongs to.

POSSESSIVE PRONOUN one of the words *mine, yours, hers, his, ours* or *theirs*, used instead of a noun to show who something belongs to.

PREPOSITION a word such as *at, for, with, into* or *from*, which is usually followed by a noun, pronoun or, in English, a word ending in *-ing*. Prepositions show how people and things relate to the rest of the sentence, for example, *She's <u>at</u> home; a tool <u>for</u> cutting grass; It's <u>from</u> David*.

PRESENT a verb form used to talk about what is true at the moment, what happens regularly, and what is happening now, for example, *I'<u>m</u> a student; I <u>travel</u> to college by train; I'<u>m studying</u> languages*.

PRESENT PARTICIPLE a verb form in English ending in *-ing*, for example, *eating, sleeping*.

PRETERITE a verb form used to talk about actions that were completed in the past in Spanish. It often corresponds to the ordinary past tense in English, for example, *I bought a new bike; Mary went to the shops on Friday; I typed two reports yesterday*.

PRONOUN a word which you use instead of a noun, when you do not need or want to name someone or something directly, for example, *it, you, none*.

PROPER NOUN the name of a person, place, organization or thing. Proper nouns are always written with a capital letter, for example, *Kevin, Glasgow, Europe, London Eye*.

QUESTION WORD a word such as *why, where, who, which* or *how* which is used to ask a question.

RADICAL-CHANGING VERBS in Spanish, verbs which change their stem or root in certain tenses and in certain persons.

REFLEXIVE PRONOUN a word ending in *-self* or *-selves*, such as *myself* or *themselves*, which refers back to the subject, for example, *He hurt <u>himself</u>; Take care of <u>yourself</u>*.

REFLEXIVE VERB a verb where the subject and object are the same, and where the action 'reflects back' on the subject. A reflexive verb is used with a reflexive pronoun such as *myself, yourself, herself*, for example, *I washed myself; He shaved himself*.

REGULAR VERB a verb whose forms follow a general pattern or the normal rules. Compare with **irregular verb**.

RELATIVE PRONOUN a word such as *that, who* or *which*, when it is used to link two parts of a sentence together.

REPORTED SPEECH see **indirect speech**.

SENTENCE a group of words which usually has a verb and a subject. In writing, a sentence begins with a capital and ends with a full stop, question mark or exclamation mark.

SIMPLE TENSE a verb tense in which the verb form is made up of one word, rather than being formed from *to have* and a past participle or *to be* and an *-ing* form; for example, *She plays tennis; He wrote a book*.

SINGULAR the form of a word which is used to refer to one person or thing. Compare with **plural**.

STEM the main part of a verb to which endings are added.

SUBJECT a noun or pronoun that refers to the person or thing doing the action or being in the state described by the verb, for example, *My cat doesn't drink milk*. Compare with object.

SUBJECT PRONOUN a word such as *I*, *he*, *she* and *they* which carries out the action described by the verb. Pronouns stand in for nouns when it is clear who is being talked about, for example, *My brother isn't here at the moment. He'll be back in an hour*. Compare with **object pronoun**.

SUBJUNCTIVE a verb form used in certain circumstances to indicate some sort of feeling, or to show doubt about whether something will happen or whether something is true. It is only used occasionally in modern English, for example, *If I were you, I wouldn't bother; So be it*.

SUPERLATIVE an adjective or adverb with *-est* on the end of it or *most* or *least* in front of it that is used to compare people, things or actions, for example, *thinnest, most quickly, least interesting*.

SYLLABLE consonant+vowel units that make up the sounds of a word, for example, *ca-the-dral (3 syllables), im-po-ssi-ble (4 syllables)*.

TENSE the form of a verb which shows whether you are referring to the past, present or future.

TRANSITIVE VERB a type of verb that takes a direct object, for example, *to spend, to raise, to waste*. Compare with **intransitive verb**.

VERB a 'doing' word which describes what someone or something does, is, or what happens to them, for example, *be, sing, live*.

VOWEL one of the letters *a, e, i, o* or *u*. Compare with **consonant**.

Nouns

What is a noun?
A **noun** is a 'naming' word for a living being, thing or idea, for example,
woman, *desk*, *happiness*, *Andrew*.

Using nouns

➤ In Spanish, all nouns are either <u>masculine</u> or <u>feminine</u>. This is called their gender. Even words for things have a <u>gender</u>.

➤ Whenever you are using a noun, you need to know whether it is masculine or feminine as this affects the form of other words used with it, such as:

- adjectives that describe it

- articles (such as **el** or **una**) that go before it

  ⇨ *For more information on **Articles** and **Adjectives**, see pages 11 and 25.*

➤ You can find information about gender by looking the word up in a dictionary. When you come across a new noun, always learn the word for *the* or *a* that goes with it to help you remember its gender.

- **el** or **un** before a noun usually tells you it is masculine

- **la** or **una** before a noun tells you it is feminine

➤ We refer to something as <u>singular</u> when we are talking about just one of them, and as <u>plural</u> when we are talking about more than one. The singular is the form of the noun you will usually find when you look a noun up in the dictionary. As in English, nouns in Spanish change their form in the plural.

➤ Adjectives, articles and pronouns are also affected by whether a noun is singular or plural.

Tip
Remember that you have to use the right word for *the*, *a* and so on according to the gender of the Spanish noun.

Gender

Nouns referring to people

➤ Most nouns referring to men and boys are <u>masculine</u>.
<u>el</u> **hombre**   the man
<u>el</u> **rey**   the king

➤ Most nouns referring to women and girls are <u>feminine</u>.

la mujer	the woman
la reina	the queen

➤ When the same word is used to refer to either men/boys or women/girls, its gender usually changes depending on the sex of the person it refers to.

el estudiante	the (male) student
la estudiante	the (female) student
el belga	the Belgian (man)
la belga	the Belgian (woman)

Grammar Extra!
Some words for people have only <u>one</u> possible gender, whether they refer to a male or a female.

la persona	the (male *or* female) person
la víctima	the (male *or* female) victim

➤ In English, we can sometimes make a word masculine or feminine by changing the ending, for example, *English<u>man</u>* and *English<u>woman</u>* or *prince* and *prin<u>cess</u>*. In Spanish, very often the ending of a noun changes depending on whether it refers to a man or a woman.

el camarero	the waiter
la camarera	the waitress
el empleado	the employee (*male*)
la empleada	the employee (*female*)
el inglés	the Englishman
la inglesa	the Englishwoman

> *Tip*
> Note that a noun ending in **-o** is usually <u>masculine</u>, and a noun ending in **-a** is usually <u>feminine</u>.

⇨ *For more information on **Masculine and feminine forms of words**, see page 4.*

Nouns referring to animals

➤ In English we can choose between words like *bull* or *cow*, depending on the sex of the animal. In Spanish too there are sometimes separate words for male and female animals.

el toro	the bull
la vaca	the cow

➤ Sometimes, the same word with different endings is used for male and female animals.

el perro	the (male) dog
la perra	the (female) dog, bitch
el gato	the (male) cat
la gata	the (female) cat

> *Tip*
> When you do not know or care what sex the animal is, you can usually use the masculine form as a general word.

➤ Words for other animals don't change according to the sex of the animal. Just learn the Spanish word with its gender, which is always the same.

el sapo	the toad
el hámster	the hamster
la cobaya	the guinea pig
la tortuga	the tortoise

Nouns referring to things

➤ In English, we call all things – for example, *table, car, book, apple* – 'it'. In Spanish, however, things are either <u>masculine</u> or <u>feminine</u>. As things don't divide into sexes the way humans and animals do, there are no physical clues to help you with their gender in Spanish. Try to learn the gender as you learn the word.

➤ There are lots of rules to help you. Certain endings are usually found on masculine nouns, while other endings are usually found on feminine nouns.

➤ The following ending is usually found on <u>masculine nouns</u>.

Masculine ending	Examples	
-o	**el libro** the book **el periódico** the newspaper	BUT: **la mano** the hand **la foto** the photo **la moto** the motorbike **la radio** the radio *(although in parts of Latin America, it is* **el radio**)

➤ The following types of word are also masculine.

- names of the days of the week and the months of the year
  Te veré <u>el lunes</u>. I'll see you on Monday.

- the names of languages
  el inglés English
  el español Spanish
  Estudio <u>el español</u>. I'm studying Spanish.

- the names of rivers, mountains amd seas
  el Ebro the Ebro
  el Everest Everest
  el Atlántico the Atlantic

➤ The following endings are usually found on <u>feminine nouns</u>.

Feminine ending	Examples	
-a	**la casa** the house **la cara** the face	BUT: **el día** the day **el mapa** the map **el planeta** the planet **el tranvía** the tram and many words ending in **-ma** (**el problema** the problem, **el programa** the programme, **el sistema** the system, **el clima** the climate)
-ción	**la lección** the lesson	
-sión	**la estación** the station **la expresión** the expression	
-dad	**la ciudad** the city	
-tad	**la libertad** freedom	
-tud	**la multitud** the crowd	

Grammar Extra!
Some words have different meanings depending on whether they are masculine or feminine.

Masculine	Meaning	Feminine	Meaning
el capital	the capital (meaning *money*)	**la capital**	the capital (meaning *city*)
el cometa	the comet	**la cometa**	the kite
el cura	the priest	**la cura**	the cure
el guía	the guide (*man*)	**la guía**	the guidebook; the guide (*woman*)

Invirtieron mucho capital.   They invested a lot of capital.
Viven en la capital.   They live in the capital.

Masculine and feminine forms of words

➤ Like English, Spanish sometimes has very different words for males and females.
el hombre   the man
la mujer   the woman
el rey   the king
la reina   the queen

➤ Many Spanish words can be used to talk about men or women simply by changing the ending. For example, if the word for the male ends in -o, you can almost always make it feminine by changing the -o to -a.

el amigo	the (male) friend
la amiga	the (female) friend
el hermano	the brother
la hermana	the sister
el empleado	the (male) employee
la empleada	the (female) employee
el viudo	the widower
la viuda	the widow

ⓘ Note that some words referring to people end in **-a** in the masculine as well as in the feminine. Only the article (**el** or **la**, **un** or **una**) can tell you what gender the noun is.

el dentista	the (male) dentist
la dentista	the (female) dentist
el deportista	the sportsman
la deportista	the sportswoman

➤ Many masculine nouns ending in a consonant (any letter other than a vowel) become feminine by adding an **-a**.

el español	the Spanish man
la española	the Spanish woman
el profesor	the (male) teacher
la profesora	the (female) teacher

> *Tip*
>
> If the last vowel of the masculine word has an accent, this is dropped in the feminine form.
>
> | | |
> |---|---|
> | **un inglés** | an Englishman |
> | **una inglesa** | an Englishwoman |
> | **un francés** | a Frenchman |
> | **una francesa** | a Frenchwoman |

⇨ *For more information about **Spelling** and **Stress**, see pages 263 and 266.*

KEY POINTS

✔ The ending of a Spanish word often helps you work out its gender: for instance, if a word ends in **-o**, it is probably masculine; if it ends in **-a**, it is probably feminine.

✔ These endings generally mean that the noun is feminine:
  -ción, -sión, -dad, -tad, -tud

✔ Days of the week and months of the year are masculine. So are languages, mountains and seas.

✔ You can change the ending of some nouns from **-o** to **-a** to make a masculine noun feminine.

Test yourself

1 **Complete the phrase by adding the feminine form of the noun. Don't forget to include the article.**

a el rey y ....

b el inglés y ....

c el empleado y ....

d el príncipe y ....

e el hermano y ....

f el dentista y ....

g el profesor y ....

h el estudiante y ....

i el actor y ....

j el hombre y ....

2 **Replace the highlighted masculine nouns with the feminine form.**

a Es **el amigo** de mi hermano. ....

b Viene **el rey**. ....

c ¿Cómo se llama **el profesor** de matemáticas? ....

d Es **el estudiante** mejor de la clase. ....

e Vive con **un inglés**. ....

f Nos lleva **el padre** de Carlos. ....

g Se casa con **el príncipe**. ....

h Es para **hombre**. ....

i Trabaja de **camarero**. ....

j Soy **un empleado**. ....

3 **Match the two columns.**

a **La capital**   extranjero ayuda mucho en este país.

b **El cura**   lleva los turistas por la ciudad.

c **La guía**   de España es Madrid.

d **El guía**   dice misa.

e **El capital**   incluye un glosario.

Forming plurals

Plurals ending in -s and -es

➤ In English we usually make nouns plural by adding an -s to the end (*garden→gardens*; *house → houses*), although we do have some nouns which are <u>irregular</u> and do not follow this pattern (*mouse →mice*; *child → children*).

> *Tip*
> Remember that you have to use **los** (for <u>masculine nouns</u>) or **las** (for <u>feminine nouns</u>) with plural nouns in Spanish. Any adjective that goes with the noun also has to agree with it, as does any pronoun that replaces it.
>
> ➪ *For more information on **Articles, Adjectives** and **Pronouns**, see pages 11, 25 and 55.*

➤ To form the plural in Spanish, add **-s** to most nouns ending in a vowel (*a, e, i, o* or *u*) which doesn't have an accent.

el libro	the book
los libros	the books
el hombre	the man
los hombres	the men
la profesora	the (female) teacher
las profesoras	the (female) teachers

➤ Add **-es** to singular nouns ending in a consonant (any letter other than a vowel).

el profesor	the (male) teacher
los profesores	the (male/male and female) teachers
la ciudad	the town/city
las ciudades	the towns/cities

> ⓘ Note that some foreign words (that is, words which have come from another language, such as English) ending in a consonant just add **-s**.
>
> | | |
> |---|---|
> | **el jersey** | the jersey |
> | **los jerseys** | the jerseys |

➤ Words ending in **-s** which have an unstressed final vowel do not change in the plural.

el paraguas	the umbrella
los paraguas	the umbrellas
el lunes	(on) Monday
los lunes	(on) Mondays

➪ *For more information on **Stress**, see page 266.*

➤ Some singular nouns ending in an accented vowel add **-es** in the plural while other very common ones add **-s**.

el jabalí	the boar
los jabalíes	the boars
el café	coffee/the café
los cafés	coffees/the cafés
el sofá	the sofa
los sofás	the sofas

Grammar Extra!

When nouns are made up of two separate words, they are called <u>compound nouns</u>, for example, **el abrelatas** (meaning *the tin-opener*) and **el hombre rana** (meaning *the frogman*). Some of these nouns don't change in the plural, for example, **los abrelatas**, while others do, for example, **los hombres rana**. It is always best to check in a dictionary to see what the plural is.

Spelling changes with plurals ending in -es

➤ Singular nouns which end in an accented vowel and either **-n** or **-s** drop the accent in the plural.

la canción	the song
las canciones	the songs
el autobús	the bus
los autobuses	the buses

➤ Singular nouns of more than one syllable which end in **-en** and don't already have an accent, add one in the plural.

el examen	the exam
los exámenes	the exams
el joven	the youth
los jóvenes	young people

➤ Singular nouns ending in **-z** change to **-c** in the plural.

la luz	the light
las luces	the lights
la vez	the times
las veces	the times

⇨ *For further information on **Spelling** and **Stress**, see pages 263 and 266.*

Plural versus singular

➤ A few words relating to clothing that are plural in English can be singular in Spanish.

una braga	(a pair of) knickers
un slip	(a pair of) underpants
un pantalón	(a pair of) trousers

➤ A few common words behave differently in Spanish from the way they behave in English.

un mueble	a piece of furniture
unos muebles	some furniture
una noticia	a piece of news
unas noticias	some news
un consejo	a piece of advice
unos consejos	some advice

KEY POINTS

✔ Add **-s** to form the plural of a noun ending in an unaccented vowel.

✔ Add **-es** to form the plural of most nouns ending in a consonant.

✔ Drop the accent when adding plural **-es** to nouns ending in an accented vowel + **-n** or **-s**.

✔ Add an accent when adding plural **-es** to words of more than one syllable ending in **-en**.

✔ Change **-z** to **-c** when forming the plural of words like **luz**.

✔ A few common words are plural in English but not in Spanish.

Test yourself

4 **Replace the highlighted words with the plural form.**

a Quiero comprar **el libro**. ....

b Cantamos **una canción** de Enrique Iglesias. ....

c Siempre desayuno con **una tostada**. ....

d Tengo que darle **una noticia**. ....

e Apaga **la luz**. ....

f Tienes que estudiar mucho para **el examen**. ....

g La película trata de **un hombre-lobo**. ....

h Siempre me regalan **un jersey**. ....

i **El lunes** voy al centro. ....

j Necesito **un mueble** para el salón. ....

5 **Cross out the nouns which the article(s) cannot refer to.**

a **el** niño/día/televisión/dentista/mano/sistema/mediterráneo/marzo

b **la** camarera/mujer/profesor/hermana/solicitud/lunes/ciudad/estación

c **un** madre/caballo/inglesa/príncipe/estudiante/moto/mapa/español

d **una** coche/casa/planeta/padre/principiante/guía

e **los** niños/días/televisiones/dentistas/manos/sistemas

f **las** camareras/mujeres/profesores/hermanas/solicitudes/lunes/ciudades/
estaciones

g **unos** madres/caballos/inglesas/príncipes/estudiantes/motos/mapas/españoles

h **unas** coches/casas/planetas/padres/principiantes/guías

i **el/un** niño/día/televisión/dentista/mano/sistema/mediterráneo/marzo

j **la/una** camarera/mujer/profesor/hermana/solicitud/lunes/ciudad/estación

6 **Complete the phrase with un or una as required.**

a Tengo .... amigo.

b Tiene .... amiga.

c .... empleado de mi padre

d .... francés

e .... francesa

f .... hombre

g .... mujer

h .... mueble

i .... pantalón

j .... estudiante

Articles

What is an article?

In English, an **article** is one of the words *the, a,* and *an* which is given in front of a noun.

Different types of article

➤ There are two types of article:

- the <u>definite</u> article: *the* in English. This is used to identify a particular thing or person.
  I'm going to <u>the</u> supermarket.
  That's <u>the</u> woman I was talking to.

- the <u>indefinite</u> article: *a* or *an* in English, whose plural is *some* or *any* (or no word at all). This is used to refer to something unspecific, or that you do not really know about.
  Is there <u>a</u> supermarket near here?
  I need <u>a</u> day off.

The definite article: el, la, los and las

The basic rules

➤ In English, there is only <u>one</u> definite article: *the*. In Spanish, you have to choose between <u>four</u> definite articles: **el, la, los** and **las**. Which one you choose depends on the noun which follows.

➤ In Spanish, all nouns (including words for things) are either masculine or feminine – this is called their <u>gender</u>. And just as in English, they can also be either singular or plural. You must bear this in mind when deciding which Spanish word to use for *the*.

   ⇨ *For more information on* **Nouns,** *see page* 1.

➤ **el** is used before <u>masculine singular nouns</u>.
  el niño   the boy
  el periódico   the newspaper

➤ **la** is used before <u>feminine singular nouns</u>.
  la niña   the girl
  la revista   the magazine

> *Tip*
>
> To help you produce correct Spanish, always learn the <u>article</u> or the <u>gender</u> together with the noun when learning words.

➤ **los** and **las** are used before <u>plural nouns</u>. **los** is used with masculine plural words, and **las** is used with feminine plural words.
  los niños   the boys
  las niñas   the girls

los periódicos	the newspapers
las revistas	the magazines

> 🛈 Note that you use **el** instead of **la** immediately before a feminine singular word beginning with **a** or **ha** when the stress falls on the beginning of the word. This is because **la** sounds wrong before the '*a*' sound and the use of **el** does not affect the feminine gender of the noun. <u>BUT</u> if you add an adjective in front of the noun, you use **la** instead, since the two 'a' sounds do not come next to each other.

el agua limpia	the clean water
el hacha	the axe
la misma agua	the same water
la mejor hacha	the best axe

a and de with the definite article

> ➤ If **a** is followed by **el**, the two words become **al**.

al cine	to the cinema
al empleado	to the employee
al hospital	to the hospital
Vio al camarero.	He saw the waiter.

> ➤ If **de** is followed by **el**, the two words become **del**.

del departamento	of/from the department
del autor	of/from the author
del presidente	of/from the president

Using the definite article

> ➤ **el**, **la**, **los** and **las** are often used in Spanish in the same way as *the* is used in English. However, there are some cases where the article is used in Spanish but not in English.

> ➤ The definite article <u>IS</u> used in Spanish:

- when talking about people, animals and things in a general way

Me gustan los animales.	I like animals.
Están subiendo los precios.	Prices are going up.
Me gusta el chocolate.	I like chocolate.
No me gusta el café.	I don't like coffee.
El azúcar es dulce.	Sugar is sweet.

- when talking about abstract qualities, for example, *time, hope, darkness, violence*

El tiempo es oro.	Time is money.
Admiro la sinceridad en la gente.	I admire honesty in people.

> 🛈 Note that the definite article is <u>NOT</u> used in certain set phrases consisting of **tener** and a noun or after certain prepositions.

tener hambre	to be hungry (*literally: to have hunger*)
sin duda	no doubt (*literally: without doubt*)
con cuidado	carefully (*literally: with care*)

> ➪ *For more information on* **Prepositions***, see page 244.*

For further explanation of grammatical terms, please see pages viii-xii.

- when talking about colours
  El azul es mi color favorito.   Blue is my favourite colour.

- when talking about parts of the body – you do not use *my, your, his* and so on as you would in English
  Tiene <u>los</u> ojos verdes.   He's got green eyes.
  No puedo mover <u>las</u> piernas.   I can't move my legs.

☒ Note that possession is often shown by a personal pronoun in Spanish.

     La cabeza <u>me</u> da vueltas.   <u>My</u> head is spinning.
     Láva<u>te</u> las manos.   Wash <u>your</u> hands.

⇨ *For more information on **Personal pronouns**, see page 55.*

- when using someone's title – for example, *Doctor, Mr* – but talking <u>ABOUT</u> someone rather than to them.
  El doctor Vidal no está.   Dr Vidal isn't here.
  El señor Pelayo vive aquí.   Mr Pelayo lives here.

- when talking about institutions, such as school or church
  en <u>el</u> colegio   at school
  en <u>la</u> universidad   at university
  en <u>la</u> iglesia   at church
  en <u>el</u> hospital   in hospital
  en <u>la</u> cárcel   in prison

- when talking about meals, games or sports
  <u>La</u> cena es a las nueve.   Dinner is at nine o'clock.
  Me gusta <u>el</u> tenis.   I like tennis.
  No me gusta <u>el</u> ajedrez.   I don't like chess.

- when talking about days of the week and dates, where we use the preposition *on* in English
  Te veo <u>el</u> lunes.   I'll see you <u>on</u> Monday.
  <u>Los</u> lunes tenemos muchos deberes.   We have a lot of homework <u>on</u> Mondays.
  Nací <u>el</u> 17 de marzo.   I was born <u>on</u> 17 March.

- when talking about the time
  Es <u>la</u> una.   It's one o'clock.
  Son <u>las</u> tres.   It's three o'clock.
  Son <u>las</u> cuatro y media.   It's half past four.

- when talking about prices and rates
  Cuesta dos euros <u>el</u> kilo.   It costs two euros a kilo.
  20 euros <u>la</u> hora   20 euros an hour

> ## KEY POINTS
> ✔ Before masculine singular nouns → use **el**.
> ✔ Before feminine singular nouns→use **la**.
> ✔ Before feminine singular nouns starting with stressed **a** or **ha** → use **el**.
> ✔ Before masculine plural nouns → use **los**.
> ✔ Before feminine plural nouns → use **las**.
> ✔ **a + el → al**
> ✔ **de + el → del**
> ✔ There are some important cases when you would use a definite article in Spanish when you wouldn't in English; for example, when talking about:
> • things in a general way
> • abstract qualities
> • colours
> • parts of the body
> • someone with a title in front of their name
> • institutions
> • meals, games or sports
> • the time, days of the week and dates (*using the preposition* <u>on</u> *in English*)
> • prices and rates

Test yourself

1 **Cross out the nouns which the article cannot go with.**

a **el** niño/mano/agua/cine/revista/hospital/dentista/precio/chocolate/cabeza/azúcar/doctor/cárcel/tenis

b **la** chica/desayuno/hambre/casa/universidad/lunes/verde/mano/fútbol/carne/jardín

c **los** brazos/precios/manos/ojos/sábados/ciudades/empleados/peces/mesas/miércoles/zapatillas

d **las** deberes/piernas/luces/dulces/colores/chocolates/plantas/animales/autobuses/llaves/ratones/sillas

e **un** niño/mano /revista/hospital/dentista/chocolate/cabeza/doctor/cárcel

f **una** chica/desayuno/casa/universidad/lunes/mano/jardín

g **unos** brazos/precios/manos/ojos /ciudades/empleados/peces/mesas/zapatillas

h **unas** deberes/piernas/luces/dulces/colores/plantas/animales/autobuses/llaves/sillas

i **los/unos** niños/manos/revistas/dentistas/precios/cabezas/cárceles

j **las/unas** chicas/desayunos/casas/manos/jardines/ratones/pijamas

2 **Complete the following sentences with the correct article.**

a Está en .... colegio.

b Estudia en .... universidad de Valencia.

c Trabajo en .... hospital.

d Se casaron por .... iglesia.

e .... agua está fría.

f .... rosa te sienta muy bien.

g No le gustan .... patatas fritas.

h .... árboles están todos en flor.

i Ponte el sombrero y .... gafas de sol.

j Voy a ponerme .... sandalias rosa.

Test yourself

3 Translate the following sentences into Spanish.

a I like animals. ....

b I don't like meat. ....

c I like red. ....

d She's got blue eyes. ....

e Wash your face. ....

f Breakfast is between 7 and 9. ....

g I work on Tuesdays and Thursdays. ....

h He's the doctor's son. ....

i We went to the cinema on Saturday. ....

j They're 5 euros a kilo. ....

The indefinite article: un, una, unos and unas

The basic rules

➤ In English, the indefinite article is *a*, which changes to *an* when it comes before a vowel or a vowel sound, for example, *an apple*. In the plural, we use *some* or *any*.

➤ In Spanish, you have to choose between <u>four</u> indefinite articles: **un**, **una**, **unos** and **unas**. Which one you choose depends on the noun that follows.

➤ In Spanish, all nouns (including words for things) are either masculine or feminine – this is called their <u>gender</u>. And, just as in English, they can also be either singular or plural. You must bear this in mind when deciding which Spanish word to use for *a*.

⇨ *For more information on **Nouns**, see page* 1.

➤ **un** is used before <u>masculine singular nouns</u>.
un niño	a boy
un periódico	a newspaper

➤ **una** is used before <u>feminine singular nouns</u>.
una niña	a girl
una revista	a magazine

➤ **unos** is used before <u>masculine plural nouns</u>.
unos niños	some boys
unos periódicos	some newspapers

➤ **unas** is used before <u>feminine plural nouns</u>.
unas niñas	some girls
unas revistas	some magazines

> ⓘ Note that you use **un** instead of **una** immediately before a feminine singular word beginning with **a** or **ha** when the stress falls on the beginning of the word. This is because **una** sounds wrong before the '*a*' sound.
>
> **un ave**   a bird

Using the indefinite article

➤ The indefinite article is often used in Spanish in the same way as it is in English. However, there are some cases where the article is not used in Spanish but is in English, and vice versa.

➤ The indefinite article is <u>NOT</u> used in Spanish:

- when you say what someone's job is
Es profesor.	He's a teacher.
Mi madre es enfermera.	My mother is a nurse.

- after **tener**, **buscar**, or **llevar (puesto)** when you are only likely *to have, be looking for* or *be wearing* one of the items in question
No tengo coche.	I haven't got a car.
¿Llevaba sombrero?	Was he wearing a hat?

[¿] Note that when you use an adjective to describe the noun, you <u>DO</u> use an article in Spanish too.

Es <u>un</u> buen médico.	He's <u>a</u> good doctor.
Tiene <u>una</u> novia española.	He has a Spanish girlfriend.
Busca <u>un</u> piso pequeño.	He's looking for a little flat.

➤ The indefinite article is <u>NOT</u> used in Spanish with the words **otro**, **cierto**, **cien**, **mil**, **sin**, and **qué**.

otro libro	another book
cierta calle	<u>a</u> certain street
cien soldados	<u>a</u> hundred soldiers
mil años	<u>a</u> thousand years
sin casa	without <u>a</u> house
¡Qué sorpresa!	What <u>a</u> surprise!

➤ The indefinite article <u>IS</u> used in Spanish but <u>NOT</u> in English when an abstract noun, such as **inteligencia** (meaning *intelligence*) or **tiempo** (meaning *time*) has an adjective with it.

Posee <u>una</u> gran inteligencia.	He possesses great intelligence.

KEY POINTS

✔ Before masculine singular nouns → use **un**.
✔ Before feminine singular nouns → use **una**.
✔ Before feminine singular nouns starting with stressed **a** or **ha** → use **un**.
✔ Before masculine plural nouns → use **unos**.
✔ Before feminine plural nouns → use **unas**.
✔ You do not use an indefinite article in Spanish for saying what someone's job is.
✔ You do not use an indefinite article in Spanish with the words **otro**, **cierto**, **cien**, **mil**, **sin**, and **qué**.

For further explanation of grammatical terms, please see pages viii-xii.

Test yourself

4 **Complete the following sentences with the correct indefinite article.**

a Compré .... revista.

b Tenemos .... coche rojo.

c Tiene .... novio francés.

d Vivimos en .... piso pequeño.

e Lleva .... zapatos negros.

f Es .... ave gris.

g Es .... parque muy grande.

h Galicia tiene .... playas muy bonitas.

i Cenamos en .... restaurante español.

j ¿Quieres .... uvas?

5 **Add an indefinite article un, una, unos, o unas if the sentence needs it.**

a Leo .... libro cada semana.

b Es .... actor.

c No tenemos .... jardín.

d Es .... autora famosa.

e Tiene .... novia inglesa.

f Buscamos .... piso en el centro.

g Comemos .... uvas.

h Juega con .... amigas de la escuela.

i ¿Tienes .... coche?

j Soy .... profesora de inglés.

6 **Match the two columns.**

a	**Mi madre**	viven en un piso.
b	**Su padre**	no tiene coche.
c	**Mis padres**	un coche rojo.
d	**Tenemos**	es un actor famoso.
e	**Jaime**	es doctora.

Test yourself

7 Translate the following sentences into Spanish.

a I'm an actor. ....

b My mother is a doctor. ....

c She's a good nurse. ....

d I want to read another book. ....

e They don't have a garden. ....

f My brother is a student. ....

g He's a famous artist. ....

h We have Australian neighbours. ....

i She has an American boyfriend. ....

j I don't have a boyfriend. ....

The article lo

➤ Unlike the other Spanish articles, and articles in English, **lo** is <u>NOT</u> used with a noun.

➤ **lo** can be used with a masculine singular adjective or past participle (the **-ado** and **-ido** forms of regular verbs) to form a noun.

<u>Lo único</u> que no me gusta ...	The only thing I don't like ...
Esto es <u>lo importante</u>.	That's the important thing.
<u>Lo bueno</u> de eso es que ...	The good thing about it is that ...
Sentimos mucho <u>lo ocurrido</u>.	We are very sorry about what happened.

⇨ *For more information on the **Past participle**, see page 164.*

➤ **lo** is also used in a number of very common phrases:

- **a lo mejor**   maybe, perhaps
  <u>A lo mejor</u> ha salido.   Perhaps he's gone out.

- **por lo menos**   at least
  Hubo <u>por lo menos</u> cincuenta heridos.   At least fifty people were injured.

- **por lo general**   generally
  <u>Por lo general</u> me acuesto temprano.   I generally go to bed early.

➤ **lo** can also be used with **que** to make **lo que** (meaning *what*).

Vi <u>lo que</u> pasó.	I saw what happened.
<u>Lo que</u> más me gusta es nadar.	What I like best is swimming.

Grammar Extra!
lo can be used with **de** followed by a noun phrase to refer back to something the speaker and listener both know about.

<u>Lo de tu hermano</u> me preocupa mucho.	I'm very worried about <u>that business with your brother</u>.
<u>Lo de ayer</u> es mejor que lo olvides.	It would be best to forget <u>what happened yesterday</u>.

lo can be used with an adjective followed by **que** to emphasize how big/small/ beautiful and so on something is or was. The adjective must agree with the noun it describes.

No sabíamos <u>lo pequeña que</u> era la casa.	We didn't know <u>how small</u> the house was.
No te imaginas <u>lo simpáticos</u> que son.	You can't imagine <u>how nice</u> they are.

lo can also be used in a similar way with an adverb followed by **que**.

Sé <u>lo mucho que te</u> gusta la música.	I know <u>how much</u> you like music.

> ## KEY POINTS
> ✔ **lo** is classed as an article in Spanish, but is not used with nouns.
> ✔ You can use **lo** with a masculine adjective or past participle to form a noun.
> ✔ You also use **lo** in a number of common phrases.
> ✔ **lo que** can be used to mean *what* in English.

Test yourself

8 Match the Spanish with its English translation.

a	por lo menos	that business with your sister
b	a lo mejor	how good they are
c	lo que dice tu hermana	at least
d	lo buenos que son	what your sister says
e	lo de tu hermana	maybe

9 Complete the following sentences with lo, lo de, or lo que.

a Eso es .... más importante.

b .... más me gusta es la catedral.

c .... mejor de la fiesta es la comida.

d A .... mejor viene mañana.

e Lo conozco mejor de .... piensa.

f Hay por .... menos 150 personas.

g No sé bien .... pasa ahí.

h Es peor de .... parece.

i ....Alberto es muy triste.

j Dime .... te pasa.

10 Match the two columns.

a	Por lo general	es ir de tiendas.
b	A lo mejor	es que no quiere venir.
c	Lo de tu primo	no vienen.
d	Lo que más me gusta	cenamos temprano.
e	Lo que pasa	me sorprende mucho.

Test yourself

11 **Translate the following sentences into English.**

a Eso es lo más importante.

....

b Lo importante es ser feliz.

....

c Lo bueno es que es barato.

....

d A lo mejor vienen mañana.

....

e Por lo general como a las dos.

....

f Lo único es que es muy caro.

....

g Por lo menos come algo.

....

h Vienen por lo menos 20 personas.

....

i Lo que más me gusta es ir al cine.

....

j Lo de Isabel me sorprende mucho.

....

Adjectives

Using adjectives

➤ Adjectives are words like *clever*, *expensive* and *silly* that tell you more about a noun (a living being, thing or idea). They can also tell you more about a pronoun, such as *he* or *they*. Adjectives are sometimes called 'describing words'. They can be used right next to a noun they are describing, or can be separated from the noun by a verb like *be*, *look*, *feel* and so on.

    a <u>clever</u> girl
    an <u>expensive</u> coat
    a <u>silly</u> idea
    He's just being <u>silly</u>.

  ⇨ *For more information on* **Nouns** *and* **Pronouns**, *see pages 1 and 55.*

➤ In English, the only time an adjective changes its form is when you are making a comparison.

    She's <u>cleverer</u> than her brother.
    That's the <u>silliest</u> idea I've ever heard!

➤ In Spanish, however, most adjectives <u>agree</u> with what they are describing. This means that their endings change depending on whether the person or thing you are referring to is masculine or feminine, singular or plural.

    un chico <u>rubio</u>   a fair boy
    una chica <u>rubia</u>   a fair girl
    unos chicos <u>rubios</u>   some fair boys
    unas chicas <u>rubias</u>   some fair girls

➤ In English, adjectives come <u>BEFORE</u> the noun they describe, but in Spanish you usually put them <u>AFTER</u> it.

    una casa <u>blanca</u>   a <u>white</u> house

  ⇨ For more information on **Word order with adjectives**, see page 31.

Making adjectives agree

Forming feminine adjectives

➤ The form of the adjective shown in dictionaries is generally the masculine singular form. This means that you need to know how to change its form to make it agree with the person or thing it is describing.

➤ Adjectives ending in **-o** in the masculine change to **-a** for the feminine.

    mi hermano <u>pequeño</u>   my little brother
    mi hermana <u>pequeña</u>   my little sister

➤ Adjectives ending in any vowel other than **-o** (that is: *a*, *e*, *i* or *u*) or ending in a vowel with an accent on it do <u>NOT</u> change for the feminine.

el vestido <u>verde</u>	the green dress
la blusa <u>verde</u>	the green blouse
un pantalón <u>caqui</u>	some khaki trousers
una camisa <u>caqui</u>	a khaki shirt
un médico <u>iraquí</u>	an Iraqi doctor
una familia <u>iraquí</u>	an Iraqi family

➤ Adjectives ending in a consonant (any letter other than a vowel) do <u>NOT</u> change for the feminine except in the following cases:

● Adjectives of nationality or place ending in a consonant add **-a** for the feminine. If there is an accent on the final vowel in the masculine, they lose this in the feminine.

un periódico <u>inglés</u>	an English newspaper
una revista <u>inglesa</u>	an English magazine
el equipo <u>francés</u>	the French team
la cocina <u>francesa</u>	French cooking
el vino <u>español</u>	Spanish wine
la lengua <u>española</u>	the Spanish language

[¿] Note that these adjectives do not start with a capital letter in Spanish.

● Adjectives ending in **-or** in the masculine usually change to **-ora** for the feminine.

un niño <u>encantador</u>	a charming little boy
una niña <u>encantadora</u>	a charming little girl

[¿] Note that a few adjectives ending in **-or** used in comparisons – such as **mejor** (meaning *better, best*), **peor** (meaning *worse, worst*), **mayor** (meaning *older, bigger*), **superior** (meaning *upper, top*), **inferior** (meaning *lower, inferior*) as well as **exterior** (meaning *outside, foreign*) and **posterior** (meaning *rear*) do not change in the feminine.

● Adjectives ending in **-án**, **-ón** and **-ín** in the masculine change to **-ana**, **-ona** and **-ina** (without an accent) in the feminine.

un gesto <u>burlón</u>	a mocking gesture
una sonrisa <u>burlona</u>	a mocking smile
un hombre <u>parlanchín</u>	a chatty man
una mujer <u>parlanchina</u>	a chatty woman

➤ Adjectives ending in a consonant but which do not fall into the above categories do <u>NOT</u> change in the feminine.

un chico <u>joven</u>	a young boy
una chica <u>joven</u>	a young girl
un final <u>feliz</u>	a happy ending
una infancia <u>feliz</u>	a happy childhood

Forming plural adjectives

➤ Adjectives ending in an unaccented vowel (*a*, *e*, *i*, *o* or *u*) in the singular add **-s** in the plural.

el <u>último</u> tren	the last train
los <u>últimos</u> trenes	the last trains
una <u>casa</u> vieja	an old house
unas casas <u>viejas</u>	some old houses

For further explanation of grammatical terms, please see pages viii-xii.

una chica muy <u>habladora</u>	a very chatty girl
unas chicas muy <u>habladoras</u>	some very chatty girls
una pintora <u>francesa</u>	a French (woman) painter
unas pintoras <u>francesas</u>	some French (women) painters
una mesa <u>verde</u>	a green table
unas mesas <u>verdes</u>	some green tables

➤ Adjectives ending in a consonant in the masculine or feminine singular add **-es** in the plural. If there is an accent on the <u>FINAL</u> syllable in the singular, they lose it in the plural.

un chico muy <u>hablador</u>	a very chatty boy
unos chicos muy <u>habladores</u>	some very chatty boys
un pintor <u>francés</u>	a French painter
unos pintores <u>franceses</u>	some French painters
un examen <u>fácil</u>	an easy exam
unos exámenes <u>fáciles</u>	some easy exams
la tendencia <u>actual</u>	the current trend
las tendencias <u>actuales</u>	the current trends

➤ **-z** at the end of a singular adjective changes to **-ces** in the plural.

un día <u>feliz</u>	a happy day
unos días <u>felices</u>	happy days

Tip

When an adjective describes a mixture of both masculine and feminine nouns, use the <u>masculine plural</u> form of the adjective.

El pan y la fruta son baratos.   Bread and fruit are cheap.

Grammar Extra!

Adjectives ending in an accented vowel in the singular add **-es** in the plural.

un médico iraní	an Iranian doctor
unos médicos iraníes	some Iranian doctors

Invariable adjectives

➤ A small number of adjectives do not change in the feminine or plural. They are called <u>invariable</u> because their form <u>NEVER</u> changes, no matter what they are describing. These adjectives are often made up of more than one word – for example **azul marino** (meaning *navy blue*) – or come from the names of things – for example **naranja** (meaning *orange*).

las chaquetas <u>azul marino</u>	navy-blue jackets
los vestidos <u>naranja</u>	orange dresses

Short forms for adjectives

➤ The following adjectives drop the final **-o** before a <u>masculine singular noun</u>.

bueno	→	buen →	un <u>buen</u> libro	a good book
malo	→	mal →	<u>mal</u> tiempo	bad weather
alguno	→	algún →	<u>algún</u> libro	some book
ninguno	→	ningún→	<u>ningún</u> hombre	no man
uno	→	un →	<u>un</u> día	one day
primero	→	primer→	el <u>primer</u> hijo	the first child
tercero	→	tercer →	el <u>tercer</u> hijo	the third child

[¿] Note that the adjectives **alguno** and **ninguno** add accents when they are shortened to become **algún** and **ningún**.

➤ **grande** (meaning *big, great*) is shortened to **gran** before a <u>singular noun</u>.

un gran actor	a great actor
una gran sorpresa	a big surprise

➤ **ciento** (meaning *a hundred*) changes to **cien** before all <u>plural nouns</u> as well as before **mil** (meaning *thousand*) and **millones** (meaning *millions*).

cien años	a hundred years
cien millones	a hundred million
cien mil euros	a hundred thousand euros

[¿] Note that you use the form **ciento** before other numbers.

ciento tres	one hundred and three

⇨ *For more information on* **Numbers**, *see page 272.*

Grammar Extra!
➤ **cualquiera** drops the final **a** before any noun.

<u>cualquier</u> día	any day
a <u>cualquier</u> hora	any time

> ### KEY POINTS
> ✔ Most Spanish adjectives change their form according to whether the person or thing they are describing is masculine or feminine, singular or plural.
> ✔ In Spanish, adjectives usually go after the noun they describe.
> ✔ Don't forget to make adjectives agree with the person or thing they describe – they change for the feminine and plural forms:
> un chico español
> una chica española
> unos chicos españoles
> unas chicas españolas
> ✔ Some adjectives never change their form.
> ✔ Some adjectives drop the final **-o** before a masculine singular noun.
> ✔ **grande** and **ciento** also change before certain nouns.

For further explanation of grammatical terms, please see pages viii-xii.

Test yourself

1 **Replace the highlighted words with the correct form of the adjective. Some may already be correct.**

a un abrigo **caro** ....

b una idea **tonto** ....

c unas chicas **alto** ....

d una chaqueta **azul** ....

e mi hermana **pequeño** ....

f mi hermana **mayor** ....

g una señora **inglés** ....

h la cocina **español** ....

i unas camisas **blanco** ....

j unas mujeres muy **charlatán** ....

2 **Cross out the adjectives that do not go with the noun(s).**

a **una madre**   feliz/encantador/joven

b **unas chicas**   jóvenes/guapas/encantadores/tontas

c **unos zapatos**   verdes/altos/nuevo/bonitos/rojo oscuro

d **unos vecinos**   irlandeses/simpáticos

e **un examen**   difícil/fáciles/largo

f **una bolsa**   azul marino/roja/pequeño/grande

g **una familia**   española/iraquí

h **chicos y chicas**   ingleses/americanas/felices/ricos

i **una casa y un jardín** bonita/grande/preciosos

j **una chaqueta y pantalón** rosa/negros/nuevas/modernos

Test yourself

3 Complete the following sentences with the correct form of the adjective.

a   Es un .... amigo. **(bueno)**

b   Viven en una casa .... **(grande)**

c   Fue una .... sorpresa. **(grande)**

d   Está de .... humor. **(malo)**

e   Ha ganado el .... premio. **(tercero)**

f   No había .... hombre en la reunión. **(ninguno)**

g   No practica .... deporte. **(ninguno)**

h   No me creo .... de sus historias. **(ninguno)**

i   No voy a .... parte. **(ninguno)**

j   .... día aparecerán por casa. **(cualquiera)**

4 Match the two columns.

a   **Hace**   de buen humor.

b   **Hace una semana**   a cualquier hora.

c   **Ven**   gran pena.

d   **Es una**   de gran calor.

e   **Está**   mal tiempo.

Word order with adjectives

➤ When adjectives are used right beside the noun they are describing, they go <u>BEFORE</u> it in English. Spanish adjectives usually go <u>AFTER</u> the noun.

una corbata <u>azul</u>	a <u>blue</u> tie
una palabra <u>española</u>	a <u>Spanish</u> word
la página <u>siguiente</u>	the <u>following</u> page
la hora <u>exacta</u>	the <u>precise</u> time

➤ When you have two or more adjectives after the noun, you use **y** (meaning *and*) between the last two.

un hombre alto **y** delgado	a tall, slim man

➤ A number of types of Spanish adjectives go <u>BEFORE</u> the noun:

- demonstrative adjectives
  <u>este</u> sombrero   this hat

- possessive adjectives (**mi**, **tu**, **su** and so on)
  <u>mi</u> padre   my father

- numbers
  <u>tres</u> días   three days

- interrogative adjectives
  ¿<u>qué</u> hombre?   which man?

- adjectives used in exclamations
  ¡<u>Qué</u> lástima!   What a pity!

- indefinite adjectives
  <u>cada</u> día   every day

- shortened adjectives
  <u>mal</u> tiempo   bad weather

➤ Some adjectives can go both <u>BEFORE</u> and <u>AFTER</u> the noun, but their meaning changes depending on where they go.

Adjective	Before Noun	Examples	After Noun	Examples
antiguo	former	**un antiguo colega** a former colleague	old, ancient	**la historia antigua** ancient history
diferente	various	**diferentes idiomas** various languages	different	**personas diferentes** different people
grande	great	**un gran pintor** a great painter	big	**una casa grande** a big house
medio	half	**medio melón** half a melon	average	**la nota media** the average mark
mismo	same	**la misma respuesta** the same answer	self, very, precisely	**yo mismo** myself **eso mismo** precisely that
nuevo	new	**mi nuevo coche** my new car (= *new to me*)	brand new	**unos zapatos nuevos** some (brand) new shoes
pobre	poor (= *wretched*)	**esa pobre mujer** that poor woman	poor (= *not rich*)	**un país pobre** a poor country
viejo	old (= *long-standing*)	**un viejo amigo** an old friend	old (= *aged*)	**esas toallas viejas** those old towels

---

KEY POINTS
- ✔ Most Spanish adjectives go after the noun.
- ✔ Certain types of adjectives in Spanish go before the noun.
- ✔ Some adjectives can go before or after the noun – the meaning changes according to the position in the sentence.

For further explanation of grammatical terms, please see pages viii-xii.

5 **Match the Spanish with its English translation.**

a	Es mi antiguo jefe.	It's a very poor country.
b	La capilla es muy antigua.	She told me herself.
c	¡Pobre de ti!	He's my old boss.
d	Es un país muy pobre.	The chapel is very old.
e	Me lo dijo ella misma.	Poor you!

6 **Cross out the adjectives that do not go with the noun.**

a	los ojos	grandes/azul/azules/verde/negros
b	el pelo	rubio/blanca/largo/corto/grasos
c	unos guantes	gris/blancas/naranja/rojo oscuro/ amarillas/beige/negros/rosa
d	un día	feliz/mala/horrorosa/caliente/fría
e	un restaurante	español/mala/caro/barata
f	una pregunta	impertinente/difícil/tonto/retórica
g	un vaso y una botella	llenas/vacíos/verdes
h	los coches	nuevos/grandes/viejas/alemanes/ naranja/pequeñas/carroza/caros
i	una noche	feliz/larga/precioso/fría
j	una chaqueta y unos pantalones	nuevos/rosa/viejas/azul marino/nueva

7 **Complete the phrase with the correct form of the adjective.**

a las mujeres .... **(español)**

b unos estudiantes .... **(inglés)**

c un día .... **(frío)**

d los países .... **(pobre)**

e unos pantalones .... **(negro)**

f agua .... **(frío)**

g idiomas .... **(difícil)**

h un chico y una chica .... **(alto)**

i unas palabras .... **(cruel)**

j las páginas .... **(siguiente)**

Test yourself

8   Match the noun to an appropriate adjective.

a	una chaqueta	inglesas
b	la hora	difícil
c	un examen	españoles
d	las costumbres	exacta
e	los hombres	azul marino

Comparatives and superlatives of adjectives

Making comparisons using comparative adjectives

> **What is a comparative adjective?**
> A **comparative adjective** in English is one with *-er* on the end of it or *more* or *less*
> in front of it, that is used to compare people or things, for example,
> *cleverer, less important, more beautiful*.

➤ In Spanish, to say something is *cheaper, more expensive* and so on, you use **más** (meaning *more*) before the adjective.

Esta bicicleta es <u>más barata</u>.	This bicycle is cheaper.
La verde es <u>más cara</u>.	The green one is more expensive.

➤ To say something is *less expensive, less beautiful* and so on, you use **menos** (meaning *less*) before the adjective.

La verde es <u>menos cara</u>.	The green one is less expensive.

➤ To introduce the person or thing you are making the comparison with, use **que** (meaning *than*).

Es <u>más</u> alto <u>que</u> yo/mi hermano.	He's taller than me/my brother.
La otra bicicleta es <u>más</u> cara <u>que</u> esta.	The other bicycle is more expensive than this one.
Esta bicicleta es <u>menos</u> cara <u>que</u> la otra.	This bicycle is less expensive than the other one.

Grammar Extra!
When *than* in English is followed by a verbal construction, use **<u>de lo que</u>** rather than **que** alone.

Está <u>más</u> cansada <u>de lo que</u> parece.	She is more tired than she seems.

Making comparisons using superlative adjectives

> **What is a superlative adjective?**
> A **superlative adjective** in English is one with *-est* on the end of it or most or least in
> front of it, that is used to compare people or things, for example, <u>thinnest</u>,
> <u>most beautiful</u>, <u>least interesting</u>.

➤ In Spanish, to say something is *the cheapest*, the *most expensive* and so on, you use **el/la/ los/las** (+ noun) + **más** + adjective.

<u>el</u> caballo <u>más viejo</u>	the oldest horse
<u>la</u> casa <u>más pequeña</u>	the smallest house
<u>los</u> hoteles <u>más baratos</u>	the cheapest hotels
<u>las</u> manzanas <u>más caras</u>	the most expensive apples
¿Quién es <u>el más alto</u>?	Who's the tallest?

➤ To say something is *the least expensive*, *the least intelligent* and so on, you use **el/la/los/las** (+ noun) + **menos** + adjective.

el hombre **menos simpático**	the least likeable man
la niña **menos habladora**	the least talkative girl
los cuadros **menos bonitos**	the least attractive paintings
las empleadas **menos trabajadoras**	the least hardworking (female) employees
¿Quién es **el menos trabajador?**	Who's the least hardworking?

> *Tip*
>
> In phrases like *the cleverest girl in the school* and *the tallest man in the world*, you use **de** to translate *in*.
>
> **el hombre más alto del mundo**　　the tallest man *in* the world

Irregular comparatives and superlatives

➤ Just as English has some irregular comparative and superlative forms – *better* instead of *'more good'*, and *worst* instead of *'most bad'* – Spanish also has a few irregular forms.

Adjective	Meaning	Comparative	Meaning	Superlative	Meaning
bueno	good	**mejor**	better	**el mejor**	the best
malo	bad	**peor**	worse	**el peor**	the worst
grande	big	**mayor**	older	**el mayor**	the oldest
pequeño	small	**menor**	younger	**el menor**	the youngest

Este es **mejor** que el otro.	This one is better than the other one.
Es **el mejor** de todos.	It's the best of the lot.
Hoy me siento **peor**.	I feel worse today.
la peor alumna de la clase	the worst student in the class

ⓘ Note that **mejor**, **peor**, **mayor** and **menor** don't change their endings in the feminine. In the plural, they become **mejores**, **peores**, **mayores** and **menores**. Don't forget to use **el**, **la**, **los** or **las** as appropriate, depending on whether the person or thing described is masculine or feminine, singular or plural.

> *Tip*
>
> **más grande** and **más pequeño** are used mainly to talk about the actual size of something.
>
> | | |
> |---|---|
> | Este plato es **más grande** que aquél. | This plate is bigger than that one. |
> | Mi casa es **más pequeña** que la tuya. | My house is smaller than yours. |
>
> **mayor** and **menor** are used mainly to talk about age.
>
> | | |
> |---|---|
> | mis hermanos **mayores** | my older brothers |
> | la hija **menor** | the youngest daughter |

For further explanation of grammatical terms, please see pages viii-xii.

Other ways of making comparisons

➤ To say *as ... as* (for example, *as pretty as, not as pretty as*) you use **tan ... como** in Spanish.

Pedro es <u>tan</u> alto <u>como</u> Miguel.	Pedro is as tall as Miguel.
No es <u>tan</u> guapa <u>como</u> su madre.	She isn't as pretty as her mother.
No es <u>tan</u> grande <u>como</u> yo creía.	It isn't as big as I thought.

Grammar Extra!

You use **tanto** with a noun rather than **tan** with an adjective in some expressions. This is because in Spanish you would use a noun where in English we would use an adjective.

Pablo tiene <u>tanto</u> miedo <u>como</u> yo.	Pablo is as frightened as I am.
Yo no tengo <u>tanta</u> hambre <u>como</u> tú.	I'm not as hungry as you are.

➤ To make an adjective stronger, you can use **muy** (meaning *very*).

Este libro es <u>muy</u> interesante.	This book is very interesting.

Grammar Extra!

For even more emphasis, you can add **-ísimo** (meaning *really, extremely*) to the end of an adjective. Take off the final vowel if the adjective already ends in one. For example, **delgado** (meaning *thin*) becomes **delgadísimo** (meaning *really thin*).

Se ha comprado un coche <u>carísimo</u>.	He's bought himself a really expensive car.
Está <u>delgadísima</u>.	She's looking really thin.

If you add **-ísimo**, you need to take off any other accent. For example, **fácil** (meaning *easy*) becomes **facilísimo** (meaning *extremely easy*) and **rápido** (meaning *fast*) becomes **rapidísimo** (meaning *extremely fast*).

Es <u>facilísimo</u> de hacer.	It's really easy to make.
un coche <u>rapidísimo</u>	an extremely fast car

When the adjective ends in **-co**, **-go** or **-z**, spelling changes are required to keep the same sound. For example, **rico** (meaning *rich*) becomes **riquísimo** (meaning *extremely rich*) and **feroz** (meaning *fierce*) becomes **ferocísimo** (meaning *extremely fierce*).

Se hizo <u>riquísimo</u>.	He became extremely rich.
un tigre <u>ferocísimo</u>	an extremely fierce tiger

⇨ *For more information on **Spelling** and **Stress**, see pages 263 and 266.*

KEY POINTS

✔ Comparative adjectives in Spanish are formed by:
- **más** + adjective + **que**
- **menos** + adjective + **que**

✔ Superlative adjectives in Spanish are formed by:
- **el/la/los/las** + **más** + adjective
- **el/la/los/las** + **menos** + adjective

✔ There are a few irregular comparative and superlative forms in Spanish.

✔ You can use **tan ... como** to say *as ... as*.

✔ To make an adjective stronger, use **muy**.

Test yourself

9 **Make comparisons, using es (=is) and más … que or menos … que, according to whether the sentence has a +, or - at the end. The first one has been done for you.**

a Juan/alto/mi hermano/+

Juan es más alto que mi hermano.

....

b Mi padre/viejo/el tuyo/+

....

c Belén/alta/tú/+ ....

d Este hotel/barato/ese/+

....

e Pedro/trabajador/Pepe/- ....

f Lucía/guapa/su hermana/+ ....

g Nuestro jardín/pequeño/el vuestro/+

....

h La película/interesante/el libro/-

....

i La verde/bonita/la azul/+...

j Mi tía/nerviosa/mi madre/-

....

10 **Complete the following sentences with the correct form: tan or tanto/tanta.**

a Soy .... inteligente como tú.

b Tenemos .... dinero como ellos.

c Es .... tonto como su padre.

d Tengo .... hambre como él.

e Marta es .... guapa como su madre.

f Es .... caro como el otro.

g No tiene .... paciencia como yo.

h Me da .... vergüenza como a ti.

i Es .... mala como su hermana.

j No bebo .... leche como antes.

Test yourself

11 **Replace the highlighted adjective with the form ending in -ísimo, etc. Be careful with any accent or spelling changes!**

a Ese examen es **fácil**. ....

b Mi prima es **delgada**. ....

c Mi tío es **rico**. ....

d Compramos un coche **viejo**. ....

e Tiene unos pendientes **caros**. ....

f Ese abrigo es **feo**. ....

g Estos exámenes son **difíciles**. ....

h Tienen un jardín **bonito**. ....

i Tengo **mucha** hambre. ....

j La tarta está **buena**. ....

12 **Translate the following superlative phrases into Spanish.**

a the tallest man ....

b the most expensive cars ....

c the cheapest hotels ....

d the least hardworking employees ....

e the smallest gardens ....

f the biggest schools ....

g the youngest daughter ....

h the oldest son ....

i the worst day ....

j the best of the lot ....

Demonstrative adjectives

> ## What is a demonstrative adjective?
> A **demonstrative adjective** is one of the words *this*, *that*, *these* and *those* used
> with a noun in English to point out a particular thing or person, for example,
> *this* woman, *that* dog.

Using demonstrative adjectives

➤ Just as in English, Spanish demonstrative adjectives go <u>BEFORE</u> the noun. Like other
adjectives in Spanish, they have to change for the feminine and plural forms.

	Masculine	Feminine	Meaning
Singular	este	esta	this
	ese	esa	that *(close by)*
	aquel	aquella	that *(further away)*
Plural	estos	estas	these
	esos	esas	those *(close by)*
	aquellos	aquellas	those *(further away)*

➤ Use **este/esta/estos/estas** (meaning *this/these*) to talk about things and people that are
near <u>you</u>.

<u>Este</u> bolígrafo no escribe.   This pen isn't working.
Me he comprado <u>estos</u> libros.   I've bought myself these books.

➤ Use **ese/esa/esos/esas** and **aquel/aquella/aquellos/aquellas** (meaning *that/those*)
to talk about things that are further away.

<u>Esa</u> revista es muy mala.   That magazine is very bad.
¿Conoces a <u>esos</u> señores?   Do you know those men?
No le gusta <u>aquella</u> muñeca.   She doesn't like that doll.
Siga usted hasta <u>aquellos</u> árboles.   Carry on until you reach those trees
  (over there).

ese or aquel?

➤ In English we use *that* and *those* to talk about anything that is not close by, but in Spanish
you need to be a bit more precise.

➤ Use **ese/esa/esos/esas**:

- to talk about things and people that are nearer to the person you are talking to than
to you
<u>ese</u> papel en el que escribes   that paper you're writing on
¿Por qué te has puesto <u>esas</u> medias?   Why are you wearing those tights?

- to talk about things and people that aren't very far away
No me gustan <u>esos</u> cuadros.   I don't like those pictures.

➤ Use **aquel/aquella/aquellos/aquellas** to talk about things that are further away.

Me gusta más <u>aquella</u> mesa.	I prefer that table (over there).

Grammar Extra!

You should use **ese/esa/esos/esas** when you are talking about a definite date, month or year.

¿1999? No me acuerdo de dónde pasamos las vacaciones <u>ese</u> año.	1999? I can't remember where we went on holiday that year.

You should use **aquel/aquella/aquellos/aquellas** when you are talking about something in the past and not mentioning a definite date.

<u>**aquellas**</u> **vacaciones que pasamos en Francia**	that holiday we had in France

---

KEY POINTS

✔ this + noun = **este/esta** + noun
✔ these + noun = **estos/estas** + noun
✔ that + noun = **ese/esa** + noun (*when the object is not far away from you or the person you're talking to*)
✔ that + noun = **aquel/aquella** + noun (*when the object is more distant*)
✔ those + noun = **esos/esas** + noun (*when the objects are not far away from you or the person you're talking to*)
✔ those + noun = **aquellos/aquellas** + noun (*when the objects are more distant*)

Test yourself

13 Cross out the nouns that the demonstrative adjective cannot go with.

a este   periódico/coche/revista/tiempo/serpiente/mes/agua/ciudad

b esta   revista/casa/año/mujer/situación/sistema/agua/moto

c estos   zapatillas/zapatos/botones/habitaciones/edificios/exámenes/televisiones

d estas   exámenes/cursos/ventanas/plantas/radios

e ese   reloj/hombre/tienda/habitación/tren

f esa   camarera/mujer/profesor/hermana/solicitud/sistema/ciudad/estación

g esos   médicos/profesores/planetas/padres/aviones

h esas   llaves/ordenadores/madres/amigas/trenes/canciones

i aquel   calle/profesor/sillón/mesa/banco/parque/señor

j aquella puerta/lápiz/calle/silla/restaurantes

14 Fill the gap with the correct form of the demonstrative adjective.

a .... bolsa es más cara que esa.

b .... proyecto es más fácil que el último.

c .... examen es más difícil que el del lunes.

d .... libros están más baratos que eses.

e .... hotel de la esquina es el mejor.

f Viven en .... casas al otro lado del parque.

g ¿Cuánto valen .... tomates?

h ¿De quién es .... niño de allí?

i ¿De quién es .... libro que estás leyendo?

j ¿Conoces a .... mujeres en esa mesa?

15 Translate the sentence into Spanish.

a   This garden is beautiful. ....

b   I don't like that colour. ....

c   This hospital is big. ....

d   I live in that house over there.

....

e   These trousers are very expensive.

....

f   That film is really bad. ....

g   I want to buy that book. ....

h   Do you want these roses or those flowers over there?

....

i   I want this shirt and those shoes.

....

j   Do you like those colours?

....

Interrogative adjectives

What is an interrogative adjective?
An **interrogative adjective** is one of the question words and expressions used with a noun such as *which*, *what*, *how much* and *how many*; for example,
Which shirt are you going to wear?; *How much time have we got?*

➤ In Spanish the interrogative adjectives are **qué** (meaning *which* or *what*) and **cuánto/cuánta/cuántos/cuántas** (meaning *how much/how many*). Note that like all other Spanish question words, **qué** and **cuánto** have accents on them.

➤ **¿qué?** (meaning *which?* or *what?*) doesn't change for the feminine and plural forms.

¿Qué libro te gusta más?	Which book do you like best?
¿Qué clase de diccionario necesitas?	What kind of dictionary do you need?
¿Qué instrumentos tocas?	What instruments do you play?
¿Qué ofertas has recibido?	What offers have you received?

➤ **¿cuánto?** means the same as *how much?* in English. It changes to **¿cuánta?** in the feminine form.

¿Cuánto dinero te queda?	How much money have you got left?
¿Cuánta lluvia ha caído?	How much rain have we had?

i Note that with **gente** (meaning *people*), which is a feminine singular noun, **cuánta** must be used.

¿Cuánta gente ha venido?	How many people came?

➤ **¿cuántos?** means the same as *how many?* in English. It changes to **¿cuántas?** in the feminine plural.

¿Cuántos bolígrafos quieres?	How many pens would you like?
¿Cuántas personas van a venir?	How many people are coming?

Tip
Don't forget to add the opening upside-down question mark in Spanish questions.

Grammar Extra!
In English we can say, *Tell me what time it is*, *He asked me how much sugar there was* and *I don't know which dress to choose* to express doubt, report a question, or ask a question in a roundabout or indirect way. In Spanish you can use **qué** and **cuánto/cuánta/cuántos/cuántas** in the same way.

Dime qué hora es.	Tell me what time it is.
Me preguntó cuánto azúcar había.	He asked me how much sugar there was.
No sé qué vestido escoger.	I don't know which dress to choose.
No sé a qué hora llegó.	I don't know what time she arrived.
Dime cuántas postales quieres.	Tell me how many postcards you'd like.

Adjectives used in exclamations

➤ In Spanish ¡qué…! is often used where we might say *What a …!* in English.

¡Qué lástima!	What a pity!
¡Qué sorpresa!	What a surprise!

> *Tip*
> Don't forget to add the opening upside-down exclamation mark in Spanish exclamations.

Grammar Extra!

¡qué…! combines with **tan** or **más** and an adjective in Spanish to mean *What (a)…!* in English.

¡Qué día tan *or* **más bonito!**	What a lovely day!
¡Qué tiempo tan *or* **más malo!**	What awful weather!
¡Qué pasteles tan *or* **más ricos!**	What delicious cakes!

In Spanish **cuánto/cuánta/cuántos/cuántas** can be used to mean *What a lot of…!* in English.

¡Cuánto dinero!	What a lot of money!
¡Cuánta gente!	What a lot of people!
¡Cuántos autobuses!	What a lot of buses!
¡Cuánto tiempo!	What a long time!

Possessive adjectives (1)

> ### What is a possessive adjective?
> In English a **possessive adjective** is one of the words *my, your, his, her, its, our* or *their* used with a noun to show that one person or thing belongs to another.

➤ Like other adjectives in Spanish, possessive adjectives have to change for the feminine and plural forms.

Singular masculine	feminine	Plural masculine	feminine	Meaning
mi	mi	mis	mis	my
tu	tu	tus	tus	your (*belonging to someone you address as* **tú**)
su	su	sus	sus	his; her; its; your (*belonging to someone you address as* **usted**)
nuestro	nuestra	nuestros	nuestras	our
vuestro	vuestra	vuestros	vuestras	your (*belonging to people you address as* **vosotros/vosotras**)
su	su	sus	sus	their; your (*belonging to people you address as* **ustedes**)

⇨ *For more information on **Ways of saying 'you' in Spanish**, see page 57.*

¿Dónde está <u>tu</u> hermana?	Where's your sister?
José ha perdido <u>su</u> cartera.	José has lost his wallet.
¿Dónde están <u>nuestros</u> pasaportes?	Where are our passports?
¿Por qué no traéis a <u>vuestros</u> hijos?	Why don't you bring your children?
Mis tíos están vendiendo <u>su</u> casa.	My uncle and aunt are selling their house.

> *Tip*
> Possessive adjectives agree with what they describe <u>NOT</u> with the person who owns that thing.
>
> **Pablo ha perdido <u>su</u> bolígrafo.**   Pablo has lost his pen.
> **Pablo ha perdido <u>sus</u> bolígrafos.**   Pablo has lost his pens.

[i] Note that possessive adjectives aren't normally used with parts of the body. You usually use the definite article instead.

Tiene <u>los</u> ojos verdes.	He's got green eyes.
No puedo mover <u>las</u> piernas.	I can't move my legs.

⇨ *For more information on **Articles**, see page 11.*

Tip

As **su** and **sus** can mean *his*, *her*, *its*, *your* or *their*, it can sometimes be a bit confusing. When you need to avoid confusion, you can say the Spanish equivalent of *of him* and so on.

<u>su</u> casa	→	la casa <u>de él</u>	his house (*literally: the house of him*)
<u>sus</u> amigos	→	los amigos <u>de usted</u>	your friends (*literally: the friends of you*)
<u>sus</u> coches	→	los coches <u>de ellos</u>	their cars (*literally: the cars of them*)
<u>su</u> abrigo	→	el abrigo <u>de ella</u>	her coat (*literally: the coat of her*)

⇨ *For more information on* **Personal pronouns,** *see page* 55.

KEY POINTS

✔ The Spanish possessive adjectives are:
  • **mi/tu/su/nuestro/vuestro/su** with a masculine singular noun
  • **mi/tu/su/nuestra/vuestra/su** with a feminine singular noun
  • **mis/tus/sus/nuestros/vuestros/sus** with a masculine plural noun
  • **mis/tus/sus/nuestras/vuestras/sus** with a feminine plural noun
✔ Possessive adjectives come before the noun they refer to. They agree with what they describe, rather than with the person who owns that thing.
✔ Possessive adjectives are not usually used with parts of the body. Use **el/la/los** or **las** as appropriate instead.
✔ To avoid confusion, it is sometimes clearer to use **el coche de él/ella/ellas/ellos/usted** and so on rather than **su coche**.

Test yourself

16 Match the two columns.

a	¡Cuánto tiempo lleva!	What's the weather like?
b	¿Cuánto tiempo lleva?	It's lovely weather!
c	¿Qué tiempo hace?	How long does it take?
d	¡Qué tiempo tan bueno hace!	How much does he earn?
e	¿Cuánto gana?	It takes such a long time!

17 Complete the following sentences with the correct form of the possessive adjective. Some may already be in the correct form.

a ¿Conoces a .... hermanas? **(mi)**

b ¿Cómo se llama .... padre? **(su)**

c .... padres trabajan en el hospital. **(mi)**

d ¿En qué universidad estudian .... hijas? **(vuestro)**

e Nos preguntaron .... nombres. **(nuestro)**

f ¿Me dejas .... bicicleta? **(tu)**

g Me gustan .... zapatos. **(tu)**

h .... hijos están en Londres. **(nuestro)**

i Quiero hablar con .... profesora. **(su)**

j Los sábados salgo con .... amigas. **(mi)**

18 Fill the gap with the correct possessive adjective.

a mi marido y .... hijos

b .... hermano y mi hermana

c tu madre y .... tía

d tu bolso y .... zapatos

e su abrigo y .... botas

f nuestra casa y .... jardín

g vuestro futuro y el de .... hijos

h vuestras preguntas y .... sugerencias

i nuestros colegas y .... jefa

j su familia y .... amigos

Possessive adjectives (2)

➤ In Spanish, there is a second set of possessive adjectives, which mean (of) mine, (of) yours and so on. Like other adjectives in Spanish, they change in the feminine and plural forms.

Singular masculine	feminine	Plural masculine	feminine	Meaning
mío	mía	míos	mías	mine/of mine
tuyo	tuya	tuyos	tuyas	yours/of yours (belonging to tú)
suyo	suya	suyos	suyas	his/of his; hers/of hers; of its; yours/of yours (belonging to usted)
nuestro	nuestra	nuestros	nuestras	ours/of ours
vuestro	vuestra	vuestros	vuestras	yours/of yours (belonging to vosotros/as)
suyo	suya	suyos	suyas	theirs/of theirs; yours/of yours (belonging to ustedes)

⇨ For more information on **Ways of saying 'you' in Spanish**, see page 57.

un amigo <u>mío</u>	a (male) friend of mine, one of my (male) friends
una revista <u>tuya</u>	a magazine of yours, one of your magazines
una tía <u>suya</u>	an aunt of his/hers/theirs/yours, one of his/her/their/your aunts
una amiga <u>nuestra</u>	a (female) friend of ours, one of our friends
¿De quién es esta bufanda? — Es <u>mía</u>.	Whose scarf is this? — It's mine.

ⓘ Note that unlike the other possessive adjectives, these adjectives go <u>AFTER</u> the noun they describe.

un amigo <u>vuestro</u>	a (male) friend of yours, one of your friends

> *Tip*
> Possessive adjectives agree with what they describe <u>NOT</u> with the person who owns that thing.
>
> **Estos apuntes son <u>míos</u>.**　　　These notes are mine.

Grammar Extra!
mío/mía and so on are also used in exclamations and when addressing someone. In this case they mean the same as *my* in English.

¡Dios <u>mío</u>!	My God!
amor <u>mío</u>	my love
Muy señor <u>mío</u>	Dear Sir
hija <u>mía</u>	my dear daughter

For further explanation of grammatical terms, please see pages viii-xii.

Indefinite adjectives

What is an indefinite adjective?
An **indefinite adjective** is one of a small group of adjectives used to talk about people or things in a general way without saying exactly who or what they are, for example, *several*, *all*, *every*.

➤ In English, indefinite adjectives do not change, but in Spanish most indefinite adjectives change for the feminine and plural forms.

Singular masculine	feminine	Plural masculine	feminine	Meaning
algún	alguna	algunos	algunas	some; any
cada	cada			each; every
mismo	misma	mismos	mismas	same
mucho	mucha	muchos	muchas	a lot of
otro	otra	otros	otras	another; other
poco	poca	pocos	pocas	little; few
tanto	tanta	tantos	tantas	so much; so many
todo	toda	todos varios	todas varias	all; every several

algún día	some day
el **mismo** día	the same day
las **mismas** películas	the same films
mucha gente	a lot of people
otro coche	another car
otra manzana	another apple
pocos amigos	few friends

ℹ️ Note that you can never use **otro** (meaning *other* or *another*) with **un** or **una**.

¿Me das otra manzana?	Will you give me another apple?
¿Tienes otro jersey?	Have you got another jumper?

Tip
Some and *any* are usually not translated before nouns that you can't count like bread, butter, water.

Hay pan en la mesa.	There's some bread on the table.
¿Quieres café?	Would you like some coffee?
¿Hay leche?	Is there any milk?
No hay mantequilla.	There isn't any butter.

➤ todo/toda/todos/todas (meaning *all* or *every*) can be followed by:

- a definite article (**el**, **la**, **los**, **las**)
  Han estudiado durante <u>toda la</u> noche.   They've been studying all night.
  Vienen <u>todos los</u> días.   They come every day.

- a demonstrative adjective (**este**, **ese**, **aquel** and so on)
  Ha llovido <u>toda esta</u> semana.   It has rained all this week.

- a possessive adjective (**mi**, **tu**, **su** and so on)
  Pondré en orden <u>todos mis</u> libros.   I'll sort out all my books.

- a place name.
  Lo sabe <u>todo Madrid</u>.   The whole of Madrid knows it.

⇨ *For more information on **Articles**, **Demonstrative adjectives** and **Possessive adjectives**, see pages 11, 41 and 46.*

➤ As in English, Spanish indefinite adjectives come <u>BEFORE</u> the noun they describe.
  las <u>mismas</u> películas   the same films

KEY POINTS

✔ Like other adjectives, Spanish indefinite adjectives (such as **otro** and **todo**) must agree with what they describe.
✔ They go before the noun to which they relate.

Test yourself

19 Complete the following sentences with the correct form of the indefinite adjective.

a Quedan .... manzanas. **(poco)**

b Siempre lleva las .... botas. **(mismo)**

c Se lo he dicho .... veces. **(mucho)**

d Tengo .... ganas de ir a Londres. **(mucho)**

e Tiene muy .... paciencia. **(poco)**

f Hay .... gente. **(mucho)**

g Nos vemos .... veces. **(algún)**

h Su madre la llama .... los días. **(todo)**

i Nos gustan las .... cosas. **(mismo)**

j Contesta .... las preguntas. **(todo)**

20 Translate the following sentences into Spanish.

a Do you want another piece of toast?

....

b I need to buy another book. ....

c I've got a lot of friends. ....

d We want to go to Australia some day.

....

e We start on the same day. ....

f We see each other every day.

....

g Do you want another coffee?

....

h Would you like some water?

....

i Do we have any bread? ....

j Do we need any milk? ....

Test yourself

21 Cross out the noun which the adjective cannot go with.

a toda Londres/España/la noche/el día

b algún tiempo/día/nube/hotel

c poco tiempo/paciencia/dinero

d muchos amigos/problemas/flores/tíos/zapatos

e cada persona/decisión/casas/uno/día/niño/familias

f todos los días/mis hermanos/las familias/las noches

g pocas veces/gente/oportunidades/días

h varias veces/posibilidades/personas/hoteles

i otra día/vez/persona/color

j la misma coche/película/hotel/talla

Pronouns

➤ There are several different types of pronoun:

- <u>Personal pronouns</u> such as *I*, *you*, *he*, *her* and *they*, which are used to refer to you, the person you are talking to, or other people and things. They can be either subject pronouns (*I*, *you*, *he* and so on) or <u>object pronouns</u> (*him*, *her*, *them*, and so on).

- <u>Possessive pronouns</u> like *mine* and *yours*, which show who someone or something belongs to.

- <u>Indefinite pronouns</u> like *someone* or *nothing*, which refer to people or things in a general way without saying exactly who or what they are.

- <u>Relative pronouns</u> like *who*, *which* or *that*, which link two parts of a sentence together.

- <u>Interrogative pronouns</u> like *who*, *what* or *which*, which are used in questions.

- <u>Demonstrative pronouns</u> like *this* or *those*, which point things or people out.

- <u>Reflexive pronouns</u>, a type of object pronoun that forms part of Spanish reflexive verbs like **lavarse** (meaning *to wash*) or **llamarse** (meaning *to be called*).

  ⇨ *For more information on **Reflexive verbs**, see page 131.*

➤ Pronouns often stand in for a noun to save repeating it.
  I finished my homework and gave <u>it</u> to my teacher.
  Do you remember Jack? I saw <u>him</u> at the weekend.

➤ Word order with personal pronouns is usually different in Spanish and English.

Personal pronouns: subject

Using subject pronouns

➤ Here are the Spanish subject pronouns:

Singular	Meaning	Plural	Meaning
yo	I	nosotros (*masculine*)	we
tú	you	nosotras (*feminine*)	we
él	he	vosotros (*masculine*)	you
ella	she	vosotras (*feminine*)	you
usted (Vd.)	you	ellos (*masculine*) ellas (*feminine*) ustedes (Vds.)	they they you

[i] Note that there is an accent on **tú** (*you*) and **él** (*he*) so that they are not confused with **tu** (*your*) and **el** (*the*).

> *Tip*
> The abbreviations **Vd**. and **Vds**. are often used instead of **usted** and **ustedes**.

➤ In English, we use subject pronouns all the time – *I walk, you eat, they are going*. In Spanish, you don't need them if the verb endings and context make it clear who the subject is. For example **hablo español** can only mean *I speak Spanish* since the **-o** ending on the verb is only used with *I*. Similarly, **hablamos francés** can only mean *we speak French* since the **-amos** ending is only used with *we*. So the subject pronouns are not needed in these examples.

Tengo un hermano.	I've got a brother.
Tenemos dos coches.	We've got two cars.

[i] Note that **usted/Vd**. and **ustedes/Vds**. are often used for politeness, even if they are not really needed.

¿Conoce <u>usted</u> al señor Martín?	Do you know Mr Martín?
Pasen <u>ustedes</u> por aquí.	Please come this way.

⇨ *For more information on **Ways of saying 'you' in Spanish**, see page 57.*

➤ Spanish subject pronouns are normally only used:

- for emphasis

¿Y <u>tú</u> qué piensas?	What do <u>you</u> think about it?
<u>Ellos</u> sí que llegaron tarde.	<u>They</u> really did arrive late

- for contrast or clarity

<u>Yo</u> estudio español pero <u>él</u> estudia francés.	I study Spanish but <u>he</u> studies French.
<u>Él</u> lo hizo pero <u>ella</u> no.	<u>He</u> did it but <u>she</u> didn't.

- after **ser** (meaning *to be*)
  Soy <u>yo</u>.   It's <u>me</u>.
  ¿Eres <u>tú</u>?   Is that <u>you</u>?

- in comparisons after **que** and **como**
  Enrique es más alto que <u>yo</u>.   Enrique is taller than <u>I</u> am *or* than me.
  Antonio no es tan alto como <u>tú</u>. Antonio isn't as tall as <u>you</u> (are).

⇨ *For more information on **Making comparisons**, see page 35.*

- on their own without a verb
  ¿Quién dijo eso? — <u>Él</u>.   Who said that? — <u>He</u> did.
  ¿Quién quiere venir? — <u>Yo</u>.   Who wants to come? — <u>I</u> do.

- after certain prepositions
  Es para <u>ella</u>.   It's for <u>her</u>.

⇨ *For more information on **Pronouns after prepositions**, see page 73.*

☑ Note that *it* used as the subject, and *they* referring to things, are <u>NEVER</u> translated into Spanish.

¿Qué es? — Es una sorpresa.   What is it? — <u>It's a</u> surprise.
¿Qué son? — Son abrelatas.   What are they? — <u>They</u> are tin openers.

Ways of saying 'you' in Spanish

➤ In English, we have only <u>one</u> way of saying *you*. In Spanish, there are <u>several</u> words to choose from. The word you use depends on:

- whether you are talking to one person or more than one person

- whether you are talking to a friend or family member, or someone else.

➤ If you are talking to one person <u>you know well</u>, such as a friend, a young person or a relative, use **tú**.

➤ If you are talking to one person <u>you do not know so well</u>, such as your teacher, your boss or a stranger, use the polite form **usted**.

➤ If you are talking to <u>more than one person</u> you know well, use **vosotros** (or **vosotras**, if you are talking to women only) in Spain. Use **ustedes** instead in Latin America.

➤ Use **ustedes** if you are talking to more than one person <u>you do not know so well</u>.

> *Tip*
> Remember that adjectives describing **tú** and **usted** should be feminine if you're talking to a woman or girl, while adjectives describing **ustedes** should be feminine plural if you're talking to women or girls only.

Using the plural subject pronouns

➤ When you are talking about males only, use **nosotros**, **vosotros** or **ellos**.

    Nosotros no somos italianos.   <u>We</u> are not Italian.

➤ When you are talking about females only, use **nosotras**, **vosotras** or **ellas**.

    Hablé con mis hermanas.   I spoke to my sisters.
    <u>Ellas</u> estaban de acuerdo conmigo.   <u>They</u> agreed with me.

➤ When you are talking about both males and females, use **nosotros**, **vosotros** or **ellos**.

    <u>Ellos</u> sí que llegaron tarde.   <u>They</u> really did arrive late.

KEY POINTS

✔ The Spanish subject pronouns are: **yo**, **tú**, **él**, **ella**, **usted** in the singular, and **nosotros/nosotras**, **vosotros/vosotras**, **ellos/ellas**, **ustedes** in the plural.

✔ Don't use the subject pronouns (other than **usted** and **ustedes**) with verbs except for emphasis or clarity.

✔ Make sure you choose the correct form of the verb.

✔ Do use the subject pronouns:
    • after **ser** (meaning *to be*)
    • in comparisons after **que** and **como**
    • in one-word answers to questions.

✔ Choose the word for *you* carefully. Remember to think about how many people you are talking to and your relationship with them when deciding between **tú**, **vosotros**, **vosotras**, **usted** and **ustedes**.

✔ *It* as the subject of the verb, and *they* when it refers to things are NOT translated in Spanish.

✔ Use masculine plural forms (**nosotros**, **vosotros**, **ellos**) for groups made up of men and women.

✔ Remember to make any adjectives describing the subject agree.

Test yourself

1 **Cross out the pronouns that do not work in the sentence.**

a **Mi hermano es más alto que**   mi/yo/él/ti/tú.

b **Somos tan ricos como**   nosotros/ellos/ustedes/ti/tú/vosotros.

c **La carta es para**   yo/mí/vosotros.

d **No comes tanto como**   él/ustedes/vosotros/yo/mí.

e **Baila mejor que**   tú/ti/mi/usted.

f **Trabajamos más que**   ellos/vosotros/ti/tú/él.

g **Es más guapa que**   mí/yo/tu.

h **Este regalo es para**   él/mi /mí/yo/tu.

i **Dale esto a**   ella/mi/ellos/él.

j **Estoy más cansada que**   ellos/vosotros/ti/tú/él.

2 **Translate the following sentences into Spanish.**

a I've got a new car. ....

b Do you have any brothers and sisters?

....

c How old are you? ....

d We've got a dog. ....

e They have two cats. ....

f She has blonde hair. ....

g It's us. ....

h He can't swim. ....

i She speaks English. ....

j They eat a lot. ....

Test yourself

3 **Replace the highlighted words with the correct pronoun.**

a Necesito hablar con **tus padres**. ....

b Quiero casarme con **Pablo**. ....

c Nos vamos de vacaciones con **Rita y mi hermana.**

....

d Puedes venir **conmigo y mi hermano**.

....

e Es tan tonto como **su padre**. ....

f Es más listo que **su hermana**. ....

g Anda siempre con **sus amigos**. ....

h Siempre veranean en casa de **sus tíos**.

....

i Gasta más que **su hermano**. ....

j Es un regalo para **mí y mi hermano**. ....

4 **Match the noun to the pronoun that would replace it.**

a mi madre   ellos

b Samuel y yo   vosotros

c el hermano de Pablo ella

d mis primos   él

e para ti y tus padres nosotros

Personal pronouns: direct object

> **What is a direct object pronoun?**
> A **direct object pronoun** is a word such as *me*, *him*, *us* and *them*, which is used instead of the noun to stand in for the person or thing most directly affected by the action expressed by the verb.

Using direct object pronouns

➤ Direct object pronouns stand in for nouns when it is clear who or what is being talked about, and save having to repeat the noun.

> I've lost my glasses. Have you seen <u>them</u>?
> 'Have you met Jo?' — 'Yes, I really like <u>her</u>!'

➤ Here are the Spanish direct object pronouns:

Singular	Meaning	Plural	Meaning
me	me	**nos**	us
te	you (*relating to* **tú**)	**os**	you (*relating to* **vosotros/vosotras**)
lo	him it (*masculine*) you (*relating to* **usted** – *masculine*)	**los**	them (*masculine*) you (*relating to* **ustedes** – *masculine*)
la	her it (*feminine*) you (*relating to* **usted**– *feminine*)	**las**	them (*feminine*) you (*relating to* **ustedes** – *feminine*)

Te quiero.	I love you.
No los toques.	Don't touch them.

⚠ Note that you cannot use the Spanish direct object pronouns on their own without a verb or after a preposition such as **a** or **de**.

⇨ *For more information on* **Pronouns after prepositions**, *see page 73.*

Word order with direct object pronouns

➤ The direct object pronoun usually comes <u>BEFORE</u> the verb.

¿Las ve usted?	Can you see them?
¿No me oís?	Can't you hear me?
Tu hija no nos conoce.	Your daughter doesn't know us.
¿Lo has visto?	Have you seen it?

➤ In orders and instructions telling someone <u>TO DO</u> something, the pronoun joins onto the end of the verb to form one word.

Ayúda<u>me</u>.	Help me.
Acompáña<u>nos</u>.	Come with us.

> ⓘ Note that you will often need to add a written accent to preserve the spoken stress when adding pronouns to the end of verbs.

⇨ *For more information on **Stress**, see page 266.*

➤ In orders and instructions telling someone <u>NOT TO DO</u> something, the pronoun does <u>NOT</u> join onto the end of the verb.

No <u>los</u> toques.	Don't touch them.

➤ If the pronoun is the object of an infinitive (the *to* form of the verb) or a gerund (the *-ing* form of the verb), you always add the pronoun to the end of the verb to form one word, unless the infinitive or gerund follows another verb. Again, you may have to add a written accent to preserve the stress.

Se fue después de arreglar<u>lo</u>.	He left after fixing it.
Practicándo<u>lo</u>, aprenderás.	You'll learn by practising it.

⇨ *For more information on **Verbs** and **Gerunds**, see pages 99 and 180.*

➤ Where an infinitive or gerund follows another verb, you can put the pronoun either at the end of the infinitive or gerund, or before the other verb.

Vienen a ver<u>nos</u> *or* **<u>Nos</u> vienen a ver.**	They are coming to see us.
Está comiéndo<u>lo</u> *or* **<u>Lo</u> está comiendo.**	He's eating it.

⇨ *For further information on the **Order of object pronouns**, see page 70.*

Special use of lo

➤ **lo** is sometimes used to refer back to an idea or information that has already been given. The word *it* is often missed out in English.

¿Va a venir María? — No <u>lo</u> sé.	Is María coming? — I don't know.
Habían comido ya pero no nos <u>lo</u> dijeron.	They had already eaten, but they didn't tell us.
Yo dibujo bien pero él <u>lo</u> hace mejor.	I'm good at drawing but he's better.

KEY POINTS

✔ The Spanish direct object pronouns are: **me**, **te**, **lo**, **la** in the singular, and **nos**, **os**, **los**, **las** in the plural.
✔ The object pronoun usually comes before the verb.
✔ Object pronouns are joined to the end of infinitives, gerunds or verbs instructing someone to do something.
✔ If an infinitive or gerund follows another verb, you can choose whether to add the object pronoun to the end of the infinitive or gerund or to put it before the first verb.
✔ **lo** is sometimes used to refer back to an idea or information that has already been given.

For further explanation of grammatical terms, please see pages viii-xii.

Test yourself

5 **Rewrite using object pronouns instead of the highlighted words.**

a   ¿Dónde compras **la fruta**? ....

b   ¿Quién te hace **la comida**? ....

c   Comimos toda **la fruta**. ....

d   No comas todas **las manzanas**. ....

e   Nunca veo a **tus padres**. ....

f   Acompaña a **Cristina y Mario**. ....

g   Ayuda a **tu madre**. ....

h   Veo a **mi novia** todos los días. ....

i   No tires **las uvas**. ....

j   Compra **el periódico**. ....

6 **Match the two columns.**

a   **No sé dónde viven.**   Los vamos a visitar.

b   **Estamos arreglando la casa.**   Cuéntamelo.

c   **Vamos a visitar a los abuelos.**   No lo sé.

d   **Cuéntame el asunto.**   Comprémoslas.

e   **Compremos estas fresas.**   La estamos arreglando.

7 **Fill the gap with the correct direct object pronoun.**

a   ¿Ves a esa chica? — Sí, ... veo.

b   ¿Quieres estos zapatos? — Sí, ... quiero.

c   ¿Me entiendes? — Sí, ... entiendo.

d   ¿Te escribe? — Sí, ... escribe.

e   ¡Escúchame! — Muy bien, ... escucho.

f   ¿Llamas a tu padre? — Sí, ... llamo a menudo.

g   ¿Os ayudan algo? — Sí, ... ayudan mucho.

h   ¿Quieres esta manzana? — No, no .... quiero.

i   ¿Conoces a mis primos? — No, no .... conozco.

j   ¿Quién es Susana? No .... conozco.

Test yourself

8 Translate the following sentences into Spanish.

a You see that bird? — Yes, I see it.

....

b Do you like football? — No, I hate it!

....

c Can you hear him?

....

d It's raining. — I know.

....

e Enrique and María are in the garden. — Yes, I can see them.

....

f Do you want this banana? — No, I don't want it.

....

g My cousin lives there. You can visit him.

....

h Help me!

....

i I like that bag. — Buy it!

....

j I can't find my keys. Can you see them?

....

Personal pronouns: indirect object

What is an indirect object pronoun?

An **indirect object pronoun** is used instead of a noun to show the person or thing an action is intended to benefit or harm, for example, *me* in *He gave me a book.*; *Can you get me a towel?*; *He wrote to me.*

Using indirect object pronouns

➤ It is important to understand the difference between direct and indirect object pronouns in English, as they can have different forms in Spanish.

➤ You can usually test whether an object is a direct object or an indirect one by asking questions about the action using *what* and *who*:

- an indirect object answers the question *who ... to?* or *who ... for?*, equally *what ... to?* or *what ... for?*
  He gave me a book. → *Who did he give the book to?* → me (*=indirect object pronoun*)
  Can you get me a towel? → *Who can you get a towel for?* → me (*=indirect object pronoun*)
  We got some varnish for it. → *What did you get the varnish for?* → it (*=indirect object pronoun*)

- if something answers the question *what* or *who*, then it is the direct object and NOT the indirect object.
  He gave me a book. → *What did he give me?* → a book (*=direct object*)
  I saw Mandy. → *Who did you see?* → Mandy (*=direct object*)
  We got some varnish for it. → *What did you get?* → some varnish (*=direct object*)

[i] Note that a verb won't necessarily have both a direct and an indirect object.

➤ Here are the Spanish indirect object pronouns:

Singular	Meaning	Plural	Meaning
me	me, to me, for me	**nos**	us, to us, for us
te	you, to you, for you (*relating to* **tú**)	**os**	you, to you, for you (*relating to* **vosotros/vosotras**)
le	him, to him, for him her, to her, for her, it, to it, for it, you, to you, for you (*relating to* **usted**)	**les**	them, to them, for them, you, to you, for you (*relating to* **ustedes**)

➤ The pronouns shown in the table are used instead of using the preposition **a** with a noun.

Estoy escribiendo a Teresa.	I am writing to Teresa.
Le estoy escribiendo.	I am writing to her.
Compra un regalo a los niños.	Buy the children a present.
Cómprales un regalo.	Buy them a present.

➤ Some Spanish verbs like **mirar** (meaning *to look at*), **esperar** (meaning *to wait for*) and **buscar** (meaning *to look for*) take a direct object, because the Spanish construction is different from the English.

Grammar Extra!
You should usually use direct object pronouns rather than indirect object
pronouns when replacing personal **a** + <u>noun</u>.

Vi <u>a Teresa</u>. → <u>**La**</u> **vi.**   I saw Teresa. → I saw her.

⇨ For more information on *Personal* a, see page 246.

Word order with indirect object pronouns

➤ The indirect object pronoun usually comes <u>BEFORE</u> the verb.
Sofía <u>os</u> ha escrito.	Sophie has written to you.
¿<u>Os</u> ha escrito Sofía?	Has Sofía written to you?
Carlos no <u>nos</u> habla.	Carlos doesn't speak to us.
¿Qué <u>te</u> pedían?	What were they asking you for?

➤ In orders and instructions telling someone <u>TO DO</u> something, the pronoun goes on the end
of the verb to form one word.
Respónde<u>me</u>.	Answer me.
Di<u>me</u> la respuesta.	Tell me the answer.

ⓘ Note that you will often need to add a written accent to preserve the spoken stress.

⇨ *For more information on* **Stress**, *see page 266.*

➤ In orders and instructions telling someone <u>NOT TO DO</u> something, the pronoun does not
join onto the end of the verb.
No <u>me</u> digas la respuesta.	Don't tell me the answer.

➤ If the pronoun is the object of an infinitive (the to form of the verb) or a gerund (the -ing
form of the verb), you always add the pronoun to the end of the verb to form one word,
unless the infinitive or gerund follows another verb. Again, you may have to add a written
accent to preserve the stress.
Eso de dar<u>le</u> tu dirección no fue muy prudente.	It wasn't very wise to give him your address.
Gritándo<u>le</u> tanto lo vas a asustar.	You'll frighten him by shouting at him like that.

➤ Where an infinitive or gerund follows another verb, you can put the pronoun either at the
end of the infinitive or gerund, or before the other verb.
Quiero decir<u>te</u> algo. *or* **<u>Te</u> quiero decir algo.**	I want to tell you something.
Estoy escribiéndo<u>le</u>. *or* **<u>Le</u> estoy escribiendo.**	I am writing to him/her.

⇨ *For further information on the* **Order of object pronouns***, see page 70.*

KEY POINTS

✔ The Spanish indirect object pronouns are: **me**, **te**, **le** in the singular, and **nos**, **os**, **les** in the plural.

✔ They can replace the preposition **a** (meaning *to*) + noun.

✔ Like the direct object pronoun, the indirect object pronoun usually comes before the verb.

✔ Object pronouns are joined to the end of infinitives, gerunds or verbs instructing someone to do something.

✔ If an infinitive or gerund follows another verb, you can choose whether to add the object pronoun to the end of the infinitive or gerund or to put it before the first verb.

Test yourself

9 Replace the highlighted words with the correct indirect object pronoun. Remember to think about word order.

a Juan envía un correo **a sus padres**. ....

b ¿Por qué no escribes una postal a **tu tía**? ....

c Envía este paquete **a tus tíos**. ....

d Pablo da un consejo **a su hijo**. ....

e Carlos dice adiós **a la profesora**. ....

f Dedico este poema **a mis pardres**. ....

g No prestes la bici **a tu hermano**. ....

h Da un beso **a tu abuela**. ....

i Di la verdad **a tus amigos**. ....

j Haz una foto **a tu perro**. ....

10 Translate the following sentences into Spanish.

a Tell me the truth. ....

b Bring me a chair. ....

c Answer him right now. ....

d Why don't you make her an omelette? ....

e Give him an apple. ....

f Give them the keys. ....

g She always brings him with her.

....

h I send them some money every week.

....

i I read her a page every night. ....

j Does she give you any advice? ....

Test yourself

11 **Change the following orders into questions by changing the word order and putting the verb into present tense.**

a ¡Tráeme un vaso! ....

b ¡Tráele un vaso de leche! ....

c ¡Tráenos la cuenta! ....

d ¡Tráeles unas sillas! ....

e ¡Dame eso! ....

f ¡Dale la pelota! ....

g ¡Dame un beso! ....

h ¡Ayúdanos con esto! ....

i ¡Llámalos esta tarde! ....

j ¡Llámame mañana! ....

Order of object pronouns

➤ Two object pronouns are often used together in the same sentence; for example: *he gave me them* or *he gave them to me*. In Spanish, you should always put the indirect object pronoun BEFORE the direct object pronoun.

Indirect		Direct
me	BEFORE	lo
te		la
nos		los
os		las

Ana os lo mandará mañana.	Ana will send it to you tomorrow.
¿Te los ha enseñado mi hermana?	Has my sister shown them to you?
No me lo digas.	Don't tell me (that).
Todos estaban pidiéndotelo.	They were all asking you for it.
No quiere prestárnosla.	He won't lend it to us.

➤ You have to use **se** instead of **le** (*to him, to her, to you*) and **les** (*to them, to you*), when you are using the object pronouns **lo**, **la**, **los**, or **las**.

Se lo di ayer.	I gave it to him/her/you/them yesterday.
Se las enviaré.	I'll send them to him/her/you/them.

Grammar Extra!
Spanish often uses pronouns in combination with nouns in a way that seems redundant to English native speakers. Note the use of indirect object pronouns as well as noun direct objects in the following:

Se lo he dado a tu novio.	I've given it to your boyfriend.
Les voy a decir a mis hermanos que no es justo.	I'm going to tell my brothers and sisters that it isn't fair.

> ### KEY POINTS
> ✔ When combining two object pronouns, put the indirect object pronoun before the direct object pronoun.
> ✔ Use **se** as the indirect object pronoun rather than **le** or **les** when there is more than one object pronoun.

For further explanation of grammatical terms, please see pages viii–xii.

Test yourself

12 **Replace the highlighted words with the direct object pronoun paying attention to word order.**

a Maruja me explicó **el problema**. ....

b Ana os dará **los papeles** mañana. ....

c ¿Tu hermano te presta **la bici**? ....

d No quiero pedirle **dinero**. ....

e Mañana le doy **el regalo**. ....

f Enséñame **los zapatos nuevos**. ....

g No quiere dejarme **el coche**. ....

h Nunca dice **la verdad** a sus padres. ....

i ¿Cuándo le damos **el regalo** a Javier? ....

j ¿Cuándo les vas a decir a tus padres **que te casas**?

....

13 **Translate the following sentences into Spanish. Pay attention to the order of the pronouns.**

a My sister gave them to me. ....

b Will you buy it for me? ....

c Lend it to him. ....

d Send it to her by email. ....

e Show me it. ....

f Give it to us. ....

g He lends it to everybody. ....

h Everyone asks me for it. ....

i Why don't you ask him for it? ....

j They promised us (it). ....

Test yourself

14 Match the English with its Spanish translation.

a	I will give it to him.	No se lo digas.
b	Show me them.	Me los manda todas las semanas.
c	Don't tell him that.	Se lo doy yo.
d	Don't buy it for her.	Enséñamelos.
e	She sends me them every week.	No se lo compres.

Further information on object pronouns

➤ The object pronoun **le** can mean *(to) him, (to) her* and *(to) you;* **les** can mean *(to) them* and *(to) you*, and **se** can mean all of these things, which could lead to some confusion.

➤ To make it clear which one is meant, **a él** (meaning *to him*), **a ella** (meaning *to her*), **a usted** (meaning *to you*) and so on can be added to the phrase.

A ella le escriben mucho.	They write to her often.
A ellos se lo van a mandar pronto.	They will be sending it to them soon.

➤ When a noun object comes before the verb, the corresponding object pronoun must be used too.

A tu hermano lo conozco bien.	I know your brother well.
(literally: Your brother I know him well.)	
A María la vemos algunas veces.	We sometimes see María.
(literally: María we see her sometimes.)	

➤ Indirect object pronouns are often used in constructions with the definite article with parts of the body or items of clothing to show who they belong to. In English, we'd use a possessive adjective.

La chaqueta le estaba ancha.	His jacket was too loose.
Me duele el tobillo.	My ankle's sore.

⇨ *For more information on* **The definite article** *and* **Possessive adjectives***, see pages 11, 46 and 50.*

➤ Indirect object pronouns can also be used in certain common phrases which use reflexive verbs.

Se me ha perdido el bolígrafo.	I have lost my pen.

⇨ *For more information on* **Reflexive verbs***, see page 131.*

Ⓘ Note that in Spain, you will often hear **le** and **les** used instead of **lo** and **los** as direct object pronouns when referring to men and boys. It is probably better not to copy this practice since it is considered incorrect in some varieties of Spanish, particularly Latin American ones.

Pronouns after prepositions

➤ In English, we use *me, you, him* and so on after a preposition, for example, *he came towards me; it's for you; books by him*. In Spanish, there is a special set of pronouns which are used after prepositions.

➤ The pronouns used after a preposition in Spanish are the same as the subject pronouns, except for the forms **mí** (meaning *me*) **ti** (meaning *you*), and **sí** (meaning *himself, herself, yourself, themselves, yourselves*).

Singular	Meaning	Plural	Meaning
mí	me	**nosotros**	us (masculine)
ti	you	**nosotras**	us (*feminine*)
él	him	**vosotros**	you (*masculine*)
ella	her	**vosotras**	you (*feminine*)
usted (Vd.)	you	**ellos**	them (*masculine*)
sí	himself	**ellas**	them (feminine)
	herself	**ustedes (Vds.)**	you
	yourself	**sí**	themselves, yourselves

Pienso <u>en ti</u>.	I think about you.
¿Son <u>para mí</u>?	Are they for me?
No he sabido nada <u>de él</u>.	I haven't heard from him.
Es <u>para ella</u>.	It's for her.
Iban <u>hacia ellos</u>.	They were going towards them.
Volveréis <u>sin nosotros</u>.	You'll come back without us.
Volaban <u>sobre vosotros.</u>	They were flying above you.

[i] Note that **mí**, **sí** and **él** each have an accent, to distinguish them from **mi** (meaning *my*), **si** (meaning *if*), and **el** (meaning *the*), but **ti** does not have an accent.

➤ These pronouns are often used for emphasis.
¿A <u>ti</u> no te escriben?	Don't they write to you?
Me lo manda a <u>mí</u>, no a <u>ti</u>.	She's sending it to me, not to you.

➤ **con** (meaning *with*) combines with **mí**, **ti** and **sí** to form:

- **conmigo**   with me
  Ven <u>conmigo</u>.   Come with me.

- **contigo**   with you
  Me gusta estar <u>contigo</u>.   I like being with <u>you</u>.

- **consigo**   with himself/herself/yourself/themselves/yourselves
  Lo trajeron <u>consigo</u>.   They brought it with them.

➤ **entre, hasta, salvo, menos** and **según** are always used with the <u>subject pronouns</u> (**yo** and **tú**), rather than with the object pronouns (**mí** and **ti**).

- **entre**   between, among
  <u>entre</u> tú y yo   between you and me

- **hasta**   even, including
  <u>Hasta</u> yo puedo hacerlo.   Even I can do it.

- **menos**   except
  todos <u>menos</u> yo   everybody except me

- **salvo**   except
  todos <u>salvo</u> yo   everyone except me

- **según**   according to
  <u>**según**</u> **tú**   according to you

⇨ *For more information on **Subject pronouns**, see page 55.*

KEY POINTS

✔ Most prepositions are followed by the forms: **mí**, **ti**, **sí** and so on.
✔ **con** combines with **mí**, **ti** and **sí** to form **conmigo**, **contigo** and **consigo**.
✔ **entre**, **hasta**, **menos**, **salvo** and **según** are followed by the subject pronouns **yo** and **tú**.

15 Complete the following sentences with the correct object pronoun. Don't forget that direct object pronouns correspond to personal a + noun while indirect object pronouns correspond to the other uses of a + noun.

a A Pilar no .... veo casi nada.

b A tus padres .... invito yo.

c A Mario y yo no .... lo dijeron.

d ¿A vosotros .... avisaron?

e A ellos no .... invitaron.

f A Lola .... conocen todos.

g A los abuelos .... vemos todos los veranos.

h A nuestras primas .... llamamos todas a la boda.

i A Lucía y Antonio .... compraron un ordenador a cada uno.

j ¿A vosotros quién .... ha dicho eso?

16 Cross out the pronouns that do not apply in the following sentences.

a Me recuerdo mucho de   tú/ti/él/mí/ustedes.

b Esos chocolates son para   me/mí/tú/yo/ti/ellos.

c No tenemos noticias de   tú/ella/sí/ellos.

d Hace tiempo que no sé nada de   tú/ti/vosotras/mí/sí.

e Me lo ha pedido a mí, no a   él/tú/ellos/ti/sí/ustedes.

f Quiere ir conmigo, no   contigo/consigo/con él/con vosotros/con tú/con ti.

g Se lo llevó   consigo/con él/contigo/con ella.

h Lo trajo   con ella/consigo/con ellos.

i Fueron todos menos   mí/yo/él/nosotros/ti/tú.

j No hay nada entre yo y   él/ti/tú/ellos.

Test yourself

17 **Replace the highlighted words with the relevant object pronoun.**

a Invitamos a **Javier y Patricia**.

....

b ¿Por qué no llevas a **tu hermano** contigo?

....

c ¿Cuándo llamaron a **María**?

....

d Vamos a esperar a **mis padres** al aeropuerto.

....

e Quiero llevar a **mi amiga** conmigo.

....

f Quiero acompañar a **mi prima** al teatro.

....

g ¿Te apetece acompañar a **José y Sofía** al cine.

....

h No conozco a **Cristina**.

....

i Llamo a **mis padres** todas las noches.

....

j ¿Quién lleva a **tus tíos**?

....

18 **Match the two columns.**

a **Lo llevaré**   consigo.

b **Se lo lleva**   con nosotros.

c **Los llevan**   contigo.

d **Queremos llevarlos**   conmigo.

e **Llévatelo**   con ellos.

Possessive pronouns

> ## What is a possessive pronoun?
> A **possessive pronoun** is one of the words *mine, yours, hers, his, ours* or *theirs*, which are used instead of a noun to show that one person or thing belongs to another, for example, *Ask Carole if this pen is <u>hers</u>.; <u>Mine's the blue one</u>*.

➤ Here are the Spanish possessive pronouns:

Masculine singular	Feminine singular	Masculine plural	Feminine plural	Meaning
el mío	la mía	los míos	las mías	mine
el tuyo	la tuya	los tuyos	las tuyas	yours (*belonging to* **tú**)
el suyo	la suya	los suyos	las suyas	his; hers; its; yours (*belonging to* **usted**)
el nuestro	la nuestra	los nuestros	las nuestras	ours
el vuestro	la vuestra	los vuestros	las vuestras	yours (*belonging to* **vosotros/ vosotras**)
el suyo	la suya	los suyos	las suyas	theirs; yours (*belonging to* **ustedes**)

⇨ *For more information on **Ways of saying 'you' in Spanish**, see page 57.*

¿Qué equipo ha ganado, <u>el suyo</u> o <u>el nuestro</u>?	Which team won — theirs or ours?
Mi perro es más joven que <u>el tuyo</u>.	My dog is younger than yours.
Si no tienes lápices, te prestaré <u>los míos</u>.	If you haven't got any pencils, I'll lend you mine.
Las habitaciones son más pequeñas que <u>las vuestras</u>.	The rooms are smaller than yours.

> *Tip*
> In Spanish, possessive pronouns agree with what they describe, <u>NOT with</u> the person who owns that thing. For example, **el suyo** can mean *his, hers, yours* or *theirs*, but can only be used to replace a masculine singular noun.

➤ After **ser** use **mío, tuyo**, etc adjectivally without the article to mean *mine, yours*, etc.
　　—¿De quién es la tele? —Es mía.　　Whose TV is it? It's mine.

⇨ *For more information on this kind of Possessive adjective see page 50.*

➤ Only use the article after **ser** when the sense is *my one*, *your one*, etc. Compare:

Pregunta a Cristina si este bolígrafo es suyo.	Ask Cristina if this pen is hers.

And:

Pregunta a Cristina si este bolígrafo es el suyo.	Ask Cristina if this pen is her one.

Similarly:

Daniel pensó que estos libros eran suyos.	Daniel thought these books were his.
Daniel pensó que estos libros eran los suyos.	Daniel thought these books were his ones.

[¿] Note that the prepositions **a** and **de** combine with the article **el** to form **al** and **del**, for example, **a + el mío** becomes **al mío**, and **de + el mío** becomes **del mío**.

Prefiero tu coche <u>al mío</u>.	I prefer your car to mine.
Su coche se parece <u>al vuestro</u>.	His/Her/Their car looks like yours.
Mi piso está encima <u>del tuyo</u>.	My flat is above yours.
Su colegio está cerca <u>del nuestro</u>.	His/Her/Your/Their school is near ours.

➤ Instead of **el suyo/la suya/los suyos/las suyas**, it is sometimes clearer to say **el/la/los/las de usted**, **el/la/los/las de ustedes**, **el/la/los/las de ellos** and so on. You choose between **el/la/los/las** to agree with the noun referred to.

mi libro y <u>el de</u> usted	my book and yours

➤ **el/la/los/las de** can also be used with a name or other noun referring to somebody.

Juan tiene un coche bonito pero yo prefiero <u>el de</u> Ana.	Juan's got a nice car, but I prefer Ana's.
Ellos tienen una casa bonita pero yo prefiero <u>la del</u> médico.	They've got a nice house, but I prefer the doctor's.

KEY POINTS

✔ The Spanish possessive pronouns are **el mío**, **el tuyo**, **el suyo**, **el nuestro**, **el vuestro** and **el suyo** when they stand in for a masculine noun. If they stand in for a feminine or a plural noun, their forms change accordingly.

✔ In Spanish, the pronoun you choose has to agree with the noun it replaces, and <u>not</u> with the person who owns that thing.

✔ **el/la/los/las de** are used with a noun or pronoun to mean the *one(s) belonging to* ...

Test yourself

19 Complete the following sentences with the correct possessive form.

a   Nuestro coche es más grande que .... tu padre.

b   Estas sandalias son bonitas pero prefiero .... Ana.

c   Este vestido es más azul que .... Nuria.

d   Nuestras maletas pesan más que .... ustedes.

e   Sus hijos son más mayores que .... su amiga.

f   Esta fruta es más cara que .... la otra tienda.

g   Esa película me gusta pero prefiero .... anoche.

h   Nuestras plantas han crecido pero no tanto como .... ustedes.

i   Nuestra casa esta más lejos del centro que .... vuestros padres.

j   Hemos comprado un coche más barato que .... mis tíos.

20 Replace the highlighted words with the correct possessive pronoun.

a   Nuestro jardín es más pequeño que **el de los vecinos**.

....

b   Esta casa es **la de Carmen y su hermano**.

....

c   Esa escuela es **la mía y de mis hermanos**.

....

d   ¿Ese coche es el tuyo o **el de tu madre**?

....

e   Esta parte de la huerta es nuestra y esa es **la tuya y de tu familia**.

....

f   Estos zapatos no me gustan. Prefiero **los de Alba**.

....

g   La tortilla de mi madre está mejor que **la de mi tía**.

....

h   Mi pueblo está más cerca de la playa que **el de ustedes**.

....

i   Han comprado un piso debajo **del de Maricarmen y Jorge**.

....

j   Estas plantas están más crecidas que **las de la vecina**.

....

Test yourself

21 Translate the following sentences into Spanish using the relevant possessive pronoun.

   a   These pencils are yours. ....

   b   Those boots are mine. ....

   c   These seats here are yours. ....

   d   Those bikes over there are ours.

       ....

   e   Are these books yours or mine?

       ....

   f   That house over there is ours. ....

   g   I like your house more than theirs. ....

   h   Are these our seats or yours [plural]?

       ....

   i   Is this my newspaper or yours? ....

   j   I've seen my bag but not hers. ....

Indefinite pronouns

What is an indefinite pronoun?

An **indefinite pronoun** is one of a small group of pronouns such as *everything*, *nobody* and *something* which are used to refer to people or things in a general way without saying exactly who or what they are.

➤ Here are the most common Spanish indefinite pronouns:

- **algo**   something, anything
Tengo <u>algo</u> para ti.	I have something for you.
¿Viste <u>algo</u>?	Did you see anything?

- **alguien**   somebody, anybody
<u>Alguien</u> me lo ha dicho.	Somebody told me.
¿Has visto a <u>alguien</u>?	Have you seen anybody?

> *Tip*
>
> Don't forget to use personal a before indefinite pronouns referring to people when they are the object of a verb.
>
> | **¿Viste <u>a</u> alguien?** | Did you see anybody? |
> |---|---|
> | **No vi <u>a</u> nadie.** | I didn't see anybody. |
>
> ⇨ For more information on **Personal a**, see page 246.

- **alguno/alguna/algunos/algunas**   some, a few
<u>Algunos</u> de los niños ya saben leer.	Some of the children can already read.

- **cada uno/una**   each (one), everybody
Le dio una manzana a <u>cada uno</u>.	She gave each one an apple.
¡<u>Cada uno</u> a su casa!	Everybody home!

- **cualquiera**   anybody; any
<u>Cualquiera</u> puede hacerlo.	Anybody can do it.
<u>Cualquiera</u> de las explicaciones vale.	Any of the explanations is valid.

- **mucho/mucha/muchos/muchas**   much; many
<u>Muchas</u> de las casas no tenían jardín.	Many of the houses didn't have a garden.

- **nada**   nothing, anything
¿Qué tienes en la mano? — <u>Nada</u>.	What have you got in your hand? — Nothing.
No dijo <u>nada</u>.	He didn't say anything.

- **nadie**   nobody, anybody
¿A quién ves? — <u>A nadie</u>.	Who can you see? — Nobody.
No quiere ver <u>a nadie</u>.	He doesn't want to see anybody.

For further explanation of grammatical terms, please see pages viii-xii.

- **ninguno/ninguna**   none, any (referring to countable things)
  ¿Cuántas tienes? — <u>Ninguna</u>.   How many have you got? — None.
  No me queda <u>ninguno</u>.   I haven't any left *or* I have none left.

- **otro/otra/otros/otras**   another one; others
  No me gusta este modelo. ¿Tienes <u>otro</u>?   I don't like this model. Have you got another?

[¿] Note that you can never put **un** or **una** before **otro** or **otra**.

- **poco/poca/pocos/pocas**   little; few
  solo unos <u>pocos</u>   only a few

- **tanto/tanta/tantos/tantas**   so much; so many
  ¿Se oía mucho ruido?– No <u>tanto</u>. Was there a lot of noise? — Not so much.

- **todo/toda/todos/todas**   all; everything
  Lo ha estropeado <u>todo</u>.   He has spoiled everything.
  <u>Todo</u> va bien.   It's all going well.

- **uno ... el otro/una ... la otra**   (the) one ... the other
  <u>Uno</u> dijo que sí y <u>el otro</u> que no.   One said yes while the other said no.

- **unos ... los otros/unas ... las otras**   some ... the others
  <u>Unos</u> cuestan 30 euros,   Some cost 30 euros, the others 40 euros.
  <u>los otros</u> 40 euros.

- **varios/varias**   several
  <u>Varios</u> de ellos me gustan mucho.   I like several of them very much.

[¿] Note that **algo**, **alguien** and **alguno** can <u>NEVER</u> be used after a negative such as **no**.
Instead you must use the appropriate negative pronouns, **nada**, **nadie**, **ninguno**.

<u>No</u> veo a <u>nadie</u>.   I can't see anybody.
<u>No</u> tengo <u>nada</u> que hacer.   I haven't got anything to do.

➤ You use **nada**, **nadie** and **ninguno** on their own without **no** to answer questions.

¿Qué pasa? — <u>Nada</u>.	What's happening? — Nothing.
¿Quién habló? — <u>Nadie</u>.	Who spoke? — Nobody.
¿Cuántos quedan? — <u>Ninguno</u>.	How many are there left? — None.

➤ You also use **nada**, **nadie** and **ninguno** on their own without **no** when they come before a verb.

<u>Nada</u> lo asusta.	Nothing frightens him.
<u>Nadie</u> habló.	Nobody spoke.
<u>Ninguno</u> de mis amigos quiso venir.	None of my friends wanted to come.

⇨ *For more information on **Negatives**, see page 215.*

KEY POINTS

✔ Where indefinite pronouns have alternative endings, they must agree with the noun they refer to.

✔ *Anything* is usually translated by **algo** in questions and by **nada** in sentences containing **no**.

✔ *Anybody* is usually translated by **alguien** in questions and by **nadie** in sentences containing **no**.

✔ When **nada**, **nadie** or **ninguno** come <u>after</u> the verb, remember to put **no** before it. When they come <u>before</u> the verb, don't use **no**.

Test yourself

22 Match the two columns.

a	Ninguno	Poca.
b	Todos	Muchas.
c	¿Había mucha gente?	va bien.
d	Todo	de ellos vino a la fiesta.
e	¿Cuántas tienes?	están estropeados.

23 In the following sentences, add personal 'a' if it is needed. Leave the gap blank if it is not needed.

a   No vimos .... nadie.

b   No conozco .... nadie allí.

c   Me lo dijo .... alguien.

d   No se lo he dicho .... nadie.

e   Todavía no hemos invitado .... nadie.

f   No sé si .... alguien vendrá.

g   Pues no me lo había dicho .... nadie.

h   Jamás se lo diría .... nadie.

i   Nunca se lo había dicho .... nadie.

j   Creo que .... alguien debería decírselo.

24 Cross out the wrong alternative.

a	No he visto	a alguien/a nadie.
b	No quiero	algo/nada.
c	¿Quién te lo dijo?	A alguien/Alguien.
d	No quiero llamar a	nadie/alguien.
e	Prefiero no contárselo	a alguien/a nadie.
f	Tengo que decírselo	a alguien/alguien.
g	Tengo que dárselo	alguien/a alguien.
h	No quiero dárselo	a nadie/a alguien.
i	No queremos invitar	a alguien/a nadie.
j	No me debes	nada/algo.

Test yourself

25 Translate the following into Spanish.

   a   Nobody is coming. ....

   b   I don't want anything. ....

   c   Do you want anything? ....

   d   We are not inviting anyone. ....

   e   Who knows? — No one. ....

   f   What are you buying? — Nothing. ....

   g   I don't have any. ....

   h   Do you want any of these? ....

   i   No one tells me anything. ....

   j   Anyone can do it. ....

Relative pronouns

> ### What is a relative pronoun?
> In English, a **relative pronoun** is one of the words *who*, *which* and *that* (and the more formal *whom*) which can be used to introduce information that makes it clear which person or thing is being talked about, for example, *The man who has just come in is Ann's boyfriend.*; *The vase that you broke was quite valuable.*
>
> Relative pronouns can also introduce further information about someone or something, for example, *Peter, who is a brilliant painter, wants to study art.*; *Jane's house, which was built in 1890, needs a lot of repairs.*

Relative pronouns referring to people

➤ In English, we use the relative pronouns *who*, *whom* and *that* to talk about people. In Spanish, **que** is used.

el hombre <u>que</u> vino ayer	the man <u>who</u> came yesterday
Mi hermano, <u>que</u> tiene veinte años, es mecánico.	My brother, <u>who</u> is twenty, is a mechanic.
el hombre <u>que</u> vi en la calle	the man (<u>that</u>) I saw in the street

> *Tip*
> In English we often miss out the relative pronouns *who*, *whom* and *that*. For example, we can say both *the friends that I see most*, or *the friends I see most*. In Spanish, you can <u>NEVER</u> miss out **que** in this way.

➤ When the relative pronoun is used with a preposition, use **el/la/los/las que** or **quien/quienes** which must agree with the noun it replaces; **el que** changes for the feminine and plural forms, **quien** changes only in the plural.

➤ Here are the Spanish relative pronouns referring to people that are used after a preposition:

	Masculine	Feminine	Meaning
Singular	el que, quien	la que, quien	who, that, whom
Plural	los que, quienes	las que, quienes	who, that, whom

las mujeres con <u>las que</u> *or* **con <u>quienes</u> estaba hablando**	the women (that) she was talking to
La chica de <u>la que</u> *or* **de <u>quien</u> te hablé llega mañana.**	The girl (that) I told you about is coming tomorrow.
los niños de <u>los que</u> *or* **de <u>quienes</u> se ocupa usted**	the children (that) you look after

> 🛈 Note that when **de** is used with **el que**, they combine to become **del que**. When **a** is used with **el que**, they combine to become **al que**.

el chico <u>del que</u> te hablé	the boy I told you about
Vive con un hombre <u>al que</u> adora.	She lives with a man she adores.

> **Tip**
> In English, we often put prepositions at the end of the sentence, for example, *the man she was talking to*. In Spanish, you can <u>never</u> put a preposition at the end of a sentence.

> **el hombre con el que** *or*
>   **con quien estaba hablando**

the man she was talking to

⇨ For more information on **Prepositions**, see page 244.

Relative pronouns referring to things

➤ In English, we use the relative pronouns *which* and *that* to talk about things. In Spanish, **que** is used.

> **la novela <u>que</u> ganó el premio**   the novel <u>that</u> *or* <u>which</u> won the prize
> **el coche <u>que</u> compré**   the car (<u>that</u> *or* <u>which</u>) I bought

> **Tip**
> In English, we often miss out the relative pronouns *which* and *that*.
> For example, we can say both *the house <u>which</u> we want to buy*, or *the house we want to buy*.
> In Spanish, you can <u>NEVER</u> miss out **que** in this way.

➤ When the relative pronoun is used with a preposition, use **el/la/los/las que**, which must agree with the noun it replaces. Here are the Spanish relative pronouns referring to things that are used after a preposition:

	Masculine	Feminine	Meaning
Singular	el que	la que	which, that
Plural	los que	las que	which, that

> **la tienda a <u>la que</u> siempre va** the shop (that *or* which) she always goes to
> **los temas de <u>los que</u> habla**   the subjects he talks about

ⓘ Note that when **de** is used with **el que**, they combine to become **del que**. When **a** is used with **el que**, they combine to become **al que**.

> **el programa <u>del que</u> te hablé**   the programme I told you about
> **el banco <u>al que</u> fuiste**   the bank you went to

➤ The neuter form **lo que** is used when referring to the whole of the previous part of the sentence.

> **Todo estaba en silencio, <u>lo que</u>**   All was silent, which I thought was odd.
>   **me pareció raro.**

⇨ *For more information on* **lo que**, *see page 21.*

For further explanation of grammatical terms, please see pages viii-xii.

> *Tip*
> In English, we often put prepositions at the end of the sentence,
> for example, *the shop she always goes to*. In Spanish, you can <u>never</u> put a
> preposition at the end of a sentence.
>
> **la tienda <u>a la que</u> siempre va**   the shop she always goes to
> **la película <u>de la que</u> te hablaba**   the film I was telling you about

---

Grammar Extra!
In English we can use *whose* to show possession, for example, *the woman whose son is ill*. In Spanish you use **cuyo/cuya/cuyos/cuyas**; **cuyo** is actually an adjective and must agree with the noun it describes <u>NOT</u> with the person who owns that thing.

La mujer, <u>cuyo</u> nombre era Antonia,   The woman, whose name was
  estaba jubilada.   Antonia, was retired.
el señor en <u>cuya</u> casa me alojé   the gentleman whose house I stayed in

In your reading, you may come across the forms **el cual/la cual/los cuales/las cuales** which are a more formal alternative to **el que/la que/los que/las que** after a preposition.

las mujeres con <u>las cuales</u> estaba   the women (that *or* who) she was
  hablando   talking to
la ventana desde <u>la cual</u> nos   the window from which they were
  observaban   watching us

el cual/la cual/los cuales/las cuales are also useful to make it clear who you are talking about in other cases where the pronoun does not immediately follow the person or thing it refers to.

El padre de Elena, <u>el cual</u> tiene   Elena's father, who has a lot of money,
  mucho dinero, es ...   is ...

Other uses of <u>el que, la que, los que, las que</u>

➤ You can use **el que, la que, los que, las que** to mean *the one(s) (who/which)* or *those who*.
  Esa película es <u>la que</u> quiero ver.   That film is the one I want to see.
  <u>los que</u> quieren irse   those who want to leave

> ## KEY POINTS
> ✔ **que** can refer to both people and things in Spanish.
> ✔ In English we often miss out the relative pronouns *who*, *which* and *that*, but in Spanish you can never miss out **que**.
> ✔ After a preposition you use **el que/la que/los que/las que** or **quien/quienes** if you are referring to people; you use **el que/la que/los que/las que** if you are referring to things. **el que** and **quien** agree with the nouns they replace.
> ✔ **a + el que → al que**
> **de + el que → del que**
> ✔ <u>Never</u> put the preposition at the end of the sentence in Spanish.
> ✔ **el que/la que/los que** and **las que** are also used to mean *the one(s) who/which or those who*.

Test yourself

26 Complete the following phrases with the relevant relative pronoun.

a   Esa es la mujer .... me lo contó.

b   las chicas con .... trabajo

c   ¿Es ese el chico de .... me hablabas?

d   Se lo preguntamos a .... trabajan aquí.

e   El vestido .... compré ya no me sirve.

f   la casa en .... vivíamos antes

g   el colegio a .... fui

h   no me entero de .... dice

i   Ese es el restaurante a .... fuimos ayer.

j   el jefe de Pedro, ... está casado con una irlandesa

27 Replace the highlighted relative pronouns with the alternative quien **form.**

a   la señora **a la que** llamamos ayer ....

b   el hombre con **el que** vive ....

c   la chica con **la que** sale ....

d   los tíos con **los que** va de vacaciones ....

e   el jefe con **el que** trabaja ....

f   los vecinos con **los que** no se habla ....

g   los tíos de Benito son **los que** nos han invitado ....

h   las primas de Amalia, **las que** viven en Inglaterra ....

i   el chico inglés con **el que** sale ....

j   la gente a **la que** invitaron ....

Test yourself

28 Translate the following phrases into Spanish.

a the woman who lives here

....

b the car I want to buy

....

c the trip she always talks about

....

d the restaurant we always go to

....

e She has a boyfriend, which is a real surprise.

....

f My cousin, whose wife is English, is coming tomorrow.

....

g What's the man she works with called?

....

h the women she works with

....

i the company, whose employees are nearly all under 30

....

j the singer she married

....

Interrogative pronouns

> **What is an interrogative pronoun?**
> In English, an **interrogative pronoun** is one of the words *who*, *which*, *whose*, *whom*, and *what* when they are used without a noun to ask questions.

➤ These are the interrogative pronouns in Spanish:

Singular	Plural	Meaning
¿qué?	¿qué?	what?
¿cuál?	¿cuáles?	which? which one(s)?; what?
¿quién?	¿quiénes?	who? (*as subject or after a preposition*)
¿cuánto?/¿cuánta?	¿cuántos?/¿cuántas?	how much? how many?

[i] Note that question words have an accent on them in Spanish.

¿qué?

➤ ¿qué? is the equivalent of *what?* in English.

¿Qué están haciendo?	What are they doing?
¿Qué dices?	What are you saying?
¿Para qué lo quieres?	What do you want it for?

➤ You can use **¿por qué?** in the same way as *why?* in English.

¿Por qué no vienes?	Why don't you come?

¿cuál?, ¿cuáles?

➤ **¿cuál?** and **¿cuáles?** are usually the equivalent of *which?* in English and are used when there is a choice between two or more things.

¿Cuál de estos vestidos te gusta más?	Which of these dresses do you like best?
¿Cuáles quieres?	Which (ones) do you want?

[i] Note that you don't use **cuál** before a noun; use **qué** instead.

¿Qué libro es más interesante?	Which book is more interesting?

➪ *For more information on **Interrogative adjectives**, see page 45.*

qué es or cuál es?

➤ You should only use ¿qué es ...? (meaning *what is...?*) and ¿qué son ...? (meaning *what are...?*) when you are asking someone to define, explain or classify something.

¿Qué es esto?	What is this?
¿Qué son los genes?	What are genes?

➤ Use ¿cuál es ...? and ¿cuáles son...? (also meaning *what is ...?* and *what are ...?*) when you want someone to specify a particular detail, number, name and so on.

¿Cuál es la capital de España?	What is the capital of Spain?
¿Cuál es tu consejo?	What's your advice?

¿quién?

➤ ¿quién? and ¿quiénes? are the equivalent of *who?* in English when it is the subject of the verb or when used with a preposition.

¿Quién ganó la carrera?	Who won the race?
¿Con quiénes los viste?	Who did you see them with?
¿A quién se lo diste?	Who did you give it to?

➤ ¿a quién? and ¿a quiénes? are the equivalent of *who(m)?* when it is the object of the verb.

¿A quién viste?	Who did you see? *or* Whom did you see?
¿A quiénes ayudaste?	Who did you help? *or* Whom did you help?

➤ ¿de quién? and ¿de quiénes? are the equivalent of *whose?* in English.

¿De quién es este libro?	Whose is this book? *or* Whose book is this?
¿De quiénes son estos coches?	Whose are these cars? *or* Whose cars are these?

¿cuánto?, ¿cuántos?

➤ ¿cuánto? (*masculine*) and ¿cuánta? (*feminine*) are the equivalent of *how much?* in English. ¿cuántos? (*masculine plural*) and ¿cuántas? (*feminine plural*) are the equivalent of *how many?*

¿Cuánto es?	How much is it?
¿Cuántos tienes?	How many have you got?

For further explanation of grammatical terms, please see pages viii-xii.

Demonstrative pronouns

What is a demonstrative pronoun?
In English a **demonstrative pronoun** is one of the words *this*, *that*, *these*, and *those* used instead of a noun to point people or things out, for example, *That* looks fun.

Using demonstrative pronouns

➤ These are the demonstrative pronouns in Spanish:

	Masculine	Feminine	Neuter	Meaning
Singular	este	esta	esto	this, this one
	ese	esa	eso	that, that one (*close by*)
	aquel	aquella	aquello	that, that one (*further away*)
Plural	estos	estas		these, these ones
	esos	esas		those, those ones (*close by*)
	aquellos	aquellas		those, those ones (*further away*)

➤ The demonstrative pronouns in Spanish have to agree with the noun that they are replacing.

¿Qué abrigo te gusta más? —	Which coat do you like best? –
Este de aquí.	This one here.
Aquella casa era más grande que <u>esta</u>.	That house was bigger than this one.
estos libros y <u>aquellos</u>	these books and those ones (over there)
Quiero estas sandalias y <u>esas</u>.	I'd like these sandals and those ones.

¿ese or aquel?

➤ In English we use *that* and *those* to talk about anything that is not close by. In Spanish, you need to be a bit more precise.

➤ Use **ese/esa** and so on to indicate things and people that are nearer to the person you're talking to than to you.

Me gusta más <u>ese</u> que tienes	I prefer the one you've got in your hand.
en la mano.	

➤ Use **ese/esa** and so on to indicate things and people that aren't very far away.

Si no te apetece este restaurante	If you don't fancy this restaurant,
podemos ir a <u>ese</u> de enfrente.	we can go to that one opposite.

➤ Use **aquel/aquella** and so on to talk about things that are further away.

<u>Aquella</u> al fondo de la calle es mi casa.	My house is that one at the end of the street.

🛈 Note that the masculine and feminine forms of demonstrative <u>pronouns</u> are sometimes written with an accent, (**éste/ésta/éstos/éstas**; **ése/ésa/ésos/ésas**; **aquél/aquélla/aquéllos/aquéllas**) to distinguish them from demonstrative <u>adjectives</u>. Compare:

este bolígrafo	this pen	**<u>éste</u>**	this one

➪ For more information on **Demonstrative adjectives**, see page 41.

➤ The neuter forms (**esto**, **eso**, **aquello**) are used to talk about an object you don't recognize or about an idea or statement.

¿Qué es <u>eso</u> que llevas en la mano?	What's that you've got in your hand?
No puedo creer que <u>esto</u> me esté pasando a mí.	I can't believe this is really happening to me.
<u>Aquello</u> sí que me gustó.	I really did like that.

ⓘ Note that the neuter forms of demonstrative pronouns do <u>NOT</u> have an accent.

KEY POINTS

✔ Spanish demonstrative pronouns agree with the noun they are replacing.

✔ Masculine and feminine demonstrative pronouns sometimes have an accent on them in both the singular and the plural.

✔ In Spanish you have to choose the correct pronoun to emphasize the difference between something that is close to you and something that is further away:

- **este/esta/estos** and **estas** (meaning *this/these*) are used to indicate things and people that are very close.
- **ese/esa/esos** and **esas** (meaning *that/those*) are used to indicate things and people that are near the person you are talking to or that aren't too far away.
- **aquel/aquella/aquellos/aquellas** (meaning *that/those*) are used to indicate things and people that are further away.

✔ The neuter pronouns (**esto**, **eso** and **aquello**) are used to talk about things you don't recognize or to refer to statements or ideas. They never have an accent.

For further explanation of grammatical terms, please see pages viii–xii.

Test yourself

29 Complete the following sentences with the correct interrogative pronoun?

a ¿ .... cuesta?

b ¿De .... es ese coche?

c ¿ .... gente había?

d ¿ .... es su casa?

e ¿ .... son los tuyos?

f ¿De .... son estos abrigos?

g ¿A .... se lo dijiste?

h ¿ .... de los invitados vendrán?

i ¿ .... churros te pongo?

j ¿Para .... es este regalo?

30 Complete the following sentences with the correct form of the interrogative pronoun. Some may be in the correct form already.

a ¿ .... de estos te pongo? **(cuánto)**

b ¿ .... son tus preferidos? **(cuál)**

c ¿ .... son aquellos hombres? **(quién)**

d A .... se lo preguntaste? **(quién)**

e Yo tengo dos hijos. ¿Tú .... tienes? **(cuánto)**

f Esos dos de ahí son mis hijas. ¿ .... son las tuyas? **(cuál)**

g ¿De .... es este libro? **(quién)**

h ¿ .... es tu coche? **(cuál)**

i ¿ .... valen? **(cuánto)**

j ¿ .... hijos tienes? **(cuánto)**

Test yourself

31 Translate the following phrases into Spanish.

  a Which ones do you prefer?

  ....

  b Who told you?

  ....

  c Who are those women over there?

  ....

  d Who are you selling your car to?

  ....

  e Who are you inviting?

  ....

  f Whose house is that?

  ....

  g How many are you buying?

  ....

  h Do you prefer this one or that one?

  ....

  i This pen writes better than that one.

  ....

  j What's that?

  ....

Verbs

What is a verb?
A **verb** is a 'doing' word which describes what someone or something does, what someone or something is, or what happens to them, for example, *be*, *sing*, *live*.

Overview of verbs

➤ Verbs are frequently used with a noun, with somebody's name or, particularly in English, with a pronoun such as *I*, *you* or *she*. They can relate to the present, the past and the future; this is called their <u>tense</u>.

⇨ *For more information on* **Nouns** *and* **Pronouns***, see pages 1 and 55.*

➤ Verbs are either:

- <u>regular</u>; their forms follow the normal rules

- <u>irregular</u>; their forms do not follow normal rules

➤ Almost all verbs have a form called the <u>infinitive</u>. This is a base form of the verb (for example, *walk*, *see*, *hear*) that hasn't had any endings added to it and doesn't relate to any particular tense. In English, the infinitive is usually shown with *to*, as in *to speak*, *to eat*, *to live*.

➤ In Spanish, the infinitive is always made up of just one word (never two as in *to speak* in English) and ends in **-ar, -er** or **-ir**: for example, **hablar** (meaning *to speak*), **comer** (meaning *to eat*) and **vivir** (meaning *to live*). All Spanish verbs belong to one of these three types, which are called <u>conjugations</u>. We will look at each of these three conjugations in turn on the next few pages.

➤ Regular English verbs have other forms apart from the infinitive: a form ending in *-s* (*walks*), a form ending in *-ing* (*walking*), and a form ending in *-ed* (*walked*).

➤ Spanish verbs have many more forms than this, which are made up of endings added to a <u>stem</u>. The stem of a verb can usually be worked out from the infinitive.

➤ Spanish verb endings change depending on who or what is doing the action and on when the action takes place. In fact, the ending is very often the only thing that shows you <u>who</u> is doing the action, as the Spanish equivalents of *I, you, he* and so on (**yo, tú, él** and so on) are not used very much. So, both **hablo** on its own and **yo hablo** mean *I speak*. Sometimes there is a name or a noun in the sentence to make it clear who is doing the action.

<u>**José** hablo español.</u>   <u>José</u> speaks Spanish.
<u>**El profesor** hablo español.</u>   <u>The teacher</u> speaks Spanish.

⇨ *For more information on* **Subject pronouns***, see page 55.*

➤ Spanish verb forms also change depending on whether you are talking about the present, past or future, so (**yo**) **hablaré** means *I will speak* while (**yo**) **hablé** means *I spoke*.

➤ Some verbs in Spanish do not follow the usual patterns. These <u>irregular verbs</u> include some very common and important verbs like **ir** (meaning *to go*), **ser** and **estar** (meaning *to be*) and **hacer** (meaning *to do* or *to make*). Other verbs are only slightly irregular, changing their stems in certain tenses.

⇨ *For **Verb Tables**, see supplement.*

KEY POINTS

✔ Spanish verbs have different forms depending on who or what is doing the action and on the tense.
✔ Spanish verb forms are made up of a stem and an ending. The stem is usually based on the infinitive of the verb. The ending depends on who or what is doing the action and on when the action takes place.
✔ Regular verbs follow the standard patterns for **-ar**, **-er** and **-ir** verbs. Irregular verbs do not.

Test yourself

1 **Complete the following sentences with the correct form of the present tense.**

    a Los hijos de Carmen .... inglés. **(hablar)**

    b Mis padres .... en España. **(vivir)**

    c Me .... Cristina. **(llamar)**

    d Se .... Xavi. **(llamar)**

    e David .... mucho. **(comer)**

    f Mis padres .... en el hospital. **(trabajar)**

    g Carlos y yo .... casarnos. **(querer)**

    h Cristina .... mucho. **(estudiar)**

    i Mis hijos siempre .... la cama. **(hacer)**

    j Siempre nos .... de vacaciones en agosto. **(ir)**

2 **Create a sentence using the elements given. Remember that, in Spanish, the subject of a verb is included in the verb form so it is not necessary to state it. Where it is not obvious, the subject of the verb is shown in square brackets to show you which verb form to use in the sentence. Remember also that when the object of the verb is a pronoun, it usually comes before the verb.**

    a cenar/fuera/a menudo/[nosotros] ....

    b dar/a él/demasiado/dinero/[vosotros] ....

    c Manuel/adora/la ....

    d siempre/regalar/un viaje/a él/[ellos] ....

    e ahora/jugar/mejor/[ellos] ....

    f preguntar/a Ana/mañana/[yo] ....

    g su amiga/venir/jugar/hoy ....

    h sus padres/trabajar/hospital ....

    i querer/descansar/un poco[nosotros] ....

    j contar/lo/a la profesora/mañana/[yo] ....

Test yourself

Translate the following into Spanish.

a   His name is Ben. ....

b   What's your name? ....

c   We live in London. ....

d   He works in an office. ....

e   I'm cold. ....

f   It's hot. ....

g   We have supper at eight. ....

h   They speak Spanish. ....

i   They live together. ....

j   I love you. ....

The present tenses

What are the present tenses?
The **present tenses** are the verb forms that are used to talk about what is true at the moment, what happens regularly and what is happening now; for example, *I'm a student*; *I travel to college by train*; *I'm studying languages*.

➤ In English, there are two tenses you can use to talk about the present:

- the <u>present simple</u> tense
  I <u>live</u> here.   They <u>get up</u> early.

- the <u>present continuous</u> tense
  He <u>is eating</u> an apple.   You <u>aren</u>'t <u>working</u> very hard.

➤ In Spanish, there is also a present simple and a present continuous tense. As in English, the present simple in Spanish is used to talk about:

- things that are generally true
  En invierno <u>hace</u> frío.   It<u>'s</u> cold in winter.

- things that are true at the moment
  Carlos no <u>come</u> carne.   Carlos <u>does</u>n't eat meat.

- things that happen at intervals
  A menudo <u>vamos</u> al cine.   We often <u>go</u> to the cinema.

➤ The <u>present continuous</u> tense in Spanish is used to talk about things that are happening right now or at the time of writing:
  Marta <u>está viendo</u> la televisión.   Marta <u>is watching</u> television.

➤ However, there are times where the use of the present tenses in the two languages is not exactly the same.

➪ *For more information on the use of the **Present tenses**, see pages 115 and 121.*

The present simple tense

Forming the present simple tense of regular -ar verbs

➤ If the infinitive of the Spanish verb ends in **-ar**, it means that the verb belongs to the <u>first conjugation</u>, for example, **hablar**, **lavar**, **llamar**.

➤ To know which form of the verb to use in Spanish, you need to work out what the stem of the verb is and then add the correct ending. The stem of regular **-ar** verbs in the present simple tense is formed by taking the <u>infinitive</u> and chopping off **-ar**.

Infinitive	Stem (without -ar)
hablar (*to speak*)	habl-
lavar (*to wash*)	lav-

➤ Now you know how to find the stem of a verb you can add the correct ending. The one you choose will depend on who or what is doing the action.

☑ Note that as the ending generally makes it clear who is doing the action, you usually don't need to add a subject pronoun such as **yo** (meaning *I*), **tú** (meaning *you*) as well.

⇨ *For more information on **Subject pronouns**, see page 55.*

➤ Here are the present simple endings for regular -**ar** verbs:

Present simple endings	Present simple of hablar	Meaning: *to speak*
-o	(yo) habl<u>o</u>	I speak
-as	(tú) habl<u>as</u>	you speak
-a	(él/ella) habl<u>a</u> (usted) habl<u>a</u>	he/she/it speaks you speak
-amos	(nosotros/nosotras) habl<u>amos</u>	we speak
-áis	(vosotros/vosotras) habl<u>áis</u>	you speak
-an	(ellos/ellas) habl<u>an</u> (ustedes) habl<u>an</u>	they speak you speak

➤ You use the **él/ella** (*third person singular*) form of the verb with nouns and with people's names when you are just talking about one person, animal or thing.

   Lydia habl<u>a</u> inglés.   Lydia speaks English.
   Mi profesor me ayud<u>a</u> mucho.   My teacher helps me a lot.

➤ You use the **ellos/ellas** (*third person plural*) form of the verb with nouns and with people's names when you are talking about more than one person, animal or thing.

   Lydia y Carlos habl<u>an</u> inglés.   Lydia and Carlos speak English.
   Mis profesores me ayud<u>an</u> mucho.   My teachers help me a lot.

☑ Note that even though you use the **él/ella** and **ellos/ellas** <u>forms</u> of the verb to talk about things in Spanish, you should <u>never</u> include the pronouns **él**, **ella**, **ellos** or **ellas** themselves in the sentence when referring to things.

   Funciona bien.   It works well.   **Funcionan bien.**   They work well.

⇨ *For more information on **Ways of saying 'you' in Spanish**, see page 57.*

KEY POINTS
✔ Verbs ending in -**ar** belong to the first conjugation. Regular -**ar** verbs form their present tense stem by losing the -**ar**.
✔ The present tense endings for regular -**ar** verbs are: -**o**, -**as**, -**a**, -**amos**, -**áis**, -**an**.
✔ You usually don't need to give a pronoun in Spanish as the ending of the verb makes it clear who or what is doing the action.

For further explanation of grammatical terms, please see pages viii-xii.

Test yourself

4 **Match the two columns.**

a	**Los niños**	todos juntos.
b	**Pepe**	estudias?
c	**No**	hablo inglés.
d	**Cenamos**	trabaja en Madrid.
e	**¿Dónde**	juegan en el patio.

5 **Complete the following sentences with the correct form of the present tense. The pronoun in brackets shows you which person to use.**

a Siempre .... la fruta en el mercado. **(comprar [yo])**

b .... el trabajo mañana. **(terminar [nosotros])**

c ¿ .... un chicle? **(dar [tú])**

d .... una coca. **(tomar [yo])**

e ¿A qué hora .... el concierto? **(terminar)**

f Nos .... sus padres. **(invitar)**

g .... en Londres. **(estudiar [ellos])**

h ¿Dónde .... ? **(trabajar [ustedes])**

i Mis padres .... inglés. **(hablar)**

j Mis hijos .... a las ocho. **(cenar)**

6 **Translate the following sentences into Spanish.**

a What's your name? ....

b Do you speak English? ....

c She works hard. ....

d He always cooks. ....

e Will you buy me this book? ....

f They go for a walk every day. ....

g We always buy the bread here. ....

h They talk to their grandparents every Sunday.

....

i Her name is Paz. ....

j She smokes too much. ....

Forming the present simple tense of regular -er verbs

➤ If the infinitive of the Spanish verb ends in -er, it means that the verb belongs to the <u>second conjugation</u>, for example, **comer**, **depender**.

➤ The stem of regular -er verbs in the present simple tense is formed by taking the <u>infinitive</u> and chopping off -er.

Infinitive	Stem (without -er)
comer (*to eat*)	com-
depender (*to depend*)	depend-

➤ Now add the correct ending, depending on who or what is doing the action.

> ⓘ Note that as the ending generally makes it clear who is doing the action, you usually don't need to add a subject pronoun such as **yo** (meaning *I*) or **tú** (meaning *you*) as well.

> ⇨ *For more information on* **Subject pronouns***, see page* 55.

➤ Here are the present simple endings for regular -er verbs:

Present simple endings	Present simple of comer	Meaning: *to eat*
-o	(yo) com<u>o</u>	I eat
-es	(tú) com<u>es</u>	you eat
-e	(él/ella) com<u>e</u> (usted) com<u>e</u>	he/she/it eats you eat
-emos	(nosotros/nosotras) com<u>emos</u>	we eat
-éis	(vosotros/vosotras) com<u>éis</u>	you eat
-en	(ellos/ellas) com<u>en</u> (ustedes) com<u>en</u>	they eat you eat

➤ You use the **él/ella** (*third person singular*) form of the verb with nouns and with people's names when you are just talking about one person, animal or thing.
  Juan com<u>e</u> demasiado.   Juan eats too much.
  Mi padre me deb<u>e</u> 15 euros.   My father owes me 15 euros.

➤ You use the **ellos/ellas** (*third person plural*) form of the verb with nouns and with people's names when you are talking about more than one person, animal or thing.
  Juan y Pedro com<u>en</u> demasiado.   Juan and Pedro eat too much.
  Mis padres me deb<u>en</u> 15 euros.   My parents owe me 15 euros.

> ⓘ Note that even though you use the **él/ella** and **ellos/ellas** forms of the verb to talk about things in Spanish, you should <u>never</u> include the pronouns **él**, **ella**, **ellos** or **ellas** themselves in the sentence when referring to things.

> **Depende.**   It depends.

> ⇨ *For more information on* **Ways of saying 'you' in Spanish***, see page* 57.

Key points

✔ Verbs ending in -er belong to the second conjugation. Regular -er verbs form their present tense stem by losing the -er.

✔ The present tense endings for regular -er verbs are: -o, -es, -e, -emos, -éis, -en.

✔ You usually don't need to give a pronoun in Spanish as the ending of the verb makes it clear who or what is doing the action.

Test yourself

7 Match the two columns.

a **Comemos**   ver la television por las noches.

b **José y Silvia**   crece mucho.

c **Nos gusta**   veo.

d **Juan**   a la una.

e **Luego te**   venden la casa.

8 Complete the following sentences with the correct form of the present tense.

a Marina nunca .... los deberes. **(hacer)**

b Esa planta .... mucho. **(crecer)**

c ¿A qué hora .... vosotros? **(comer)**

d ¿Qué se .... en esa tienda? **(vender)**

e Mi hermano .... mucho. **(leer)**

f Jorge y yo .... todas las noches. **(leer)**

g ¿Por qué no .... para quedarte a dormir? **(leer)**

h Nos .... la compra a casa. **(traer)**

i Olga siempre me .... un detalle. **(traer)**

j No se .... alcohol a menores de 18 años. **(vender)**

9 Create a sentence in the present tense using the elements given. Remember that, in Spanish, the subject of a verb is included in the verb form so it is not necessary to state it. Where it is not obvious, the subject of the verb is shown in square brackets to show you which verb form to use. Remember also that when the object of the verb is a pronoun, it usually comes before the verb.

a Laura/deber/dinero/a mí ....

b A qué hora/comer/ustedes ....

c eso/depender de/vosotros ....

d ¿meter/esto/en tu maleta/[tú]? ....

e siempre/ver/a ella/en el parque/[yo] ....

f comer/a las dos/todos los días/[ellos] ....

g Óscar/comer/muy poco ....

h siempre/meterte/en mis asuntos ....

i esa tienda/vender/ropa ....

j ¿no/temer/al profesor [tú]? ....

Forming the present simple tense of regular -ir verbs

➤ If the infinitive of the Spanish verb ends in -ir, it means that the verb belongs to the <u>third conjugation</u>, for example, **vivir**, **recibir**.

➤ The stem of regular -ir verbs in the present simple tense is formed by taking the <u>infinitive</u> and chopping off -ir.

Infinitive	Stem (without -ir)
vivir (*to live*)	**viv-**
recibir (*to receive, to get*)	**recib-**

➤ Now add the correct ending depending on who or what is doing the action.

> [i] Note that as the ending generally makes it clear who is doing the action, you usually don't need to add a subject pronoun such as **yo** (meaning *I*) or **tú** (meaning *you*) as well.

⇨ *For more information on **Subject pronouns**, see page 55.*

➤ Here are the present simple endings for regular -ir verbs:

Present simple endings	Present simple of vivir	Meaning: *to live*
-o	(yo) viv<u>o</u>	I live
-es	(tú) viv<u>es</u>	you live
-e	(él/ella) viv<u>e</u> (usted) viv<u>e</u>	he/she/it lives you live
-imos	(nosotros/nosotras) viv<u>imos</u>	we live
-ís	(vosotros/vosotras) vivís	you live
-en	(ellos/ellas) viv<u>en</u> (ustedes) viv<u>en</u>	they live you live

➤ You use the **él/ella** (*third person singular*) form of the verb with nouns and with people's names when you are just talking about one person, animal or thing.

> **Javier viv<u>e</u> aquí.**   Javier lives here.
> **Mi padre recib<u>e</u> muchas cartas.**   My father gets a lot of letters.

➤ You use the **ellos/ellas** (*third person plural*) form of the verb with nouns and with people's names, when you are talking about more than one person, animal or thing.

> **Javier y Antonia viv<u>en</u> aquí.** Javier and Antonia live here.
> **Mis padres recib<u>en</u> muchas cartas.**   My parents get a lot of letters.

> [i] Note that even though you use the **él/ella** and **ellos/ellas** forms of the verb to talk about things in Spanish, you should <u>never</u> include the pronouns **él**, **ella**, **ellos** or **ellas** themselves in the sentence when referring to things.

> **Ocurrió ayer.**   It happened yesterday.

⇨ *For more information on **Ways of saying 'you' in Spanish**, see page 57.*

> ## KEY POINTS
> ✔ Verbs ending in **-ir** belong to the third conjugation. Regular **-ir** verbs form their present tense stem by losing the **-ir**.
> ✔ The present tense endings for regular **-ir** verbs are: **- o, -es, -e, -imos, -ís, -en.**
> ✔ You usually don't need to give a pronoun in Spanish as the ending of the verb makes it clear who or what is doing the action.

Test yourself

10 **Complete the following sentences with the correct form of the present tense.**

    a   Mis padres y yo .... en Salamanca. **(vivir)**

    b   Mi hermano .... en Manchester. **(vivir)**

    c   Los tíos de Isabel .... en Barcelona. **(vivir)**

    d   ¿Dónde .... vosotros? **(vivir)**

    e   Mientras estudio, ... en Santiago. **(vivir)**

    f   ¿Quién .... la tarta? **(partir)**

    g   Felipe y yo .... muchas postales. **(recibir)**

    h   La profesora no se lo .... **(permitir)**

    i   No se lo .... sus padres. **(permitir)**

    j   Mi tía no .... ayuda de nadie. **(recibir)**

11 **Translate the following sentences into Spanish.**

    a   They live in Scotland. ....

    b   My sister lives alone. ....

    c   My mother insists. ....

    d   That isn't allowed. ....

    e   I receive a cheque every month. ....

    f   Where do your friends live? ....

    g   She always prints the invitations. ....

    h   They live near us. ....

    i   She always interrupts me. ....

    j   We get a lot of letters. ....

Test yourself

12 **Create a sentence in the present tense using the elements given. Remember that, in Spanish, the subject of a verb is included in the verb form so it is not necessary to state it. Where it is not obvious, the subject of the verb is shown in square brackets to show you which verb form to use. Remember also that when the object of the verb is a pronoun, it usually comes before the verb.**

a Antonio y yo/vivir/aquí ....

b dónde/vivir/tus amigos ....

c no se/permitir/fumar ....

d los profesores/no permitir/móviles/en clase/[a nosotros]
....

e siempre/recibir/muchos regalos/[ellos] ....

f nunca/interrumpir/la profesora/[nosotros]
....

g cuándo/recibir/la paga/[vosotros] ....

h por qué/interrumpirme/[tú] ....

i mis padres/insistir ....

j vivir/sola/[yo] ....

Forming the present simple tense of less regular verbs

➤ Many Spanish verbs do not follow the regular patterns shown previously. There are lots of verbs that change their <u>stem</u> in the present tense when the stress is on the stem. This means that all forms are affected in the present simple <u>APART FROM</u> the **nosotros** and **vosotros** forms. Such verbs are often called <u>radical-changing verbs</u>, meaning root-changing verbs.

➤ For example, some verbs containing an **-o** in the stem change it to **-ue** in the present simple for all forms <u>APART FROM</u> the **nosotros/nosotras** and **vosotros/vosotras** forms.

	encontrar *to find*	recordar *to remember*	poder *to be able*	dormir *to sleep*
(yo)	enc<u>ue</u>ntro	rec<u>ue</u>rdo	p<u>ue</u>do	d<u>ue</u>rmo
(tú)	enc<u>ue</u>ntras	rec<u>ue</u>rdas	p<u>ue</u>des	d<u>ue</u>rmes
(él/ella/ usted)	enc<u>ue</u>ntra	rec<u>ue</u>rda	p<u>ue</u>de	d<u>ue</u>rme
(nosotros/as)	enc<u>o</u>ntramos	rec<u>o</u>rdamos	p<u>o</u>demos	d<u>o</u>rmimos
(vosotros/as)	enc<u>o</u>ntráis	rec<u>o</u>rdáis	p<u>o</u>déis	d<u>o</u>rmís
(ellos/ellas/ ustedes)	enc<u>ue</u>ntran	rec<u>ue</u>rdan	p<u>ue</u>den	d<u>ue</u>rmen

➤ Other verbs containing an **-e** in the stem change it to **-ie** for all forms <u>APART FROM</u> the **nosotros/nosotras** and **vosotros/vosotras** forms.

	cerrar *to close*	pensar *to think*	entender *to understand*	perder *to lose*	preferir *to prefer*
(yo)	c<u>ie</u>rro	p<u>ie</u>nso	ent<u>ie</u>ndo	p<u>ie</u>rdo	pref<u>ie</u>ro
(tú)	c<u>ie</u>rras	p<u>ie</u>nsas	ent<u>ie</u>ndes	p<u>ie</u>rdes	pref<u>ie</u>res
(él/ella/ usted)	c<u>ie</u>rra	p<u>ie</u>nsa	ent<u>ie</u>nde	p<u>ie</u>rde	pref<u>ie</u>re
(nosotros/as)	c<u>e</u>rramos	p<u>e</u>nsamos	ent<u>e</u>ndemos	p<u>e</u>rdemos	pref<u>e</u>rimos
(vosotros/as)	c<u>e</u>rráis	p<u>e</u>nsáis	ent<u>e</u>ndéis	p<u>e</u>rdéis	pref<u>e</u>rís
(ellos/ellas/ ustedes)	c<u>ie</u>rran	p<u>ie</u>nsan	ent<u>ie</u>nden	p<u>ie</u>rden	pref<u>ie</u>ren

➤ A few **-ir** verbs containing **-e** in the stem change this to **-i** in the present simple for all forms <u>APART FROM</u> the **nosotros/nosotras** and **vosotros/ vosotras** forms.

	pedir *to ask (for)*	servir *to serve*
(yo)	p<u>i</u>do	s<u>i</u>rvo
(tú)	p<u>i</u>des	s<u>i</u>rves
(él/ella/usted)	p<u>i</u>de	s<u>i</u>rve
(nosotros/as)	p<u>e</u>dimos	s<u>e</u>rvimos
(vosotros/as)	p<u>e</u>dís	s<u>e</u>rvís
(ellos/ellas/ustedes)	p<u>i</u>den	s<u>i</u>rven

➤ If you are not sure whether a Spanish verb belongs to this group of <u>radical-changing verbs</u>, you can look up the **Verb Tables** in the supplement.

⇨ *For more information on **Spelling**, see page 263.*

Forming the present simple tense of common irregular verbs

➤ There are many other verbs that do not follow the usual patterns in Spanish. These include some very common and important verbs such as **tener** (meaning *to have*), **hacer** (meaning *to do* or *to make*) and **ir** (meaning *to go*). These verbs are shown in full on the next page.

➤ Here are the present simple tense endings for **tener**:

	tener	**Meaning: *to have***
(yo)	**tengo**	I have
(tú)	**tienes**	you have
(él/ella/usted)	**tiene**	he/she/it has, you have
(nosotros/nosotras)	**tenemos**	we have
(vosotros/vosotras)	**tenéis**	you have
(ellos/ellas/ustedes)	**tienen**	they have, you have

<u>Tengo</u> dos hermanas.   I have two sisters.
No <u>tengo</u> dinero.   I haven't any money.
¿Cuántos sellos <u>tienes</u>?   How many stamps have you got?
<u>Tiene</u> el pelo rubio.   He has blond hair.

➤ Here are the present simple tense endings for **hacer**:

	hacer	**Meaning: *to do, to make***
(yo)	**hago**	I do, I make
(tú)	**haces**	you do, you make
(él/ella/usted)	**hace**	he/she/it does, he/she/it makes, you do, you make
(nosotros/nosotras)	**hacemos**	we do, we make
(vosotros/vosotras)	**hacéis**	you do, you make
(ellos/ellas/ustedes)	**hacen**	they do, they make, you do, you make

<u>Hago</u> una tortilla.   I'm making an omelette.
No <u>hago</u> mucho deporte.   I don't do a lot of sport.
¿Qué <u>haces</u>?   What are you doing?
<u>Hace</u> calor.   It's hot.

➤ Here are the present simple tense endings for **ir**:

	ir	Meaning: *to go*
(yo)	voy	I go
(tú)	vas	you go
(él/ella/usted)	va	he/she/it goes, you go
(nosotros/nosotras)	vamos	we go
(vosotros/vosotras)	vais	you go
(ellos/ellas/ustedes)	van	they go, you go

Voy a Salamanca.   I'm going to Salamanca.
¿Adónde vas?   Where are you going?
No va al colegio.   He doesn't go to school.
No van a vender la casa.   They aren't going to sell the house.

⇨ *For other irregular verbs in the present simple tense, see* **Verb Tables** *in the supplement.*

How to use the present simple tense in Spanish

➤ The present simple tense is often used in Spanish in the same way as it is in English, although there are some differences.

➤ As in English, you use the Spanish present simple to talk about:

- things that are generally true
  En verano hace calor.   It's hot in summer.

- things that are true now
  Viven en Francia.   They live in France.

- things that happen all the time or at certain intervals or that you do as a habit
  Marta lleva gafas.   Marta wears glasses.
  Mi tío vende mariscos.   My uncle sells shellfish.

- things that you are planning to do
  El domingo jugamos en León.   We're playing in León on Sunday.
  Mañana voy a Madrid.   I am going to Madrid tomorrow.

➤ There are some instances when you would use the present simple in Spanish, but you wouldn't use it in English:

- to talk about current projects and activities that may not actually be going on right at this very minute
  Construye una casa.   He's building a house.

- when you use certain time expressions in Spanish, especially **desde** (meaning *since*) and **desde hace** (meaning *for*), to talk about activities and states that started in the past and are still going on now
  Jaime vive aquí desde hace dos años.   Jaime has been living here for two years.
  Daniel vive aquí desde 1999.   Daniel has lived here since 1999.
  Llevo horas esperando aquí.   I've been waiting here for hours.

⇨ *For more information on the use of tenses with* **desde***, see page 285.*

ser and estar

➤ In Spanish there are two irregular verbs, **ser** and **estar**, that both mean *to be*, although they are used very differently. In the present simple tense, they follow the patterns shown below.

Pronoun	ser	estar	Meaning: *to be*
(yo)	soy	estoy	I am
(tú)	eres	estás	you are
(él/ella/usted)	es	está	he/she/it is, you are
(nosotros/nosotras)	somos	estamos	we are
(vosotros/ vosotras)	sois	estáis	you are
(elllos/ellas/ustedes)	son	están	they/you are

➤ **ser** is used:

- with an adjective when talking about a characteristic or fairly permanent quality, for example, shape, size, height, colour, material, nationality.

Mi hermano es alto.	My brother is tall.
María es inteligente.	María is intelligent.
Es rubia.	She's blonde.
Es muy guapa.	She's very pretty.
Es rojo.	It's red.
Es de algodón.	It's made of cotton.
Sus padres son italianos.	His parents are Italian.
Es joven/viejo.	He's young/old.
Son muy ricos/pobres.	They're very rich/poor.

- with a following noun or pronoun that tells you what someone or something is

Miguel es camarero.	Miguel is a waiter.
Soy yo, Enrique.	It's me, Enrique.
Madrid es la capital de España.	Madrid is the capital of Spain.

- to say that something belongs to someone

La casa es de Javier.	The house belongs to Javier.
Es mío.	It's mine.

- to talk about where someone or something comes from

Yo soy de Escocia.	I'm from Scotland.
Mi mujer es de Granada.	My wife is from Granada.

- to say what time it is or what the date is

Son las tres y media.	It's half past three.
Mañana es sábado.	Tomorrow is Saturday.

- in calculations

Tres y dos son cinco.	Three and two are five.
¿Cuánto es? — Son dos euros.	How much is it? It's two euros.

- when followed by an infinitive

Lo importante es decir la verdad.	The important thing is to tell the truth.

⇨ *For more information on the **Infinitive**, see page 201.*

For further explanation of grammatical terms, please see pages viii-xii.

- to describe actions using the passive (for example *they are made, it is sold*)
  Son fabricados en España.   They are made in Spain.

- to talk about where an event is taking place
  La boda será en Madrid.   The wedding will be in Madrid.

➪ *For more information on the **Passive**, see page 175.*

➤ **estar** is used:

- to talk about where someone or something (other than an event) is
  Estoy en Madrid.   I'm in Madrid.
  ¿Dónde está Burgos?   Where's Burgos?

- with an adjective when there has been a change in the condition of someone or something or to suggest that there is something unexpected about them
  El café está frío.   The coffee's cold.
  ¡Qué guapa estás con este vestido!   How pretty you look in that dress!

➪ *For more information on **Adjectives**, see page 25.*

- with a past participle used as an adjective, to describe the state that something is in
  Las tiendas están cerradas.   The shops are closed.
  No está terminado.   It isn't finished.
  Está roto.   It's broken.

➪ *For more information on **Past participles**, see page 164.*

- when talking about someone's health
  ¿Cómo están ustedes?   How are you?
  Estamos todos bien.   We're all well.

- to form continuous tenses such as the present continuous tense
  Está comiendo.   He's eating.
  Estamos aprendiendo mucho.   We are learning a great deal.

➪ *For more information on the **Present continuous**, see page 121.*

➤ Both **ser** and **estar** can be used with certain adjectives, but the meaning changes depending on which is used.

➤ Use **ser** to talk about <u>permanent</u> qualities.
  Marta es muy joven.   Marta is very young.
  Es delgado.   He's slim.
  Viajar es cansado.   Travelling is tiring.
  La química es aburrida.   Chemistry is boring.

➤ Use **estar** to talk about <u>temporary</u> states or qualities.
  Está muy joven con ese vestido.   She looks very young in that dress.
  ¡Estás muy delgada!   You're looking very slim!
  Hoy estoy cansado.   I'm tired today.
  Estoy aburrido.   I'm bored.

➤ **ser** is used with adjectives such as **importante** (meaning *important*) and **imposible** (meaning *impossible*) when the subject is *it* in English.

Es muy interesante.	It's very interesting.
Es imposible.	It's impossible.
Es fácil.	It's easy.

➤ **ser** is used in certain set phrases.

Es igual *or* **Es lo mismo.**	It's all the same.
Es para ti.	It's for you.

➤ **estar** is also used in some set phrases.

- **estar de pie**   to be standing
Juan está de pie.	Juan is standing.

- **estar de vacaciones**   to be on holiday
¿Estás de vacaciones?	Are you on holiday?

- **estar de viaje**   to be on a trip
Mi padre está de viaje.	My father's on a trip.

- **estar de moda**   to be in fashion
Las pantallas de plasma están de moda.	Plasma screens are in fashion.

- **estar claro**   to be obvious
Está claro que no entiendes.	It's obvious that you don't understand.

Grammar Extra!
Both **ser** and **estar** can be used with past participles. Use **ser** and the past participle in passive constructions to describe an action.
Son fabricados en España.   They are made in Spain.

Use **estar** and the past participle to describe a state.
Está terminado.   It's finished.

⇨ For more information on **Past participles**, see page 164.

KEY POINTS
- ✔ **ser** and **estar** both mean *to be* in English, but are used very differently.
- ✔ **ser** and **estar** are irregular verbs. You have to learn them.
- ✔ Use **ser** with adjectives describing permanent qualities or characteristics; with nouns or pronouns telling you who or what somebody or something is; with time and dates; and to form the passive.
- ✔ Use **estar** to talk about location; health; with adjectives describing a change of state; and with past participles used as adjectives to describe states.
- ✔ **estar** is also used to form present continuous tenses.
- ✔ **ser** and **estar** can sometimes be used with the same adjectives, but the meaning changes depending on which verb is used.
- ✔ **ser** and **estar** are both used in a number of set phrases.

Test yourself

13 **Complete the following sentences with the correct form of the verbs** ser **or** estar.

a Miguel .... alto. **(ser)**

b Juan y yo .... felices. **(ser)**

c Juana .... muy guapa. **(estar)**

d No puedo ir porque .... en Sevilla. **(estar)**

e Ese .... el coche de mi jefe. **(ser)**

f Mis padres .... los dos abogados. **(ser)**

g Nuestra casa .... al otro lado del parque. **(estar)**

h Necesitamos unas vacaciones porque .... muy cansados. **(estar)**

i El agua .... fría. **(estar)**

j .... las cuatro de la tarde. **(ser)**

14 **Complete the following sentences with the correct form of** ser **or** estar.

a La piscina .... abierta de abril a octubre.

b Jorge e Isabel .... primos.

c La boda .... el sábado.

d La línea .... ocupada.

e Sofía todavía .... enfadada.

f Nuestros vecinos .... argentinos.

g ¿Dónde .... Zaragoza?

h ¿Quiénes .... esos hombres?

i Mi marido .... de Glasgow.

j Este coche .... mío.

15 **Match the two columns.**

a	**Estoy aburrido.**	Your father looks very young.
b	**Es muy aburrida.**	It's delicious.
c	**Tu padre es muy joven.**	She's very boring.
d	**Tu padre está muy joven.**	I'm bored.
e	**Está muy rica.**	Your father's very young.

PRACTICE PRACTICE PRACTICE PRACTICE PRACTICE PRACTICE

16 **Translate the following sentences into Spanish.**

a I'm tired. ....

b She's bored. ....

c The film is boring. ....

d They're on holiday. ....

e My parents are on a trip.

....

f Yoga is in fashion. ....

g This exam is easy. ....

h The programme is very interesting.

....

i This is for you. ....

j How are you *(familiar, plural)*? ....

The present continuous tense

➤ In Spanish, the present continuous tense is used to talk about something that is happening at this very moment.

➤ The Spanish present continuous tense is formed from the <u>present tense</u> of **estar** and the <u>gerund</u> of the verb. The gerund is the form of the verb that ends in **-ando** (for **-ar** verbs) or **-iendo** (for **-er** and **-ir** verbs) and is the same as the -ing form of the verb in English (for example, walking, swimming).

<u>**Estoy** trabaj<u>ando</u></u>	I'm working.
No <u>estamos</u> com<u>iendo</u>.	We aren't eating.
¿<u>Estás</u> escrib<u>iendo</u>?	Are you writing?

⇨ For more information on **estar** and the **Gerund**, see pages 116 and 180.

➤ To form the gerund of an -**ar** verb, take off the -**ar** ending of the infinitive and add -**ando**:

Infinitive	Meaning	Stem (without -**ar**)	Gerund	Meaning
hablar	to speak	habl-	habl<u>ando</u>	speaking
trabajar	to work	trabaj-	trabaj<u>ando</u>	working

➤ To form the gerund of an -**er** or -**ir** verb, take off the -**er** or -**ir** ending of the infinitive and add -**iendo**:

Infinitive	Meaning	Stem (without -**er**/-**ir**)	Gerund	Meaning
comer	to eat	com-	com<u>iendo</u>	eating
escribir	to write	escrib-	escrib<u>iendo</u>	writing

> **Tip**
>
> Only use the present continuous to talk about things that are in the middle of happening right now. Use the present simple tense instead to talk about activities which are current but which may not be happening at this minute.
>
> **María <u>trabaja</u> en el hospital.**   María works at the hospital.
>
> ⇨ For more information on the **Present simple tense**, see page 103.

> **KEY POINTS**
> ✔ Only use the present continuous in Spanish for actions that are happening right now.
> ✔ To form the present continuous tense in Spanish, take the present tense of **estar** and add the gerund of the main verb.

Test yourself

17 Replace the highlighted verb with the present continuous form.

a **Estudia** medicina. ....

b **Cenamos** en un restaurante.
....

c **Vive** en Valencia. ....

d **Escribe** un cuento infantil.
....

e **Trabajo** en un hotel. ....

f **Hablan** con la vecina. ....

g **Vemos** una película. ....

h ¿Qué **lees**? ....

i **Estudio** en Londres. ....

j **Compran** una casa en el pueblo.
....

18 Match the English and the Spanish columns.

a **Están trabajando mucho.**   They're getting very rich.

b **Los están vendiendo baratos.**   He's reading a book.

c **Están haciéndose muy ricos.**   They're laughing at me.

d **Está leyendo un libro.**   They're selling them cheap.

e **Se están riendo de mí.**   They're working a lot.

19 **Complete the following sentences with the correct form of the present continuous.**

a   No puedo ir ahora porque .... **(comer)**

b   No podemos ir de vacaciones porque .... una casa. **(comprar)**

c   .... con su madre. **(Hablar)**

d   Los niños .... la tele. **(ver)**

e   Susana .... los deberes. **(hacer)**

f   Pablo y yo .... la cocina. **(pintar)**

g   Los demás .... un refresco. **(tomar)**

h   No lo molestes porque .... **(descansar)**

i   Lucía .... en la playa. **(tomar el sol)**

j   Ahora voy. Solo .... un vaso de agua. **(beber)**

20 **Match the reply to the question.**

a   **¿Qué estás cocinando?**   Porque está contenta.

b   **¿Que queréis cenar?**   Estamos lavando el coche.

c   **¿Dónde está tu madre?**   Estoy haciendo una tortilla.

d   **¿Qué estáis haciendo?**   Pescado con ensalada.

e   **¿Por qué está cantando?**   Está haciendo la compra.

The imperative

What is the imperative?
An **imperative** is a form of the verb used when giving orders and instructions, for example, *Sit down!*; *Don't go!*; *Let's start!*

Using the imperative

➤ In Spanish, the form of the imperative that you use for giving instructions depends on:

- whether you are telling someone to do something or not to do something

- whether you are talking to one person or to more than one person

- whether you are on familiar or more formal terms with the person or people

➤ These imperative forms correspond to the familiar **tú** and **vosotros/ vosotras** and to the more formal **usted** and **ustedes**, although you don't actually say these pronouns when giving instructions.

⇨ *For more information on Ways of saying 'you' in Spanish, see page 57.*

➤ There is also a form of the imperative that corresponds to *let's* in English.

Forming the imperative: instructions not to do something

➤ In orders that tell you <u>NOT</u> to do something and that have **no** in front of them in Spanish, the imperative forms for **tú**, **usted**, **nosotros/nosotras**, **vosotros/vosotras** and **ustedes** are all taken from a verb form called the <u>present subjunctive</u>. It's easy to remember because the endings for **-ar** and **-er** verbs are the opposite of what they are in the ordinary present tense.

⇨ *For more information on the Present tense and the Subjunctive, see pages 103 and 190.*

➤ In regular -**ar** verbs, you take off the -**as**, -**a**, -**amos**, -**áis** and -**an** endings of the present tense and replace them with: -**es**, -**e**, -**emos**, -**éis** and -**en**.

-ar **verb**	**trabajar**	**to work**
tú form	¡no trabajes!	Don't work!
usted form	¡no trabaje!	Don't work!
nosotros/as form	¡no trabajemos!	Let's not work!
vosotros/as form	¡no trabajéis!	Don't work!
ustedes form	¡no trabajen!	Don't work!

➤ In regular **-er** verbs, you take off the **-es**, **-e**, **-emos**, **-éis** and **-en** endings of the present tense and replace them with **-as**, **-a**, **-amos**, **-áis** and **-an**.

-er verb	comer	to eat
tú form	¡no comas!	Don't eat!
usted form	¡no coma!	Don't eat!
nosotros/as form	¡no comamos!	Let's not eat!
vosotros/as form	¡no comáis!	Don't eat!
ustedes form	¡no coman!	Don't eat!

➤ In regular **-ir** verbs, you take off the **-es**, **-e**, **-imos**, **-ís** and **-en** endings of the present tense and replace them with **-as**, **-a**, **-amos**, **-áis** and **-an**.

-ir verb	decidir	to decide
tú form	¡no decidas!	Don't decide!
usted form	¡no decida!	Don't decide!
nosotros/as form	¡no decidamos!	Let's not decide!
vosotros/as form	¡no decidáis!	Don't decide!
ustedes form	¡no decidan!	Don't decide!

➤ A number of irregular verbs also have irregular imperative forms. These are shown in the table below.

	dar to give	decir to say	estar to be	hacer to do/make	ir to go
tú form	¡no des! don't give!	¡no digas! don't say!	¡no estés! don't be!	¡no hagas! don't do/make!	¡no vayas! don't go!
usted form	¡no dé! don't give!	¡no diga! don't say!	¡no esté! don't be!	¡no haga! don't do/make!	¡no vaya! don't go!
nosotros/as form	¡no demos! let's not give!	¡no digamos! let's not say!	¡no estemos! let's not be!	¡no hagamos! let's not do/make!	¡no vayamos! let's not go!
vosotros/as form	¡no deis! don't give!	¡no digáis! don't say!	¡no estéis! don't be!	¡no hagáis! don't do/make!	¡no vayáis! don't go!
ustedes form	¡no den! don't give!	¡no digan! don't say!	¡no estén! don't be!	¡no hagan! don't do/make!	¡no vayan! don't go!
	poner to put	**salir** to leave	**ser** to be	**tener** to have	**venir** to come
tú form	¡no pongas! don't put!	¡no salgas! don't leave!	¡no seas! don't be!	¡no tengas! don't have!	¡no vengas! don't come!
usted form	¡no ponga! don't put!	¡no salga! don't leave!	¡no sea! don't be!	¡no tenga! don't have!	¡no venga! don't come!
nosotros/as form	¡no pongamos! let's not put!	¡no salgamos! let's not leave!	¡no seamos! let's not be!	¡no tengamos! let's not have!	¡no vengamos! let's not come!
vosotros/as form	¡no pongáis! don't put!	¡no salgáis! don't leave!	¡no seáis! don't be!	¡no tengáis! don't have!	¡no vengáis! don't come!
ustedes form	¡no pongan! don't put!	¡no salgan! don't leave!	¡no sean! don't be!	¡no tengan! don't have!	¡no vengan! don't come!

i Note that if you take the **yo** form of the present tense, take off the **-o** and add the endings to this instead for instructions <u>NOT TO DO</u> something, some of these irregular forms will be more predictable.

digo	*I say*	→	negative imperative stem	→	**dig-**
hago	*I do*	→	negative imperative stem	→	**hag-**
pongo	*I put*	→	negative imperative stem	→	**pong-**
salgo	*I leave*	→	negative imperative stem	→	**salg-**
tengo	*I have*	→	negative imperative stem	→	**teng-**
vengo	*I come*	→	negative imperative stem	→	**veng-**

Forming the imperative: instructions to do something

➤ In instructions telling you <u>TO DO</u> something, the forms for **usted**, **nosotros** and **ustedes** are exactly the same as they are in negative instructions (instructions telling you not to do something) except that there isn't a **no**.

	trabajar to work	**comer** to eat	**decidir** to decide
usted form	¡Trabaje!	¡Coma!	¡Decida!
nosotros/as form	¡Trabajemos!	¡Comamos!	¡Decidamos!
ustedes form	¡Trabajen!	¡Coman!	¡Decidan!

➤ There are special forms of the imperative for **tú** and **vosotros/vosotras** in positive instructions (instructions telling you to do something).

➤ The **tú** form of the imperative is the same as the **tú** form of the ordinary present simple tense, but without the final **-s**.

trabajar	→	**¡Trabaja!**
to work		Work!
comer	→	**¡Come!**
to eat		Eat!
decidir	→	**¡Decide!**
to decide		Decide!

⇨ *For more information on the **Present simple tense**, see page 103.*

➤ The **vosotros/vosotras** form of the imperative is the same as the infinitive, except that you take off the final **-r** and add **-d** instead.

trabajar	→	**Trabajad!**
to work		Work!
comer	→	**Comed!**
to eat		Eat!
decidir	→	**Decidid!**
to decide		Decide!

➤ There are a number of imperative forms that are irregular in Spanish. The irregular imperative forms for **usted**, **nosotros/nosotras** and **ustedes** are the same as the irregular negative imperative forms without the **no**. The **tú** and **vosotros/vosotras** forms are different again.

	dar to give	**decir** to say	**estar** to be	**hacer** to do/make	**ir** to go
tú form	¡da! give!	¡di! say!	¡está! be!	¡haz! do/make!	¡ve! go!
usted form	¡dé! give!	¡diga! say!	¡esté! be!	¡haga! do/make!	¡vaya! go!
nosotros/as form	¡demos! let's give!	¡digamos! let's say!	¡estemos! let's be!	¡hagamos! let's do/make!	¡vamos! let's go!
vosotros/as form	¡dad! give!	¡decid! say!	¡estad! be!	¡haced! do/make!	¡id! go!
ustedes form	¡den! give!	¡digan! say!	¡estén! be!	¡hagan! do/make!	¡vayan! go!
	poner to put	**salir** to leave	**ser** to be	**tener** to have	**venir** to come
tú form	¡pon! put!	¡sal! leave!	¡sé! be!	¡ten! have!	¡ven! come!
usted form	¡ponga! put!	¡salga! leave!	¡sea! be!	¡tenga! have!	¡venga! come!
nosotros/as form	¡pongamos! let's put!	¡salgamos! let's leave!	¡seamos! let's be!	¡tengamos! let's have!	¡vengamos! let's come!
vosotros/as form	¡poned! put!	¡salid! leave!	¡sed! be!	¡tened! have!	¡venid! come!
ustedes form	¡pongan! put!	¡salgan! leave!	¡sean! be!	¡tengan! have!	¡vengan! come!

ⓘ Note that the **nosotros/as** form for **ir** in instructions <u>TO DO</u> something is **vamos**; in instructions <u>NOT TO DO</u> something, it is **no vayamos**.

Position of object pronouns

➤ An object pronoun is a word like **me** (meaning *me* or *to me*), **la** (meaning *her/it*) or **les** (meaning *to them/to you*) that is used instead of a noun as the object of a sentence. In orders and instructions, the position of these object pronouns in the sentence changes depending on whether you are telling someone <u>TO DO</u> something or <u>NOT TO DO</u> something.

⇨ *For more information on **Object pronouns**, see page 61.*

➤ If you are telling someone <u>NOT TO DO</u> something, the object pronouns go BEFORE the verb.

¡No <u>me lo</u> mandes!	Don't send it to me!
¡No <u>me</u> molestes!	Don't disturb me!
¡No <u>los</u> castigue!	Don't punish them!
¡No <u>se la</u> devolvamos!	Let's not give it back to him/her/them!
¡No <u>las</u> contestéis!	Don't answer them!

➤ If you are telling someone <u>TO DO</u> something, the object pronouns join on to the <u>END</u> of the verb. An accent is usually added to make sure that the stress in the imperative verb stays the same.

¡Explícamelo!	Explain it to me!
¡Perdóneme!	Excuse me!
¡Dígame!	Tell me!
¡Esperémosla!	Let's wait for her/it!

ⓘ Note that when there are two object pronouns, the indirect object pronoun always goes before the direct object pronoun.

⇨ *For more information on **Stress**, see page 266.*

Other ways of giving instructions

➤ For general instructions in instruction leaflets, recipes and so on, use the <u>infinitive</u> form instead of the imperative.

<u>Ver</u> **página 9.**	See page 9.

➤ **vamos a** with the infinitive is often used to mean *let's*.

<u>Vamos</u> **a ver.**	Let's see.
<u>Vamos</u> **a empezar.**	Let's start.

KEY POINTS

✔ In Spanish, in instructions <u>not to do</u> something, the endings are taken from the present subjunctive. They are the same as the corresponding endings for **-ar** and **-er** verbs in the ordinary present tense, except that the **-e** endings go on the **-ar** verbs and the **-a** endings go on the **-er** and **-ir** verbs.

✔ For **-ar** verbs, the forms are: **no hables** (**tú** form); **no hable** (**usted** form); **no hablemos** (**nosotros/as** form); **no habléis** (**vosotros/as** form); **no hablen** (**ustedes** form).

✔ For **-er** verbs, the forms are: **no comas** (**tú** form); **no coma** (**usted** form); **no comamos** (**nosotros/as** form); **no comáis** (**vosotros/as** form); **no coman** (**ustedes** form).

✔ For **-ir** verbs, the forms are: **no decidas** (**tú** form); **no decida** (**usted** form); **no decidamos** (**nosotros/as** form); **no decidáis** (**vosotros/as** form); **no decidan** (**ustedes** form).

✔ In instructions <u>to do</u> something, the forms for **usted**, **nosotros/as** and **ustedes** are the same as they are in instructions not to do something.

✔ The forms for **tú** and **vosotros/as** are different:
  ● the **tú** form is the same as the corresponding form in the ordinary present tense, but without the final **-s**: **trabaja**; **come**; **decide**
  ● the **vosotros/as** form is the same as the infinitive but with a final **-d** instead of the **-r**: **trabajad**; **comed**; **decidid**

✔ A number of verbs have irregular imperative forms.

✔ The object pronouns in imperatives go before the verb when telling someone not to do something; they join onto the end of the verb when telling someone to do something.

Test yourself

21 **Translate the following instructions into Spanish using the imperative forms. Where appropriate, assume you are addressing one person with whom you are on familiar terms.**

a Don't speak to me! ....

b Give me that! ....

c Tell me right now! ....

d Don't send it to them! ....

e Give them to me! ....

f Let's wait for them here. ....

g Don't touch it! ....

h Don't say that! ....

i Let's finish this exercise. ....

j Put that there! ....

22 **Give an instruction using the elements below. The subject pronouns are given to show who the instruction is for but remember you may not need to use them.**

a [tú]/trabajar/más rápido ....

b [vosotros]/comer/en silencio ....

c [nosotros]/comprar/este coche ....

d [tú]/callar/la boca ....

e [vosotros]/no/tardar ....

f [nosotros]/ir/al centro ....

g [vosotros]/esperar/a mí/ahí ....

h [tú]/no/hablar/tan alto ....

i [tú]/hablar/más bajito ....

j [vosotros]/no/hacer/tanto ruido ....

Test yourself

23 **¿Me traes un vaso? is more polite than using the imperative: ¡Tráeme un vaso!.
Change the question into an order, remembering that the order of the pronoun
may change.**

a ¿Miras esto? ....

b ¿Me escucháis, por favor? ....

c ¿Le das un poco a tu hermana?

....

d ¿Me lo cuentas? ....

e ¿Me esperas? ....

f ¿Me lo compras? ....

g ¿Les ayudáis? ....

h ¿Terminas los deberes antes de cenar?

....

i ¿Me dices lo que te pasa? ....

j ¿Me permites? ....

24 **Replace the highlighted negative command with a positive one.**

a **¡No te vayas** sin ellos! ....

b **¡No me dejes** sola! ....

c **¡No comas** el último! ....

d **¡No lo comáis** todo! ....

e **¡No me despiertes** temprano! ....

f **¡No le dejéis** el coche! ....

g **¡No le hables** a tu hermano! ....

h **¡No la llames** antes de las diez! ....

i **¡No te atrevas**! ....

j **¡No los esperemos**! ....

Reflexive verbs

What is a reflexive verb?
A **reflexive verb** is one where the subject and object are the same, and where the action 'reflects back' on the subject. It is used with a reflexive pronoun such as *myself*, *yourself* and *herself* in English, for example, *I washed myself.*; *He shaved himself.*

Using reflexive verbs

➤ In Spanish, reflexive verbs are much more common than in English, and many are used in everyday language. The infinitive form of a reflexive verb has **se** attached to the end of it, for example, **secarse** (meaning *to dry oneself*). This is the way reflexive verbs are shown in dictionaries. **se** means *himself, herself, itself, yourself, themselves, yourselves* and *oneself*. **se** is called a <u>reflexive pronoun</u>.

➤ In Spanish, reflexive verbs are often used to describe things you do to yourself every day or that involve a change of some sort, for example, going to bed, sitting down, getting angry, and so on. Some of the most common reflexive verbs in Spanish are listed here.

acostarse	to go to bed
afeitarse	to shave
bañarse	to have a bath, to have a swim
dormirse	to go to sleep
ducharse	to have a shower
enfadarse	to get angry
lavarse	to wash
levantarse	to get up
llamarse	to be called
secarse	to get dried
sentarse	to sit down
vestirse	to get dressed

Me <u>baño</u> a las siete y media.	I have a bath at half past seven.
¡<u>Duérmete</u>!	Go to sleep!
Mi hermana <u>se ducha</u>.	My sister has a shower.
Mi madre <u>se enfada</u> mucho.	My mother often gets angry.
Mi hermano no <u>se lava</u>.	My brother doesn't wash.
Me <u>levanto</u> a las siete.	I get up at seven o'clock.
¿Cómo <u>te llamas</u>?	What's your name?
¿A qué hora <u>os acostáis</u>?	What time do you go to bed?
¡<u>Sentaos</u>!	Sit down!
<u>Nos vestimos</u>.	We're getting dressed.

i Note that **se**, **me** and so on are very rarely translated as *himself, myself* and so on in English. Instead of *he dresses himself* or *they bath themselves*, in English, we are more likely to say *he gets dressed* or *they have a bath*.

➤ Some Spanish verbs can be used both as reflexive verbs and as ordinary verbs (without the reflexive pronoun). When they are used as ordinary verbs, the person or thing doing the action is not the same as the person or thing receiving the action, so the meaning is different.

Me lavo.	I wash (myself).
Lavo la ropa a mano.	I wash the clothes by hand.
Me llamo Antonio.	I'm called Antonio.
¡Llama a la policía!	Call the police!
Me acuesto a las 11.	I go to bed at 11 o'clock.
Acuesta al niño.	He puts the child to bed.

Grammar Extra!
Some verbs mean <u>ALMOST</u> the same in the reflexive as when they are used on their own.

Duermo.	I sleep.
Me duermo.	I go to sleep.
¿Quieres <u>ir</u> al cine?	Do you want to go to the cinema?
Acaba de ir<u>se</u>.	He has just left.

Forming the present tense of reflexive verbs

➤ To use a reflexive verb in Spanish, you need to decide which reflexive pronoun to use. See how the reflexive pronouns in the table on the next page correspond to the subject pronouns.

Subject pronoun	Reflexive pronoun	Meaning
(yo)	me	myself
(tú)	te	yourself
(él), (ella), (uno) (usted)	se	himself, herself, oneself, itself, yourself
(nosotros/nosotras)	nos	ourselves
(vosotros/vosotras)	os	yourselves
(ellos), (ellas) (ustedes)	se	themselves yourselves

(Yo) <u>me</u> levanto temprano.	I get up early.
(Él) <u>se</u> acuesta a las once.	He goes to bed at eleven.
Ellos no <u>se</u> afeitan.	They don't shave.

➤ The present tense forms of a reflexive verb work in just the same way as an ordinary verb, except that the reflexive pronoun is used as well.

➪ *For more information on the **Present tense**, see page 103.*

➤ The following table shows the reflexive verb **lavarse** in full.

Reflexive forms of lavarse	Meaning
(yo) **me lavo**	I wash (myself)
(tú) **te lavas**	you wash (yourself)
(él) **se lava** (ella) **se lava** (uno) **se lava, se lava** (usted) **se lava**	he washes (himself) she washes (herself) one washes (oneself), it washes (itself) you wash (yourself)
(nosotros/nosotras) **nos lavamos**	we wash (ourselves)
(vosotros/vosotras) **os laváis**	you wash (yourselves)
(ellos) **se lavan** (ellas) **se lavan** (ustedes) **se lavan**	they wash (themselves) they wash (themselves) you wash (yourselves)

➤ Some reflexive verbs, such as **acostarse**, are irregular. Some of these irregular verbs are shown in the **Verb tables** in the supplement.

Position of reflexive pronouns

➤ In ordinary tenses such as the present simple, the reflexive pronoun goes <u>BEFORE</u> the verb.
> **Me acuesto temprano.**   I go to bed early.
> **¿Cómo se llama usted?**   What's your name?

⇨ *For more information on the **Present simple tense**, see page 103.*

➤ When telling someone <u>NOT TO DO</u> something, you also put the reflexive pronoun <u>BEFORE</u> the verb.
> **No te levantes.**   Don't get up.
> **¡No os vayáis!**   Don't leave!

➤ When telling someone <u>TO DO</u> something, you join the reflexive pronoun onto the end of the verb.
> **¡Siéntense!**   Sit down!
> **¡Cállate!**   Be quiet!

⇨ *For more information on the **Imperative**, see page 124.*

Tip
When adding reflexive pronouns to the end of the imperative, you drop the final **-s** of the **nosotros** form and the final **-d** of the **vosotros** form, before the pronoun.

¡Vámonos!   Let's go!
¡Sentaos!   Sit down!

➤ You always join the reflexive pronoun onto the end of infinitives and gerunds (the **-ando** or **-iendo** forms of the verb) unless the infinitive or gerund follows another verb.

Hay que relajarse de vez en cuando.	You have to relax from time to time.
Acostándose temprano, se descansa mejor.	You feel more rested if you go to bed early.

➤ Where the infinitive or gerund follows another verb, you can put the reflexive pronoun either at the end of the infinitive or gerund or before the other verb.

Quiero bañarme or **Me quiero bañar.**	I want to have a bath.
Tienes que vestirte or **Te tienes que vestir.**	You must get dressed.
Está vistiéndose or **Se está vistiendo.**	She's getting dressed.
¿Estás duchándote? or **¿Te estás duchando?**	Are you having a shower?

⇨ *For more information on **Gerunds**, see page 180.*

[i] Note that, when adding pronouns to the ends of verb forms, you will often have to add a written accent to preserve the stress.

⇨ *For more information on **Stress**, see page 266.*

Using reflexive verbs with parts of the body and clothes

➤ In Spanish, you often talk about actions to do with your body or your clothing using a reflexive verb.

Se está secando el pelo.	She's drying her hair.
Nos lavamos los dientes.	We clean our teeth.
Se está poniendo el abrigo.	He's putting on his coat.

[i] Note that in Spanish you do not use a possessive adjective such as *my* and *her* when talking about parts of the body. You use **el, la, los** and **las** with a reflexive verb instead.

Me estoy lavando las manos.	I'm washing my hands.

⇨ *For more information on **Articles**, see page 11.*

Other uses of reflexive verbs

➤ In English we often use a passive construction, for example, *goods are transported all over the world, most of our tea is imported from India and China*. In Spanish, this construction is not used so much. Instead, very often a reflexive verb with **se** is used.

Aquí se vende café.	Coffee is sold here.
Aquí se venden muchos libros.	Lots of books are sold here.
Se habla inglés.	English is spoken here.
En Suiza se hablan tres idiomas.	Three languages are spoken in Switzerland.

[i] Note that the verb has to be singular or plural depending on whether the noun is singular or plural.

⇨ *For more information on the **Passive**, see page 175.*

For further explanation of grammatical terms, please see pages viii-xii.

➤ A reflexive verb with **se** is also used in some very common expressions.

¿Cómo <u>se dice</u> "siesta" en inglés?	How do you say "siesta" in English?
¿Cómo <u>se escribe</u> "Tarragona"?	How do you spell "Tarragona"?

➤ **se** is also used in impersonal expressions. In this case, it often corresponds to *one* (or *you*) in English.

No <u>se puede</u> entrar.	You can't go in.
No <u>se permite</u>.	You aren't *or* It isn't allowed.

⇨ *For more information on* **Impersonal verbs**, *see page* 185.

➤ **nos**, **os** and **se** are all also used to mean *each other* and *one another*.

<u>Nos</u> escribimos.	We write to one another.
<u>Nos</u> queremos.	We love each other.
Rachel y Julie <u>se</u> odian.	Rachel and Julie hate each other.
No <u>se</u> conocen.	They don't know each other.

KEY POINTS

✔ A reflexive verb is made up of a reflexive pronoun and a verb.
✔ The reflexive pronouns are: **me, te, se, nos, os, se**.
✔ The reflexive pronoun goes before the verb, except when you are telling someone to do something and with infinitives and gerunds.

Test yourself

25 **Replace the highlighted sentences with the alternative reflexive form where the pronoun is joined onto the verb. Pay attention to any accents you may need to add. The first one has been done for you.**

a ¿Te quieres duchar ahora? .... ¿Quieres ducharte ahora? ....

b Nos tenemos que ir ya. ....

c Se está arreglando para salir. ....

d Se está afeitando. ....

e Nos están llamando. ....

f Me quiero ir. ....

g ¿Os queréis sentar? ....

h Se están lavando las manos. ....

i Nos vamos a acostar pronto. ....

j No me quiero reír de ellos. ....

26 **Change the following instructions into the negative.**

a ¡Levántate! ....

b ¡Vete! ....

c ¡Quédate ahí! ....

d ¡Siéntense ahí! ....

e ¡Mírate al espejo! ....

f Relajaos del todo. ....

g Vámonos mañana. ....

h Vístete de azul. ....

i ¡Ponte el abrigo! ....

j ¡Espérame! ....

Test yourself

27 **Translate the following sentences into Spanish assuming, where appropriate, that you're addressing one person with whom you are on familiar terms.**

a What's your name?

....

b What's your brother's name?

....

c They love each other very much.

....

d We don't know each other.

....

e They don't write to each other any more.

....

f Mobile phones aren't allowed in school.

....

g What time do you go to bed?

....

h He's only 12 but he already shaves.

....

i I get up really early.

....

j Wash your hands before eating.

....

The future tense

> ## What is the future tense?
> The **future** tense is a verb tense used to talk about something that will happen or will be true in the future, for example, *He'll be here soon; I'll give you a call; What will you do?; It will be sunny tomorrow.*

Ways of talking about the future

➤ In Spanish, just as in English, you can often use the present tense to refer to something that is going to happen in the future.

Cogemos el tren de las once.	We're getting the eleven o'clock train.
Mañana voy a Madrid.	I am going to Madrid tomorrow.

➤ In English we often use *going to* with an infinitive to talk about the immediate future or our future plans. In Spanish, you can use the present tense of **ir** followed by **a** and an infinitive.

Va a perder el tren.	He's going to miss the train.
Va a llevar una media hora.	It's going to take about half an hour.
Voy a hacerlo mañana.	I'm going to do it tomorrow.

Forming the future tense

➤ In English we can form the future tense by putting *will* or its shortened form *'ll* before the verb. In Spanish you have to change the verb endings. So, just as **hablo** means *I speak*, **hablaré** means *I will speak* or *I shall speak*.

➤ To form the future tense of regular **-ar**, **-er** and **-ir** verbs, add the following endings to the infinitive of the verb: **-é, -ás, -á, -emos, -éis, -án**.

➤ The following table shows the future tense of three regular verbs: **hablar** (meaning *to speak*), **comer** (meaning *to eat*) and **vivir** (meaning *to live*).

(yo)	hablaré	comeré	viviré	I'll speak/eat/live
(tú)	hablarás	comerás	vivirás	you'll speak/eat/live
(él) (ella) (usted)	hablará	comerá	vivirá	he'll speak/eat/live she'll speak/eat/live it'll speak/eat/live you'll speak/eat/live
(nosotros/ nosotras)	hablaremos	comeremos	viviremos	we'll speak/eat/live
(vosotros/ vosotras)	hablaréis	comeréis	viviréis	you'll speak/eat/live
(ellos/ellas/ ustedes)	hablarán	comerán	vivirán	they'll/you'll speak/eat/live

Hablaré con ella.	I'll speak to her.
Comeremos en casa de José.	We'll eat at José's.

For further explanation of grammatical terms, please see pages viii-xii.

No <u>volverá</u>.	He won't come back.
¿Lo <u>entenderás</u>?	Will you understand it?

ⓘ Note that in the future tense only the **nosotros/nosotras** form doesn't have an accent.

> *Tip*
> Remember that Spanish has no direct equivalent of the word *will* in verb forms like *will* rain or *will* look and so on. You change the Spanish verb ending instead to form the future tense.

Grammar Extra!

In English, we sometimes use *will* with the meaning of be *willing* to rather than simply to express the future, for example, *Will you wait for me a moment?* In Spanish you don't use the future tense to say this; you use the verb **querer** (meaning to want) instead.

¿Me quieres esperar un momento, por favor?	Will you wait for me a moment, please?

Verbs with irregular stems in the future tense

➤ There are a few verbs that <u>DO NOT</u> use their infinitives as the stem for the future tense. Here are some of the most common.

Verb	Stem	(yo)	(tú)	(él) (ella) (usted)	(nosotros) (nosotras)	(vosotros) (vosotras)	(ellos) (ellas) (ustedes)
decir to say	dir-	dir<u>é</u>	dir<u>ás</u>	dir<u>á</u>	dir<u>emos</u>	dir<u>éis</u>	dir<u>án</u>
haber to have	habr-	habr<u>é</u>	habr<u>ás</u>	habr<u>á</u>	habr<u>emos</u>	habr<u>éis</u>	habr<u>án</u>
hacer to do/ make	har-	har<u>é</u>	har<u>ás</u>	har<u>á</u>	har<u>emos</u>	har<u>éis</u>	har<u>án</u>
poder to be able to	podr-	podr<u>é</u>	podr<u>ás</u>	podr<u>á</u>	podr<u>emos</u>	podr<u>éis</u>	podr<u>án</u>
poner to put	pondr-	pondr<u>é</u>	pondr<u>ás</u>	pondr<u>á</u>	pondr<u>emos</u>	pondr<u>éis</u>	pondr<u>án</u>
querer to want	querr-	querr<u>é</u>	querr<u>ás</u>	querr<u>á</u>	querr<u>emos</u>	querr<u>éis</u>	querr<u>án</u>
saber to know	sabr-	sabr<u>é</u>	sabr<u>ás</u>	sabr<u>á</u>	sabr<u>emos</u>	sabr<u>éis</u>	sabr<u>án</u>
salir to leave	saldr-	saldr<u>é</u>	saldr<u>ás</u>	saldr<u>á</u>	saldr<u>emos</u>	saldr<u>éis</u>	saldr<u>án</u>
tener to have	tendr-	tendr<u>é</u>	tendr<u>ás</u>	tendr<u>á</u>	tendr<u>emos</u>	tendr<u>éis</u>	tendr<u>án</u>
venir to come	vendr-	vendr<u>é</u>	vendr<u>ás</u>	vendr<u>á</u>	vendr<u>emos</u>	vendr<u>éis</u>	vendr<u>án</u>

Lo <u>haré</u> mañana.	I'll do it tomorrow.
No <u>podremos</u> hacerlo.	We won't be able to do it.
Lo <u>pondré</u> aquí.	I'll put it here.
<u>Saldrán</u> por la mañana.	They'll leave in the morning.
¿A qué hora <u>vendrás</u>?	What time will you come?

[i] Note that the verb **haber** is only used when forming other tenses, such as the perfect tense, and in the expression **hay** (meaning *there is* or *there are*).

⇨ *For more information on the* **Perfect tense** *and on* **hay**, *see pages 164 and 186.*

Reflexive verbs in the future tense

➤ The future tense of reflexive verbs is formed in just the same way as for ordinary verbs, except that you have to remember to give the reflexive pronoun (**me, te, se, nos, os, se**).

Me <u>levantaré</u> temprano.	I'll get up early.

> ### KEY POINTS
> ✔ You can use a present tense in Spanish to talk about something that will happen or be true, just as in English.
> ✔ You can use **ir a** with an infinitive to talk about things that will happen in the immediate future.
> ✔ In Spanish there is no direct equivalent of the word *will* in verb forms like *will rain* and *will look*. You change the verb endings instead.
> ✔ To form the future tense, add the endings **-é, -ás, á, -emos, -éis, -án** to the infinitive.
> ✔ Some verbs have irregular stems in the future tense. It is worth learning these.

Test yourself

28 Replace the highlighted verb with the future tense using the **ir a** construction.

a **Hablo** con mis padres. ....

b **Cenamos** pescado. ....

c **Están viendo** una película. ....

d ¿**Quieres** comer con nosotros? ....

e ¿**Vais** al cine? ....

f **Compran** una casa en el pueblo. ....

g **Estudia** en Salamanca. ....

h No **quieren** venir. ....

i **Hacemos** una fiesta el domingo. ....

j ¿**Trabajas** en un banco? ....

29 Complete the following sentences with the correct form of the future tense by adding the correct endings to the infinitive form.

a No te preocupes. Yo .... con tus padres. **(hablar)**

b Javier y yo os .... **(acompañar)**

c .... mañana porque tienen que volver a trabajar. **(irse)**

d Juan e Isabel .... por la iglesia. **(casarse)**

e Necesito un coche pero lo .... cuando tenga dinero. **(comprar)**

f Los vecinos .... con el alcalde acerca del asunto. **(hablar)**

g Mi hermano .... conmigo. **(venir)**

h ¿A qué hora .... las tiendas? **(abrir)**

i Los niños lo .... mañana. **(hacer)**

j Pregúntales a qué hora .... de viaje. **(salir)**

30 Translate the sentences into Spanish. Use the tú form for 'you' unless otherwise indicated.

a I'll do it tomorrow.

....

b Laura will be able to help you.

....

c You'll have to be careful.

....

d I will arrive at nine o'clock.

....

e I'm going to get up early tomorrow.

....

f She'll have time to read during the holidays.

....

g It's going to be hot tomorrow.

....

h When will your parents return?

....

i Do you think you'll go to the beach tomorrow?

....

j Will you [**vosotros** form] be in London on Sunday?

....

PRACTICE PRACTICE PRACTICE PRACTICE PRACTICE PRACTICE

The conditional

What is the conditional?
The **conditional** is a verb form used to talk about things that would happen or that would be true under certain conditions, for example, I <u>would</u> help you if I could. It is also used to say what you would like or need, for example, <u>Could</u> you give me the bill?

Using the conditional

➤ You can often recognize a conditional in English by the word *would* or its shortened form *'d*.
   I <u>would</u> be sad if you left.
   If you asked him, he<u>'d</u> help you.

➤ You use the conditional for:

- saying what you would like to do
  Me <u>gustaría</u> conocerlo.   I'd like to meet him.

- making suggestions
  <u>Podrías</u> alquilar una bici.   You could hire a bike.

- giving advice
  <u>Deberías</u> hacer más ejercicio.   You should do more exercise.

- saying what you would do
  Le dije que le <u>ayudaría</u>.   I said I would help him.

> *Tip*
> There is no direct Spanish translation of would in verb forms like *would be*, *would like*, *would help* and so on. You change the Spanish verb ending instead.

Forming the conditional

➤ To form the conditional of regular **-ar, -er,** and **-ir** verbs, add the following endings to the <u>infinitive</u> of the verb: **-ía, -ías, -ía, -íamos, -íais, -ían.**

➤ The following table shows the conditional tense of three regular verbs: **hablar** (meaning *to speak*), **comer** (meaning *to eat*) and **vivir** (meaning *to live*).

(yo)	hablaría	comería	viviría	I would speak/eat/live
(tú)	hablarías	comerías	vivirías	you would speak/eat/live
(él) (ella) (usted)	hablaría	comería	viviría	he would speak/eat/live she would speak/eat/live it would speak/eat/live you would speak/eat/live
(nosotros/ nosotras) (vosotros/ vosotras) (ellos/ellas) (ustedes)	hablaríamos hablaríais hablarían	comeríamos comeríais comerían	viviríamos viviríais vivirían	we would speak/eat/live you would speak/eat/live they would speak/eat/live you would speak/eat/live

Me <u>gustaría</u> ir a China.	I'd like to go to China.
Dije que <u>hablaría</u> con ella.	I said that I would speak to her.
<u>Debería</u> llamar a mis padres.	I should ring my parents.

> *Tip*
> Don't forget to put an accent on the í in the conditional.

🛈 Note that the endings in the conditional tense are identical to those of the <u>imperfect tense</u> for **-er** and **-ir** verbs. The only difference is that they are added to a different stem.

⇨ *For more information on the **Imperfect tense**, see page 157.*

Verbs with irregular stems in the conditional

➤ To form the conditional of irregular verbs, use the same stem as for the <u>future tense</u>, then add the usual endings for the conditional. The same verbs that are irregular in the future tense are irregular in the conditional.

Verb	Stem	(yo)	(tú)	(él) (ella) (usted)	(nosotros) (nosotras)	(vosotros) (vosotras)	(ellos) (ellas) (ustedes)
decir to say	dir-	diría	dirías	diría	diríamos	diríais	dirían
haber to have	habr-	habría	habrías	habría	habríamos	habríais	habrían
hacer to do/ make	har-	haría	harías	haría	haríamos	haríais	harían
poder to be able to	podr-	podría	podrías	podría	podríamos	podríais	podrían
poner to put	pondr-	pondría	pondrías	pondría	pondríamos	pondríais	pondrían
querer to want	querr-	querría	querrías	querría	querríamos	querríais	querrían
saber to know	sabr-	sabría	sabrías	sabría	sabríamos	sabríais	sabrían
salir to leave	saldr-	saldría	saldrías	saldría	saldríamos	saldríais	saldrían
tener to have	tendr-	tendría	tendrías	tendría	tendríamos	tendríais	tendrían
venir to come	vendr-	vendría	vendrías	vendría	vendríamos	vendríais	vendrían

➪ *For more information on the **Future tense**, see page 138.*

¿Qué <u>harías</u> tú en mi lugar?	What would you do if you were me?
¿<u>Podrías</u> ayudarme?	Could you help me?
Yo lo <u>pondría</u> aquí.	I would put it here.

ⓘ Note that the verb **haber** is only used when forming other tenses, such as the perfect tense, and in the expression **hay** (meaning *there is/there are*).

➪ *For more information on the **Perfect tense** and on **hay**, see pages 164 and 186.*

Reflexive verbs in the conditional

➤ The conditional of reflexive verbs is formed in just the same way as for ordinary verbs, except that you have to remember to give the reflexive pronoun (**me, te, se, nos, os, se**).

Le dije que <u>me levantaría</u> temprano.   I told him I would get up early.

KEY POINTS

✔ In Spanish, there is no direct equivalent of the word *would* in verb forms like *would go* and *would look* and so on. You change the verb ending instead.

✔ To form the conditional tense, add the endings **-ía, ías, -ía, -íamos, -íais, -ían** to the infinitive. The conditional uses the same stem as for the future.

✔ Some verbs have irregular stems which are used for both the conditional and the future. It is worth learning these.

Test yourself

31 Complete the following sentences with the correct form of the conditional tense.

a Me .... ir contigo. **(gustar)**

b Os .... si abriese la ventana. **(importar)**

c Me prometieron que me .... mañana. **(ayudar)**

d Les dije que ya se lo .... yo. **(decir)**

e Creo que eres tú quién .... decírselo. **(deber)**

f Si tuviésemos dinero .... alquilar un coche. **(poder)**

g Creo que si los invitásemos, ... **(venir)**

h Le dije que la .... tú y yo. **(acompañar)**

i .... ir a verlos antes de irme. **(Deber)**

j Me dijo que ella lo .... **(hacer)**

32 Replace the highlighted infinitive with the relevant conditional form.

a ¿Te **gustar** venir con nosotros? ....

b Tu jefe **deber** haberlo hecho. ....

c Mi tía **poder** ayudarte. ....

d Nos **gustar** ir al cine mañana. ....

e Me **encantar** conocerte. ....

f **ser** un placer acompañarlos. ....

g ¿Me **permitir** ir con vosotros? ....

h Paula **saber** cómo hacerlo. ....

i Eso no **importar**. ....

j Yo no **atreverse** a decírselo. ....

Test yourself

33 **Translate the following sentences into Spanish using the tú form for 'you' where appropriate.**

a   I would tell her.

....

b   I told him I would do it.

....

c   How would you do it?

....

d   Would you like to come with me?

....

e   I should tell them.

....

f   I told them we would eat together.

....

g   How much would you give for that car?

....

h   The children would have a good time here.

....

i   You ought to take some photos.

....

j   I would like to buy it for you but I can't.

....

The preterite

Using the preterite

➤ In English, we use the <u>simple past tense</u> to talk about actions:

- that were completed at a certain point in the past
  I <u>bought</u> a dress yesterday.

- that were part of a series of events
  I <u>went</u> to the beach, <u>undressed</u> and <u>put on</u> my swimsuit.

- that went on for a certain amount of time
  The war lasted three years.

➤ In English, we also use the <u>simple past tense</u> to describe actions which happened frequently (*Our parents <u>took</u> us swimming in the holidays*), and to describe settings (*It <u>was</u> a dark and stormy night*).

➤ In Spanish, the <u>preterite</u> is the most common tense for talking about the past. You use the preterite for actions:

- that were completed at a certain point in the past
  Ayer <u>compré</u> un vestido.   I bought a dress yesterday.

- that were part of a series of events
  <u>Fui</u> a la playa, me <u>quité</u> la ropa   I went to the beach, undressed and put on
  y me <u>puse</u> el bañador.   my swimsuit.

- that went on for a certain amount of time
  La guerra <u>duró</u> tres años.   The war lasted three years.

➤ However, you use the <u>imperfect tense</u> for actions that happened frequently (where you could use *used to* in English) and for descriptions of settings.

⇨ *For more information on the **Imperfect tense**, see page 157.*

Forming the preterite of regular verbs

➤ To form the preterite of any regular **-ar** verb, you take off the **-ar** ending to form the stem, and add the endings: **-é, -aste, -ó, -amos, -asteis, -aron**.

➤ To form the preterite of any regular **-er** or **-ir** verb, you also take off the **-er** or **-ir** ending to form the stem and add the endings: **-í, -iste, -ió, -imos, -isteis, -ieron**.

➤ The following table shows the preterite of three regular verbs: **hablar** (meaning *to speak*), **comer** (meaning *to eat*) and **vivir** (meaning *to live*).

(yo)	habl<u>é</u>	com<u>í</u>	viv<u>í</u>	I spoke/ate/lived
(tú)	habl<u>aste</u>	com<u>iste</u>	viv<u>iste</u>	you spoke/ate/lived
(él) (ella) (usted)	habl<u>ó</u>	com<u>ió</u>	viv<u>ió</u>	he spoke/ate/lived she spoke/ate/lived it spoke/ate/lived you spoke/ate/lived
(nosotros nosotras)	habl<u>amos</u>	com<u>imos</u>	viv<u>imos</u>	we spoke/ate/lived
(vosotros/ vosotras)	habl<u>asteis</u>	com<u>isteis</u>	viv<u>isteis</u>	you spoke/ate/lived
(ellos/ellas) (ustedes)	habl<u>aron</u>	com<u>ieron</u>	viv<u>ieron</u>	they spoke/ate/lived you spoke/ate/lived

<u>**Bailé**</u> **con mi hermana.**	I danced with my sister.
No <u>**hablé**</u> **con ella.**	I didn't speak to her.
<u>**Comimos**</u> **en un restaurante.**	We had lunch in a restaurant.
¿<u>**Cerraste**</u> **la ventana?**	Did you close the window?

ⓘ Note that Spanish has no direct translation of *did* or *didn't* in questions or negative sentences. You simply use a past tense and make it a question by making your voice go up at the end or changing the word order; you make it negative by adding **no**.

⇨ *For more information on* **Questions** *and* **Negatives***, see pages 220 and 215.*

> *Tip*
> Remember the accents on the **yo** and **él/ella/usted** forms of regular verbs in the preterite. Only an accent shows the difference, for example, between **hablo** I <u>speak</u> and **habló** <u>he spoke</u>.

Irregular verbs in the preterite

➤ A number of verbs have very irregular forms in the preterite. The table shows some of the most common.

Verb	(yo)	(tú)	(él) (ella) (usted)	(nosotros) (nosotras)	(vosotros) (vosotras)	(ellos) (ellas) (ustedes)
andar to walk	anduve	anduviste	anduvo	anduvimos	anduvisteis	anduvieron
conducir to drive	conduje	condujiste	condujo	condujimos	condujisteis	condujeron
dar to give	di	diste	dio	dimos	disteis	dieron
decir to say	dije	dijiste	dijo	dijimos	dijisteis	dijeron
estar to be	estuve	estuviste	estuvo	estuvimos	estuvisteis	estuvieron
hacer to do, to make	hice	hiciste	hizo	hicimos	hicisteis	hicieron
ir to go	fui	fuiste	fue	fuimos	fuisteis	fueron
poder to be able to	pude	pudiste	pudo	pudimos	pudisteis	pudieron
poner to put	puse	pusiste	puso	pusimos	pusisteis	pusieron
querer to want	quise	quisiste	quiso	quisimos	quisisteis	quisieron
saber to know	supe	supiste	supo	supimos	supisteis	supieron
ser to be	fui	fuiste	fue	fuimos	fuisteis	fueron
tener to have	tuve	tuviste	tuvo	tuvimos	tuvisteis	tuvieron
traer to bring	traje	trajiste	trajo	trajimos	trajisteis	trajeron
venir to come	vine	viniste	vino	vinimos	vinisteis	vinieron
ver to see	vi	viste	vio	vimos	visteis	vieron

🔲 Note that **hizo** (the **él/ella/usted** form of **hacer**) is spelt with a **z**.

⇨ *For more information on **Spelling**, see page 263.*

Fue a Madrid.	He went to Madrid.
Te vi en el parque.	I saw you in the park.
No vinieron.	They didn't come.
¿Qué hizo?	What did she do?
Se lo di a Teresa.	I gave it to Teresa.
Fue en 1999.	It was in 1999.

> *Tip*
> The preterite forms of **ser** (meaning *to be*) are the same as the preterite forms of **ir** (meaning *to go*).

➤ Some other verbs are regular <u>EXCEPT FOR</u> the **él/ella/usted** and **ellos/ellas/ustedes** forms (*third persons singular and plural*). In these forms the stem vowel changes.

Verb	(yo)	(tú)	(él) (ella) (usted)	(nosotros) (nosotras)	(vosotros) (vosotras)	(ellos) (ellas) (ustedes)
dormir to sleep	dormí	dormiste	durmió	dormimos	dormisteis	durmieron
morir to die	morí	moriste	murió	morimos	moristeis	murieron
pedir to ask for	pedí	pediste	pidió	pedimos	pedisteis	pidieron
reír to laugh	reí	reíste	rio	reímos	reísteis	rieron
seguir to follow	seguí	seguiste	siguió	seguimos	seguisteis	siguieron
sentir to feel	sentí	sentiste	sintió	sentimos	sentisteis	sintieron

Antonio durmió diez horas.	Antonio slept for ten hours.
Murió en 1066.	He died in 1066.
Pidió paella.	He asked for paella.
¿Los siguió?	Did she follow them?
Sintió un dolor en la pierna.	He felt a pain in his leg.
Nos reímos mucho.	We laughed a lot.
Juan no se rio.	Juan didn't laugh.

➤ **caer** (meaning *to fall*) and **leer** (meaning *to read*) have an accent in all persons apart from the **ellos/ellas/ustedes** form (*third person plural*). In addition, the vowel changes to **y** in the **él/ella/usted** and **ellos/ellas/ ustedes** forms (*third persons singular and plural*).

Verb	(yo)	(tú)	(él) (ella) (usted)	(nosotros) (nosotras)	(vosotros) (vosotras)	(ellos) (ellas) (ustedes)
caer to fall	caí	caíste	cayó	caímos	caísteis	cayeron
construir to build	construí	construiste	construyó	construimos	construisteis	construyeron
leer to read	leí	leíste	leyó	leímos	leísteis	leyeron

🛈 Note that **construir** also changes to **y** in the **él/ella/usted** and **ellos/ellas/ustedes** forms (*third persons singular and plural*), but only has accents in the **yo** and **él/ella/usted** forms.

Se cayó por la ventana.	He fell out of the window.
Ayer leí un artículo muy interesante.	I read a very interesting article yesterday.
Construyeron una nueva autopista.	They built a new motorway.

Other spelling changes in the preterite

➤ Spanish verbs that end in **-zar**, **-gar** and **-car** in the infinitive change the **z** to **c**, the **g** to **gu** and the **c** to **qu** in the **yo** form (*first person singular*).

Verb	(yo)	(tú)	(él) (ella) (usted)	(nosotros) (nosotras)	(vosotros) (vosotras)	(ellos) (ellas) (ustedes)
cruzar to cross	cru<u>c</u>é	cruzaste	cruzó	cruzamos	cruzasteis	cruzaron
empezar to begin	empe<u>c</u>é	empezaste	empezó	empezamos	empezasteis	empezaron
pagar to pay for	pa<u>gu</u>é	pagaste	pagó	pagamos	pagasteis	pagaron
sacar to follow	sa<u>qu</u>é	sacaste	sacó	sacamos	sacasteis	sacaron

<u>**Crucé**</u> **el río.**	I crossed the river.
<u>**Empecé**</u> **a hacer mis deberes.**	I began doing my homework.
No <u>**pagué**</u> **la cuenta.**	I didn't pay the bill.
Me <u>**saqué**</u> **las llaves del bolsillo.**	I took my keys out of my pocket.

🛈 *Note that the change from* **g** *to* **gu** *and* **c** *to* **qu** *before* **e** *is to keep the sound hard.*

⇨ *For more information on* **Spelling***, see page 263.*

Reflexive verbs in the preterite

➤ The preterite of reflexive verbs is formed in just the same way as for ordinary verbs, except that you have to remember to give the reflexive pronoun (**me, te, se, nos, os, se**).

    Me <u>levanté</u> a las siete.   I got up at seven.

> ### KEY POINTS
> ✔ The preterite is the most common way to talk about the past in Spanish.
> ✔ To form the preterite of regular -ar verbs, take off the -ar ending and add the endings: **-é, -aste, -ó, -amos, -asteis, -aron**.
> ✔ To form the preterite of regular -er and -ir verbs, take off the -er and -ir endings and add the endings: **-í, -iste, -ió, -imos, -isteis, -ieron**.
> ✔ There are a number of verbs which are irregular in the preterite. These forms have to be learnt.
> ✔ With some verbs, the accents and spelling change in certain forms.

Test yourself

34 **Complete the following sentences with the correct form of the preterite.**

a   La película .... casi dos horas. **(durar)**

b   Mi hermano y yo .... un piso juntos. **(comprar)**

c   ¿Cuándo .... vosotros la casa? **(comprar)**

d   Los profesores .... todos juntos en la excursión. **(comer)**

e   Pregúntale si .... la ventana. **(cerrar)**

f   Jorge .... con Susana. **(bailar)**

g   ¿Quién .... con la oficina? **(hablar)**

h   ¿En que año .... tú? **(nacer)**

i   Ya se lo .... yo a tu padre. **(comentar)**

j   Lola y Pepe .... cinco años en Londres. **(vivir)**

35 **Match the two columns.**

a   **Me**   levantamos a las ocho.

b   **Tino se**   levantasteis hoy?

c   **Nos**   levanté temprano.

d   **¿A qué hora te**   levantó a las once.

e   **¿A qué hora os**   levantaste?

36 **Complete the following sentences with the correct form of the preterite paying attention to any verbs that are irregular.**

a   ¿ .... tú o tu hermana? **(Conducir)**

b   Me lo .... mis padres. **(decir)**

c   Sara y yo .... en la playa toda la tarde. **(estar)**

d   El número se lo .... yo. **(dar)**

e   Los niños y yo .... buscándote en todo el parque. **(andar)**

f   ¿Cuándo .... vosotros en Madrid? **(estar)**

g   ¿Lo .... tú o tu hermano? **(hacer)**

h   ¿Cuándo .... la fiesta? **(ser)**

i   ¿Cuándo lo .... tus tíos? **(saber)**

j   ¡Hola Sandra! ¿Por qué no .... venir a la fiesta? **(querer)**

Test yourself

37 Translate the following sentences into Spanish.

a She gave me her phone number.

....

b I lost my passport in Spain.

....

c They won 2–1.

....

d We stayed at home yesterday.

....

e We went out last night.

....

f I bought myself a new dress on Saturday.

....

g He ordered ice cream for dessert.

....

h We had an accident.

....

i Ana bought a new mobile.

....

j The price of petrol went up yesterday.

....

The imperfect tense

What is the imperfect tense?

The **imperfect tense** is one of the verb tenses used to talk about the past, especially in descriptions, and to say what was happening or used to happen, for example, *It was sunny at the weekend; We were living in Spain at the time; I used to walk to school.*

Using the imperfect tense

➤ In Spanish, the imperfect tense is used:

- to describe what things were like and how people felt in the past

Hacía calor.	It was hot.
No teníamos mucho dinero.	We didn't have much money.
Tenía hambre.	I was hungry.

- to say what used to happen or what you used to do regularly in the past

Cada día llamaba a su madre.	He used to ring his mother every day.

- to describe what was happening or what the situation was when something else took place

Tomábamos café.	We were having coffee.
Me caí cuando cruzaba la carretera.	I fell over when I was crossing the road.

Grammar Extra!

Sometimes, instead of the ordinary imperfect tense being used to describe what was happening at a given moment in the past when something else occurred interrupting it, the continuous form is used. This is made up of the imperfect tense of **estar** (**estaba**, **estabas** and so on), followed by the **-ando/-iendo** form of the main verb. The other verb – the one that relates the event that occurred – is in the preterite.

Montse miraba la televisión *or*	Montse was watching television
Montse estaba mirando la televisión cuando sonó el teléfono.	when the telephone rang.

⇨ For further information on the *Preterite*, see page 149.

Forming the imperfect tense

➤ To form the imperfect of any regular **-ar** verb, you take off the **-ar** ending of the infinitive to form the stem and add the endings: **-aba, -abas, -aba, -ábamos, -abais, -aban.**

➤ The following table shows the imperfect tense of one regular **-ar** verb: **hablar** (meaning *to speak*).

(yo)	hablaba	I spoke, I was speaking, I used to speak
(tú)	hablabas	you spoke, you were speaking, you used to speak
(él/ella/usted)	hablaba	he/she/it/you spoke, he/she/it was speaking, you were speaking , he/she/it/you used to speak
(nosotros/nosotras)	hablábamos	we spoke, we were speaking, we used to speak
(vosotros/vosotras)	hablabais	you spoke, you were speaking, you used to speak
(ellos/ellas/ustedes)	hablaban	they/you spoke, they/you were speaking, they/you used to speak

🛈 Note that in the imperfect tense of **-ar** verbs, the only accent is on the **nosotros/nosotras** form

Hablaba francés e italiano.   He spoke French and Italian.
Cuando era joven, mi tío trabajaba mucho.   My uncle worked hard when he was young.
Estudiábamos matemáticas e inglés.   We were studying maths and English.

➤ To form the imperfect of any regular **-er** or **-ir** verb, you take off the **-er** or **-ir** ending of the infinitive to form the stem and add the endings: **-ía, -ías, -ía, -íamos, -íais, -ían.**

➤ The following table shows the imperfect of two regular verbs: **comer** (meaning *to eat*) and **vivir** (meaning *to live*).

(yo)	comía	vivía	I ate/lived, I was eating/living, I used to eat/live
(tú)	comías	vivías	you ate/lived, you were eating/living, you used to eat/live
(él/ella/ usted)	comía	vivía	he/she/it/you ate/lived, he/she/it was eating/living, you were eating/living, he/she/it was eating/living, you were eating/living
(nosotros/ nosotras)	comíamos	vivíamos	we ate/lived, we were eating/living, we used to eat/live
(vosotros/ vosotras)	comíais	vivíais	you ate/lived, you were eating/living, you used to eat/live
(ellos/ellas/ ustedes)	comían	vivían	they/you ate/lived, they/you were eating/living, they/you used to eat/live

For further explanation of grammatical terms, please see pages viii-xii.

☑ Note that in the imperfect tense of **-er** and **-ir** verbs, there's an accent on all the endings.

A veces, <u>comíamos</u> en casa de Pepe.	We sometimes used to eat at Pepe's.
<u>Vivía</u> en un piso en la Avenida de Barcelona.	She lived in a flat in Avenida de Barcelona.
Cuando llegó el médico, ya se <u>sentían</u> mejor.	They were already feeling better when the doctor arrived.

> *Tip*
> The imperfect endings for **-er** and **-ir** verbs are the same as the endings used to form the conditional for all verbs. The only difference is that, in the conditional, the endings are added to the future stem.

⇨ *For more information on the **Conditional**, see page 143.*

Irregular verbs in the imperfect tense

➤ **ser**, **ir** and **ver** are irregular in the imperfect tense.

	ser	Meaning: *to be*
(yo)	era	I was
(tú)	eras	you were
(él/ella/usted)	era	he/she/it was, you were
(nosotros/nosotras)	éramos	we were
(vosotros/vosotras)	erais	you were
(ellos/ellas/ustedes)	eran	they were/you were

<u>Era</u> un chico muy simpático.	He was a very nice boy.
Mi madre <u>era</u> profesora.	My mother was a teacher.

	ir	Meaning: *to go*
(yo)	iba	I went/used to go/was going
(tú)	ibas	you went/used to go/were going
(él/ella/usted)	iba	he/she/it went/used to go/was going, you went/used to go/were going
(nosotros/nosotras)	íbamos	we went/used to go/were going
(vosotros/vosotras)	ibais	you went/used to go/were going
(ellos/ellas/ustedes)	iban	they/you went/used to go/were going

<u>Iba</u> a la oficina cada día.	Every day he would go to the office.
¿Adónde <u>iban</u>?	Where were they going?

	ver	Meaning: *to see/to watch*
(yo)	veía	I saw/used to see, I watched/used to watch/was watching
(tú)	veías	you saw/used to see, you watched/used to watch/were watching
(él/ella/usted)	veía	he/she/it saw/used to see, he/she/it watched/used to watch/was watching, you saw/used to see, you watched/used to watch/were watching
(nosotros/nosotras)	veíamos	we saw/used to see, we watched/used to watch/were watching
(vosotros/vosotras)	veíais	you saw/used to see, you watched/used to watch/were watching
(ellos/ellas/ustedes)	veían	they/you saw/used to see, they/you watched/used to watch/were watching

Los sábados, siempre lo <u>veíamos</u>.	We always used to see him on Saturdays.
<u>Veía</u> la televisión cuando llegó mi tío.	I was watching television when my uncle arrived.

Reflexive verbs in the imperfect tense

➤ The imperfect of reflexive verbs is formed in just the same way as for ordinary verbs, except that you have to remember to give the reflexive pronoun (**me, te, se, nos, os, se**).

Antes <u>se levantaba</u> temprano.   He used to get up early.

Grammar Extra!

In Spanish, you also use the imperfect tense with certain time expressions, in particular with **desde** (meaning *since*), **desde hacía** (meaning *for*) and **hacía ... que** (meaning *for*) to talk about activities and states that had started previously and were still going on at a particular point in the past:

<u>Estaba</u> enfermo desde 2000.	He had been ill since 2000.
<u>Conducía</u> ese coche desde hacía tres meses.	He had been driving that car for three months.
Hacía mucho tiempo que <u>salían</u> juntos.	They had been going out together for a long time.
Hacía dos años que <u>vivíamos</u> en Madrid.	We had been living in Madrid for two years.

Compare the use of **desde, desde hacía** and **hacía ... que** with the imperfect with that of **desde, desde hace,** and **hace ... que** with the present.

⇨ For more information on the use of tenses with *desde*, see page 255.

KEY POINTS

✔ To form the imperfect tense of -**ar** verbs, take off the -**ar** ending and add the endings: -**aba**, -**abas**, -**aba**, -**ábamos**, -**abais**, -**aban**.

✔ To form the imperfect tense of -**er** and -**ir** verbs, take off the -**er** and -**ir** endings and add the endings: -**ía**, -**ías**, -**ía**, -**íamos**, -**íais**, -**ían**.

✔ **ser**, **ir** and **ver** are irregular in the imperfect.

Test yourself

38 Complete the following sentences with the correct form of the imperfect tense.

a   .... a sus padres todos los domingos. **(Llamar)**

b   Mis abuelos siempre .... la siesta después de comer. **(tomar)**

c   Leonor siempre .... a su madre los fines de semana. **(llamar)**

d   .... a visitarnos todos los domingos. **(vienen)**

e   Mis hijos y yo .... comiendo cuando llegaron. **(estar)**

f   En mi casa, siempre se .... a las nueve. **(cenar)**

g   Cuando erais jóvenes, ¿ .... al fútbol? **(jugar)**

h   Mi hermana y yo nos .... por teléfono todas las semanas. **(hablar)**

i   Vosotros ¿no .... en Venezuela antes? **(vivir)**

j   Los fines de semana íbamos a ver a los abuelos y .... todos juntos. **(comer)**

39 Translate the following into Spanish.

a   When we were young, our mother didn't work.

    ....

b   It was really cold. ....

c   Everyone was really tired.

    ....

d   They were watching a film.

    ....

e   There were seven of us for dinner.

    ....

f   She was prettier than her sister.

    ....

g   They said they were going to the cinema.

    ....

h   We saw each other quite often.

    ....

i   We hadn't seen each other for a long time.

    ....

Test yourself

40 Match the two columns.

a	Hacía mucho tiempo	para ducharme.
b	Cuando éramos jóvenes	para quedar a dormir.
c	Me levantaba temprano	que no venían a vernos.
d	Leía un libro	siempre les ofrecíamos algo de picar.
e	Cuando venían a visitarnos	nos gustaba ir a las fiestas.

The perfect tense

Using the perfect tense

➤ In English, we use the perfect tense (*have*, *has* or their shortened forms *'ve* and *'s* followed by a past participle such as *spoken*, *eaten*, *lived*, *been*) to talk about what has or hasn't happened today, this week, this year or in our lives up to now.

➤ The Spanish perfect tense is used in a similar way.

He terminado el libro.	I've finished the book.
¿**Has fregado** el suelo?	Have you washed the floor?
Nunca **ha estado** en Bolivia.	He's never been to Bolivia.
Ha vendido su caballo.	She has sold her horse.
Todavía no **hemos comprado** un ordenador.	We still haven't bought a computer.
Ya se **han ido**.	They've already left.

Grammar Extra!
You may also come across uses of the perfect tense in Spanish to talk about actions completed in the very recent past. In English, we'd use the past simple tense in such cases.

¿Lo has visto?	Did you see that?

Forming the perfect tense

➤ As in English, the perfect tense in Spanish has two parts to it. These are:

- the <u>present</u> tense of the verb **haber** (meaning *to have*)

- a part of the main verb called the <u>past participle</u>.

Forming the past participle

➤ To form the past participle of regular **-ar** verbs, take off the **-ar** ending of the infinitive and add **-ado**.

    hablar (*to speak*)   →   **hablado** (*spoken*)

➤ To form the past participle of regular **-er** or **-ir** verbs, take off the **-er** or **-ir** ending of the infinitive and add **-ido**.

    comer (*to eat*)   →   **comido** (*eaten*)
    vivir (*to live*)   →   **vivido** (*lived*)

For further explanation of grammatical terms, please see pages viii-xii.

The perfect tense of some regular verbs

➤ The following table shows how you can combine the present tense of **haber** with the past participle of any verb to form the perfect tense. In this case, the past participles are taken from the following regular verbs: **hablar** (meaning *to speak*); **trabajar** (meaning *to work*); **comer** (meaning *to eat*); **vender** (meaning *to sell*); **vivir** (meaning *to live*); **decidir** (meaning *to decide*).

	Present of haber	**Past participle**	**Meaning**
(yo)	he	hablado	I have spoken
(tú)	has	trabajado	you have worked
(él/ella/usted)	ha	comido	he/she/it has eaten, you have eaten
(nosotros/ nosotras)	hemos	vendido	we have sold
(vosotros/ vosotras)	habéis	vivido	you have lived
(ellos/ellas/ ustedes)	han	decidido	they/you have decided

Has trabajado mucho.	You've worked hard.
No he comido nada.	I haven't eaten anything.

[i] Note that you should not confuse **haber** with **tener.** Even though they both mean *to have*, **haber** is only used for forming tenses and in certain impersonal expressions such as **hay** and **había** meaning *there is, there are, there was, there were,* and so on.

⇨ For further information on **Impersonal verbs**, see page 185.

Verbs with irregular past participles

➤ Some past participles are irregular. There aren't too many, so try to learn them.

abrir (*to open*)	→	**abierto** (*opened*)
cubrir (*to cover*)	→	**cubierto** (*covered*)
decir (*to say*)	→	**dicho** (*said*)
escribir (*to write*)	→	**escrito** (*written*)
freír (*to fry*)	→	**frito** (*fried*)
hacer (*to do, to make*)	→	**hecho** (*done, made*)
morir (*to die*)	→	**muerto** (*died*)
oír (*to hear*)	→	**oído** (*heard*)
poner (*to put*)	→	**puesto** (*put*)
romper (*to break*)	→	**roto** (*broken*)
ver (*to see*)	→	**visto** (*seen*)
volver (*to return*)	→	**vuelto** (*returned*)

He abierto una cuenta en el banco.	I've opened a bank account.
No ha dicho nada.	He hasn't said anything.
Hoy he hecho muchas cosas.	I've done a lot today.
Todavía no he hecho los deberes.	I haven't done my homework yet.
Han muerto tres personas.	Three people have died.

¿Dónde <u>has puesto</u> mis zapatos?	Where have you put my shoes?
Carlos <u>ha roto</u> el espejo.	Carlos has broken the mirror.
Jamás <u>he visto</u> una cosa parecida.	I've never seen anything like it.
¿<u>Ha vuelto</u> Ana?	Has Ana come back?

> *Tip*
>
> he/has/ha and so on must <u>NEVER</u> be separated from the past participle.
> Any object pronouns go before the form of **haber** being used, and <u>NOT</u>
> between the form of **haber** and the past participle.
>
> | | |
> |---|---|
> | No <u>lo</u> he visto. | I haven't seen it. |
> | ¿<u>Lo</u> has hecho ya? | Have you done it yet? |

Reflexive verbs in the perfect tense

➤ The perfect tense of reflexive verbs is formed in the same way as for ordinary verbs. The reflexive pronouns (**me**, **te**, **se**, **nos**, **os**, **se**) come before **he**, **has**, **ha**, and so on. The table below shows the perfect tense of **lavarse** in full.

(Subject pronoun)	Reflexive pronoun	Present tense of haber	Past Participle	Meaning
(yo)	me	he	lavado	I have washed
(tú)	te	has	lavado	you have washed
(él) (ella) (uno) (usted)	se	ha	lavado	he has washed she has washed one has washed it has washed you have washed
(nosotros) (nosotras)	nos	hemos	lavado	we have washed we have washed
(vosotros) (vosotras)	os	habéis	lavado	you have washed you have washed
(ellos) (ellas) (ustedes)	se	han	lavado	they have washed they have washed you have washed

---

Grammar Extra!

Don't use the perfect tense with **desde, desde hace** and **hace ... que** when talking about how long something has been going on for. Use the <u>present tense</u> instead.

<u>**Está**</u> **enfermo desde julio.**	He has been ill since July.
<u>**Conduce**</u> **ese coche desde hace tres meses.**	He has been driving that car for three months.
Hace mucho tiempo que <u>**salen**</u> **juntos.**	They have been going out together for a long time.

⇨ For more information on the *Present tense*, see page 103.

➤ In European Spanish you <u>CAN</u> use the perfect tense in the negative with **desde** and **desde hace**.

No lo <u>**he visto**</u> **desde hace mucho tiempo.**	I haven't seen him for a long time.

KEY POINTS

✔ The Spanish perfect tense is formed using the present tense of **haber** and a past participle.

✔ In Spanish, the perfect tense is used very much as it is in English.

✔ The past participle of regular **-ar** verbs ends in **-ado**, and the past participle of regular **-er** and **-ir** verbs ends in **-ido**.

✔ Make sure you know the following irregular past participle forms: **abierto, cubierto, dicho, escrito, frito, hecho, muerto, oído, puesto, roto, visto, vuelto**.

Test yourself

41 Replace the highlighted verbs with the perfect tense.

a **Terminé** el trabajo. ....

b ¿**Estuviste** en Sevilla alguna vez? ....

c **Vendimos** la casa. ....

d **Se fueron** de viaje. ....

e ¿**Viste** a Javier? ....

f **Comimos** demasiado. ....

g **Abrieron** un negocio. ....

h No **hizo** los deberes. ....

i Me **puse** el vestido nuevo. ....

j ¿Quién **rompió** el vaso? ....

42 Complete the following sentences with the correct past participle.

a Los hemos .... todos. (**vender**)

b No los he .... desde el año pasado. (**ver**)

c Han ....: en muchas partes de España. (**vivir**)

d He .... la ventana un poco. (**abrir**)

e ¿Quién te ha .... eso? (**decir**)

f Está todo .... de nieve. (**cubrir**)

g ¿Quién ha .... eso? (**hacer**)

h ¿Dónde has .... las llaves? (**poner**)

i Ya han .... de las vacaciones. (**volver**)

j Esa película ya la hemos .... (**ver**)

Test yourself

43 Translate the following sentences into Spanish.

a I haven't seen her. ....

b I've already done it. ....

c Have they done it yet? ....

d We've arrived. ....

e Who broke the chair? ....

f Have you all forgotten your books? ....

g I've opened the window. ....

h Who's told you that? ....

i Have you done your homework? ....

j I haven't seen them in a long time. ....

44 Match the two columns.

a **¿Cuándo**   han muerto?

b **¿Quién te lo**   habéis puesto?

c **¿Cómo lo**   han hecho?

d **¿Cuántos**   ha dicho?

e **¿Dónde lo**   habéis vuelto?

The pluperfect or past perfect tense

Using the pluperfect tense

➤ When talking about the past, we sometimes refer to things that had happened previously. In English, we often use *had* followed by a <u>past participle</u> such as *spoken, eaten, lived* or *been* to do this. This tense is known as the <u>pluperfect</u> or <u>past perfect</u> tense.

➤ The Spanish pluperfect tense is used and formed in a similar way.

Ya **<u>habíamos comido</u>** cuando llegó.	We'd already eaten when he arrived.
Nunca lo **<u>había visto</u>** antes de aquella noche.	I'd never seen it before that night.

Forming the pluperfect tense

➤ Like the perfect tense, the pluperfect tense in Spanish has <u>two</u> parts to it:

- the imperfect tense of the verb **haber** (meaning *to have*)

- the past participle.

⇨ *For more information on the **Imperfect tense** and **Past participles**, see pages 157 and 164.*

➤ The table below shows how you can combine the imperfect tense of **haber** with the past participle of any verb to form the pluperfect tense. Here, the past participles are taken from the following regular verbs: **hablar** (meaning *to speak*); **trabajar** (meaning *to work*); **comer** (meaning *to eat*); **vender** (meaning *to sell*); **vivir** (meaning *to live*); **decidir** (meaning *to decide*).

(Subject pronoun)	Imperfect of <u>haber</u>	Past Participle	Meaning
(yo)	había	hablado	I had spoken
(tú)	habías	trabajado	you had worked
(él/ella/usted)	había	comido	he/she/it/you had eaten
(nosotros/nosotras)	habíamos	vendido	we had sold
(vosotros/vosotras)	habíais	vivido	you had lived
(ellos/ellas/ustedes)	habían	decidido	they/you had decided

No <u>**había trabajado**</u> antes.	He hadn't worked before.
<u>**Había vendido**</u> su caballo.	She had sold her horse.

For further explanation of grammatical terms, please see pages viii-xii.

➤ Remember that some very common verbs have irregular past participles.

abrir (*to open*)	→	abierto (*opened*)
cubrir (*to cover*)	→	cubierto (*covered*)
decir (*to say*)	→	dicho (*said*)
escribir (*to write*)	→	escrito (*written*)
freír (*to fry*)	→	frito (*fried*)
hacer (*to do, to make*)	→	hecho (*done, made*)
morir (*to die*)	→	muerto (*died*)
oír (*to hear*)	→	oído (*heard*)
poner (*to put*)	→	puesto (*put*)
romper (*to break*)	→	roto (*broken*)
ver (*to see*)	→	visto (*seen*)
volver (*to return*)	→	vuelto (*returned*)

No <u>había dicho</u> nada.   He hadn't said anything.
Tres personas <u>habían muerto</u>.   Three people had died.

> *Tip*
> **había/habías/habían** and so on must <u>NEVER</u> be separated from the past participle. Any object pronouns go before the form of **haber** being used, and <u>NOT</u> between the form of **haber** and the past participle.
>
> **No lo había visto.**   I hadn't seen it.

Reflexive verbs in the pluperfect tense

➤ The pluperfect tense of reflexive verbs is formed in the same way as for ordinary verbs. The reflexive pronouns (**me, te, se, nos, os, se**) come before **había, habías, había**, and so on. The table below shows the pluperfect tense of **lavarse** in full.

(Subject pronoun)	Reflexive pronoun	Imperfect tense of haber	Past Participle	Meaning
(yo)	me	había	lavado	I had washed
(tú)	te	habías	lavado	you had washed
(él) (ella) (uno) (usted)	se	había	lavado	he had washed she had washed one had washed it had washed you had washed
(nosotros) (nosotras)	nos	habíamos	lavado	we had washed we had washed
(vosotros) (vosotras)	os	habíais	lavado	you had washed you had washed
(ellos) (ellas) (ustedes)	se	habían	lavado	they had washed they had washed you had washed

---

Grammar Extra!
Don't use the pluperfect with **desde**, **desde hacía** and **hacía ... que** when talking about how long something had been going on for. Use the <u>imperfect</u> instead.

<u>Estaba</u> **enfermo desde 2000.**	He had been ill since 2000.
<u>Conducía</u> **ese coche desde hacía tres meses.**	He had been driving that car for three months.
Hacía mucho tiempo que <u>salían</u> **juntos.**	They had been going out together for a long time.

⇨ For more information on the *Imperfect tense*, see page 157.

In European Spanish you <u>CAN</u> use the pluperfect tense in the negative with **desde** and **desde hacía**.

No lo <u>había visto</u> **desde hacía mucho tiempo.**	I hadn't seen him for a long time.

KEY POINTS

✔ The Spanish pluperfect tense is formed using the imperfect tense of **haber** and a past particple.
✔ In Spanish, the pluperfect tense is used very much as it is in English.
✔ The past participle of regular -**ar** verbs ends in -**ado**, while that of regular -**er** and -**ir** verbs ends in -**ido**.
✔ Make sure you know the irregular forms: **abierto**, **cubierto**, **dicho**, **escrito**, **frito**, **hecho**, **muerto**, **oído**, **puesto**, **roto**, **visto**, **vuelto**.

Test yourself

45 **Replace the highlighted verbs with the pluperfect tense.**

a **Terminé** el trabajo. ....

b ¿**Estuviste** en Sevilla alguna vez? ....

c **Se fueron** de viaje. ....

d ¿Ya lo **viste** este verano? ....

e Ya **comimos** ahí una vez. ....

f **Abrieron** un negocio. ....

g No **hizo** los deberes. ....

h Nunca **oí** eso. ....

i Me **puse** el vestido nuevo. ....

j ¿Cuántos vasos **rompió**? ....

46 **Translate the following into Spanish.**

a We hadn't seen them in a long time.

....

b They had lived in England before.

....

c She had already decided to tell them.

....

d Had you already told him?

....

e She had never worked there before.

....

f Had you already showered in the morning? (**vosotros** form)

....

g They had never been to Scotland before.

....

h He still hadn't been to see that film.

....

i We'd already decided to sell the house.

....

j She had already taken the exam.

Test yourself

47 Create a sentence in the past perfect tense using the elements below. Where the subject of the sentence is unclear, it is shown in square brackets. Pay attention to the order of pronouns where these are required.

a Juan/ya/decir/lo del trabajo/a mí

....

b mi madre/freír/pescado/demasiado

....

c por qué/no/hacer los deberes/[vosotros]

....

d dónde/ver/a ellos/[tú]

....

e saber/quién/romper/el espejo/[tú]

....

f lavarse/las manos/ya/[nosotros]

....

g no/ver/a él/desde el verano pasado/[yo]

....

h no/oír/lo que dijo/[nosotros]

....

i cuándo/volver/de vacaciones/[vosotros]

....

j no saber/dónde/poner/las llaves/[yo]

....

The passive

> ## What is the passive?
> The **passive** is a verb form that is used when the subject of the verb is the person or thing that is affected by the action, for example, *Mary is liked by everyone; Two children were hurt in an accident; The house was sold.*

Using the passive

➤ Verbs can be either <u>active</u> or <u>passive</u>.

➤ In a normal or active sentence, the subject of the verb is the person or thing doing the action described by the verb. The object of the verb is the person or thing that the verb most directly affects.

   Peter (*subject*) wrote (*active verb*) a letter (*object*).
   Ryan (*subject*) hit (*active verb*) me (*object*).

➤ Provided the verb has an object, in English, as in Spanish, you can turn an <u>active</u> sentence round to make it a <u>passive</u> sentence by using *to be* followed by a past participle. In this case the person or thing directly affected by the action becomes the subject of the verb.

   A letter (*subject*) was written (*passive verb*).
   I (*subject*) was hit (*passive verb*).

➤ To show who or what is responsible for the action in a passive construction, in English you use *by*.

   I (*subject*) was hit (*passive verb*) <u>by</u> Ryan.

➤ You use the passive rather than the active when you want to focus attention on the person or thing <u>affected by</u> the action rather than the person or thing that carries it out.

   <u>John</u> was injured in an accident.

➤ You can also use the passive when you don't know who is responsible for the action.

   Several buses were vandalized.

Forming the passive

➤ In English we use the verb *to be* with a <u>past participle</u> (*was painted, were seen, are made*) to form the passive. In Spanish, the passive is formed in exactly the same way, using the verb **ser** (meaning *to be*) and a <u>past participle</u>. When you say who the action is or was done by, you use the preposition **por** (meaning *by*).

   ⇨ *For more information on the **Past participle**, see page 164.*

<u>Son fabricados</u> en España.	They're made in Spain.
<u>Es hecho</u> a mano.	It's made by hand *or* It's handmade.
<u>Fue escrito</u> por JK Rowling.	It was written by JK Rowling.
La casa <u>fue construida</u> en 1956.	The house was built in 1956.
El cuadro <u>fue pintado</u> por mi padre.	The picture was painted by my father.
El colegio va a <u>ser modernizado</u>.	The school is going to be modernized.

[i] Note that the ending of the past participle agrees with the subject of the verb **ser** in exactly the same way as an adjective would.

⇨ *For more information on **Adjectives**, see page 25.*

➤ Here is the preterite of the **-ar** verb **enviar** (meaning *to send*) in its passive form.

(Subject pronoun)	Preterite of ser	Past Participle	Meaning
(yo)	fui	enviado (masculine) enviada (feminine)	I was sent
(tú)	fuiste	enviado (masculine) enviada (feminine)	you were sent
(él) (ella) (usted)	fue	enviado enviada enviado (masculine) enviada (feminine)	he was sent she was sent you were sent
(nosotros) (nosotras)	fuimos fuimos	enviados enviadas	we were sent we were sent
(vosotros) (vosotras)	fuisteis	enviados enviadas	you were sent you were sent
(ellos) (ellas) (ustedes)	fueron	enviados enviadas enviados (masculine) enviadas (feminine)	they were sent they were sent you were sent you were sent

➤ You can form other tenses in the passive by changing the tense of the verb **ser**.
Future: **Serán enviados.**   They will be sent.
Perfect: **Han sido enviados.**   They have been sent.

➤ Irregular past participles are the same as they are in the perfect tense.

⇨ *For more information on **Irregular past participles**, see page 165.*

Avoiding the passive

➤ Passives are not as common in Spanish as they are in English. Spanish native speakers usually prefer to avoid using the passive by:

- using the active construction instead of the passive
  La policía <u>interrogó</u> al sospechoso.   The suspect was interrogated by the police.
  Su madre le regaló un libro.   He was given a book by his mother.

- using an active verb in the third person plural
  **<u>Ponen</u> demasiados anuncios en   Too many adverts are shown on television.
   la televisión.**

- using a reflexive construction (as long as you don't need to say who the action is done by)

Se fabrican en España.	They're made in Spain.
Se hace a mano.	It's made by hand.
La casa se construyó en 1956.	The house was built in 1956.
Todos los libros se han vendido.	All the books have been sold.

➩ *For more information on **Reflexive verbs**, see page 131.*

- using an impersonal **se** construction

Se cree que va a morir.	It is thought he will die.

➩ *For more information on the impersonal se construction, see page 188.*

Tip

Active verbs often have both a direct object and an indirect object.
He gave me (*indirect object*) a book (*direct object*).

In English, both of these objects can be made the subject of a passive verb;
I was given a book. or *A book was given to me*.

In Spanish, an indirect object can <u>NEVER</u> become the subject of a passive verb.

KEY POINTS

✔ The passive is formed using **ser** + past participle, sometimes followed by **por** (meaning *by*).
✔ The past participle must agree with the subject of **ser**.
✔ Passive constructions are not as common as they are in English. You can often avoid the passive by using the third person plural of the active verb or by using a reflexive construction.

Test yourself

48 Create a passive sentence in the past tense using the elements below.

a carta/escribir/Ramón ....

b tarta/hacer/Manuel ....

c coche/conducir/su primo

....

d tienda/destrozar/dos chicos

....

e todos/afectar/noticia

....

f juguetes/hacer/en China

....

g novela/escribir/Jane Austen

....

h película/dirigir/Almódovar

....

i cuadros/pintar/mi tío

....

j casa/alquilar/unos turistas alemanes

....

49 Replace the highlighted passive form with the more common reflexive construction using se.

a La casa **fue construida** en el año 2007. ....

b **Son fabricados** en China. ....

c **Fue anunciado** en la televisión. ....

d La carta **fue enviada** ayer. ....

e El coche **fue comprado** en Madrid. ....

f La cena **será celebrada** el sábado. ....

g El tema **será explicado**. ....

h La casa **fue comprada** hace poco. ....

i **Fue escrito** en inglés. ....

j La basura **fue tirada** al mar. ....

Test yourself

50 Translate the following passive sentences into Spanish using an active construction.

a   This wine is produced in Spain.

....

b   The film was shot in Barcelona.

....

c   He was bought a car by his father.

....

d   A lot of money is spent on the lottery.

....

e   Too many flats have been built in the area.

....

f   A lot of cars were sold last month.

....

g   Paella is served every Sunday.

....

h   He was given homework by the maths teacher.

....

i   She was invited by Mary.

....

j   It was painted by my uncle.

....

The gerund

> ### What is a gerund?
> The **gerund** is a verb form ending in -ing which is used to form verb tenses,
> and which in English may also be used as an adjective and a noun, for example,
> *What are you doing?; the setting sun; Swimming is easy!*

Using the gerund

> In Spanish, the gerund is a form of the verb that usually ends in -**ando** or -**iendo** and is used to form continuous tenses.
>
> | | |
> |---|---|
> | **Estoy trabaj<u>ando</u>.** | I'm work<u>ing</u>. |
> | **Estamos com<u>iendo</u>.** | We are eat<u>ing</u>. |

> It is used with **estar** to form continuous tenses such as:

- the present continuous

<u>**Está fregando**</u> **los platos.**	He's washing the dishes.
<u>**Estoy escribiendo**</u> **una carta.**	I'm writing a letter.

⇨ *For more information on the **Present continuous,** see page 121.*

- the imperfect continuous

<u>**Estaba reparando**</u> **el coche.**	She was fixing the car.
<u>**Estaban esperándo**</u>**nos.**	They were waiting for us.

[i] Note that continuous tenses should only be used in Spanish to describe action that is or was happening at the time you are talking about.

Grammar Extra!
Sometimes another verb, such as **ir** or **venir** is used instead of **estar** with a gerund in continuous tenses. These verbs emphasize the gradualness or the slowness of the process.

Iba anocheciendo.	It was getting dark.
Eso lo vengo diciendo desde hace tiempo.	That's what I've been saying all along.

> The gerund is also used after certain other verbs:

- **seguir haciendo algo** and **continuar haciendo algo** are both used with the meaning of *to go on doing something* or *to continue doing something*.

Siguió cantando *or* **Continuó cantando.**	He went on singing *or* He continued singing.
Siguieron leyendo *or* **Continuaron leyendo.**	They went on reading *or* They continued reading.

- **llevar** with a time expression followed by the gerund is used to talk about how long someone has been doing something:

Lleva dos años estudiando inglés.	He's been studying English for two years.
Llevo una hora esperando aquí.	I've been waiting here for an hour.

ⓘ Note that the present tense of **llevar** followed by a gerund means the same as the English *have/has been + -ing*.

➤ **pasar(se)** with a time expression followed by the gerund is used to talk about how long you've spent doing something.

Pasé *or* **Me pasé el fin de semana estudiando.**	I spent the weekend studying.
Pasamos *or* **Nos pasamos el día leyendo.**	We spent the day reading.

➤ Verbs of movement, such as **salir** (meaning *to come out* or *to go out*), **entrar** (meaning *to come in* or *to go in*), and **irse** (meaning *to leave*) are sometimes followed by a gerund such as **corriendo** (meaning *running*) or **cojeando** (meaning *limping*). The English equivalent of **salir corriendo**, **entrar corriendo** or **irse cojeando**, would be *to run out, to run in* or *to limp off* in such cases.

Salió corriendo.	He ran out.
Se fue cojeando.	He limped off.

> *Tip*
> Use a past participle not a gerund to talk about physical position.
>
> | | |
> |---|---|
> | **Estaba <u>tumbado</u> en el sofá.** | He was lying on the sofa. |
> | **Estaba <u>sentada</u>.** | She was sitting down. |
> | **Lo encontré <u>tendido</u> en el suelo.** | I found him lying on the floor. |
> | **La escalera estaba <u>apoyada</u> contra la pared.** | The ladder was leaning against the wall. |
>
> ⇨ For more information on the *Past participles,* see page 164.

➤ You will also come across the gerund used in other ways. For example:

Los vimos jugando al fútbol.	We saw them playing football.
Estudiando, aprobarás.	By studying, *or* If you study, you'll pass.

Forming the gerund of regular verbs

➤ To form the gerund of regular **-ar** verbs, take off the **-ar** ending of the infinitive to form the stem, and add **-ando**.

Infinitive	Stem	Gerund
hablar	habl-	hablando
trabajar	trabaj-	trabajando

➤ To form the gerund of regular **-er** and **-ir** verbs, take off the **-er** and **-ir** ending of the infinitive to form the stem, and add **-iendo**.

Infinitive	Stem	Gerund
comer	com-	comiendo
vivir	viv-	viviendo

The gerund of irregular verbs

➤ Some verbs have an irregular gerund form. You have to learn these.

Infinitives	Meaning	Gerund	Meaning
decir	to say	diciendo	saying
dormir	to sleep	durmiendo	sleeping
freír	to fry	friendo	frying
morir	to die	muriendo	dying
pedir	to ask for	pidiendo	asking for
poder	to be able to	pudiendo	being able to
reír	to laugh	riendo	laughing
seguir	to follow	siguiendo	following
sentir	to feel	sintiendo	feeling
venir	to come	viniendo	coming
vestir	to dress	vistiendo	dressing

➤ In the next group of verbs there is a **y** rather than the normal **i**.

Infinitives	Meaning	Gerund	Meaning
caer	to fall	cayendo	falling
creer	to believe	creyendo	believing
leer	to read	leyendo	reading
oír	to hear	oyendo	hearing
traer	to bring	trayendo	bringing
ir	to go	yendo	going

For further explanation of grammatical terms, please see pages viii-xii.

> Tip
>
> In English, we often use -ing forms as adjectives, for example, running water, shining eyes, the following day. In Spanish, you cannot use the -ando and -iendo forms like this. Instead, there are sometimes corresponding forms ending in -ante and -iente that can be used as adjectives.
>
> | | |
> |---|---|
> | agua <u>corriente</u> | running water |
> | ojos <u>brillantes</u> | shining eyes |
> | Al día <u>siguiente</u>, visitamos Toledo. | The following day we visited Toledo. |
>
> Similarly, in English, we often use the -ing forms as nouns. In Spanish you have to use the <u>infinitive</u> instead.
>
> | | |
> |---|---|
> | <u>Fumar</u> es malo para la salud. | <u>Smoking</u> is bad for you. |

Position of pronouns with the gerund

➤ Object pronouns and reflexive pronouns are usually attached to the end of the gerund, although you can also often put them before **estar** in continuous tenses.

Estoy hablándote *or*	I'm talking to you.
<u>Te</u> estoy hablando.	
Está vistiéndo<u>se</u> *or*	He's getting dressed.
<u>Se</u> está vistiendo.	
Estaban mostrándo<u>selo</u> *or*	They were showing it to him/her/
<u>Se lo</u> estaban mostrando.	them/you.

🛈 Note that you will always have to add an accent to keep the stress in the same place when adding pronouns to the end of a gerund.

⇨ *For more information on **Stress**, see page 266.*

KEY POINTS

✔ Use the gerund in continuous tenses with **estar** as well as after **seguir** and **continuar.**
✔ Gerunds for -**ar** verbs add -**ando** to the stem of the verb.
✔ Gerunds for -**er** and -**ir** verbs usually add -**iendo** to the stem of the verb.
✔ -**ando** and -**iendo** gerunds <u>cannot</u> be used as adjectives or nouns.
✔ You can attach pronouns to the end of the gerund, or sometimes put them before the previous verb.

Test yourself

51 Replace these infinitives with the gerund form. Remember some may be irregular.

a estudiar ....

b comer ....

c vivir ....

d dormir ....

e leer ....

f pedir ....

g reír ....

h creer ....

i ir ....

j oír ....

52 Complete the following sentences with the gerund.

a Sigamos .... **(trabajar)**

b Estamos .... **(comer)**

c ¿Qué estáis ....? **(hacer)**

d Nos están .... **(mirar)**

e Siguió .... **(hablar)**

f Estoy .... un libro. **(leer)**

g Estaban .... la tele. **(ver)**

h Llevamos dos años .... en Londres. **(vivir)**

i Llevo veinte minutos .... **(esperar)**

j Tengo que salir .... **(correr)**

53 Translate the following into Spanish.

a I like swimming. ....

b They were sitting down. ....

c They were playing tennis. ....

d Laughing is good for you. ....

e No Smoking. ....

f I love reading. ....

g She's getting dressed. ....

h They were telling the truth. ....

i I'm buying a flat. ....

j Riding a bike is good exercise. ....

Impersonal verbs

> ### What is an impersonal verb?
> An **impersonal verb** is a verb whose subject is *it*, but this '*it*' does not refer to any specific thing; for example, *It's going to rain; It's nine o'clock.*

Verbs that are always used impersonally

➤ There are some verbs such as **llover** (meaning *to rain*) and **nevar** (meaning *to snow*), that are only used in the '*it*' form, the infinitive, and as a gerund (the *-ing* form of the verb). These are called <u>impersonal verbs</u> because there is no person, animal or thing performing the action.

Llueve.	It's raining.
Está lloviendo.	It's raining.
Va a llover.	It's going to rain.
Nieva.	It's snowing.
Está nevando.	It's snowing.
Nevaba.	It was snowing.
Estaba nevando.	It was snowing.
Mañana nevará.	It will snow tomorrow.

Verbs that are sometimes used impersonally

➤ There are also some other very common verbs that are sometimes used as impersonal verbs, for example **hacer**, **haber** and **ser**.

➤ **hacer** is used in a number of impersonal expressions relating to the weather:

<u>Hace</u> **frío/calor.**	It's cold/hot.
Ayer <u>hacía</u> **mucho frío/calor.**	It was very cold/hot yesterday.
<u>Hace</u> **sol/viento.**	It's sunny/windy.
Va a <u>hacer</u> **sol/viento.**	It's going to be sunny/windy.
<u>Hace</u> **un tiempo estupendo/horrible.**	It's a lovely/horrible day.

➤ **hacer** is also used in combination with **que** and **desde** in impersonal time expressions, to talk about how long something has been going on for or how long it is since something happened.

<u>Hace</u> **seis meses** <u>que</u> **vivo aquí.** *or* **Vivo aquí** <u>desde hace</u> **seis meses.**	I've been living here for six months.
Hace tres años que estudio español *or* **Estudio español** <u>desde hace</u> **tres años.**	I've been studying Spanish for three years.
<u>Hace</u> **mucho tiempo** <u>que</u> **no la veo** *or* **No la veo** <u>desde hace</u> **mucho tiempo.**	I haven't seen her for ages *or* It is ages since I saw her.
<u>Hace</u> **varias semanas que no** **voy por allí** *or* **No voy por allí** <u>desde hace</u> **varias semanas.**	I haven't been there for several weeks *or* It is several weeks since I went there.

ⓘ Note the use of the <u>present simple</u> in Spanish in the above examples where in English we'd use the perfect tense or the past tense.

➤ **hacer** is also used impersonally in the expression (**me/te/le**) **hace falta**, which means *it is necessary* (*for me/you/him*).

Si <u>hace falta</u>, voy.	I'll go if necessary.
No <u>hace falta</u> llamar.	We/You/I needn't call.
Me <u>hace falta</u> otro vaso más.	I need another glass.
No <u>hace falta</u> ser un experto.	You don't need to be an expert.
No <u>hacía falta</u>.	It wasn't necessary.

> [¿] Note that not all impersonal expressions in Spanish are translated into English using impersonal expressions.

➤ **haber** too can be used impersonally with the meaning *there is/there are, there was/there were, there will be*, and so on. It has the special form **hay** in the present. For the other tenses, you take the third person singular (the '*it*' form) of **haber** in the appropriate tense.

<u>Hay</u> un cine cerca de aquí.	There's a cinema near here.
<u>Hay</u> dos supermercados.	There are two supermarkets.
No <u>hay</u> bares.	There are no bars.
<u>Había</u> mucho ruido.	There was a lot of noise.
<u>Había</u> muchos coches.	There were a lot of cars
<u>Hubo</u> un accidente.	There was an accident.
<u>Hubo</u> varios problemas.	There were several problems.
¿<u>Habrá</u> tiempo?	Will there be time?
¿<u>Habrá</u> suficientes sillas?	Will there be enough chairs?

> [¿] Note that you should <u>ALWAYS</u> use the singular form (never the plural), no matter how many things there are.

➤ **haber** is used in the construction **hay que** with an infinitive to talk about actions that need to be taken.

<u>Hay que</u> trabajar más.	We/You need to work harder.
<u>Hay que</u> ser respetuoso.	You/We/One must be respectful.
<u>Habrá</u> que decírselo.	We'll/You'll have to tell him.

➤ **ser** can be used in certain impersonal constructions with adjectives, for example:

- **es/era/fue** + adjective + infinitive

<u>Es</u> importante ahorrar dinero.	It's important to save money.
<u>Fue</u> torpe hacer eso.	It was silly to do that.
<u>Sería</u> mejor esperar.	It would be better to wait.

- **es/era/fue** + adjective + **que** + verb

<u>Es cierto que</u> tengo problemas.	It's true that I've got problems.
<u>Es verdad que</u> trabaja mucho.	It's true that he works hard.

> [¿] Note that when they are used in the negative (**no es cierto que…**; **no es verdad que…**), these expressions have to be followed by the subjunctive.

⇨ *For more information on the* **Subjunctive**, *see page* 190.

Grammar Extra!
When impersonal expressions that don't state facts are followed by **que** (meaning *that*) and a verb, this verb must be in the subjunctive. For this reason, the following non-factual impersonal expressions are all followed by the <u>subjunctive</u>:

- **Es posible que...**   It's possible that... / ...might...
  Es posible que ganen.   They might win.

- **Es imposible que...**   It's impossible that... /
                                                                   ...can't possibly...
  Es imposible que lo sepan.   They can't possibly know.

- **Es necesario que...**   It's necessary that... / ...need to...
  No es necesario que vengas.   You don't need to come.

- **Es mejor que...**   ...be better to...
  Es mejor que lo pongas aquí.   You'd better put it here.

⇨ *For more information on the **Subjunctive**, see page 190.*

➤ **ser** is also used impersonally with **de día** and **de noche** to say whether it's day or night.
  <u>Era de noche</u> cuando llegamos.   It was night when we arrived.
  Todavía <u>es de día</u> allí.   It's still day there.

⇨ *For other time expressions with **ser**, see page 116.*

➤ **basta con** is used impersonally:

- with a following <u>infinitive</u> to mean *it's enough to/all you need do is*
  <u>Basta con telefonear</u> para   All you need do is phone to reserve a seat.
  reservar un asiento.
  <u>Basta con dar</u> una vuelta por la   You only need to take a walk round
  ciudad para...   the city to ...

- with a <u>noun</u> or <u>pronoun</u> to mean *all you need is* or *all it takes is*
  <u>Basta con un error</u> para que   All it takes is one mistake to ruin everything.
  todo se estropee.

➤ **(me) parece que** is used to give opinions.
  <u>Parece que</u> va a llover.   It looks as if it's going to rain.
  <u>Me parece que</u> estás equivocado. I think that you are wrong.

☞ Note that when **(me) parece que** is used in the negative, the following verb has to be in the <u>subjunctive</u>.

⇨ *For more information on the **Subjunctive**, see page 190.*

➤ **vale la pena** is used to talk about what's worth doing.

Vale la pena.	It's worth it.
No vale la pena.	It's not worth it.
Vale la pena hacer el esfuerzo.	It's worth making the effort.
No vale la pena gastar tanto dinero.	It's not worth spending so much money.

Grammar Extra!

se is often used in impersonal expressions, especially with the verbs **creer, decir, poder,** and **tratar**. In such cases it often corresponds to *it, one* or *you* in English.

- **Se cree que...** It is thought *or* People think that...
  Se cree que es un mito. It is thought to be a myth.

- **Se dice que...** It is said *or* People say that...
  Se dice que es rico. He is said to be rich.

- **Se puede...** One can.../People can.../You can...
  Aquí se puede aparcar. One can park here.

- **Se trata de...** It's a question of.../It's about...
  No se trata de dinero. It isn't a question of money.
  Se trata de resolverlo. We must solve it.

⇨ *For more information on* **Reflexive verbs**, *see page* 131.

KEY POINTS

✔ Impersonal verbs and expressions can only be used in the '*it*' form, the infinitive and the gerund.
✔ Impersonal expressions relating to the weather are very common.
✔ Although in English we use *there is* or *there are* depending on the number of people or things that there are, in Spanish **hay**, **había**, **hubo** and so on are used in the singular form only.
✔ Some very common ordinary verbs are also used as impersonal verbs.

Test yourself

54 Translate the following sentences into Spanish.

a   It's cold. ....

b   It was very hot. ....

c   It's going to be sunny tomorrow. ....

d   The weather was lovely. ....

e   It's raining. ....

f   It's going to snow. ....

g   It was very windy. ....

h   What's the weather like? ....

i   Tomorrow will be sunny. ....

j   It's going to rain. ....

55 Match the two columns.

a   **Es posible que**   vendrán.

b   **No vale la pena**   unos mil euros.

c   **Parece que**   vengan.

d   **Se dice que**   decírselo.

e   **Se trata de**   son muy ricos.

56 Translate the following sentences into Spanish.

a   There's a school in the village. ....

b   There isn't a park near here. ....

c   There were a lot of people at the party.

   ....

d   There was a meeting yesterday. ....

e   Will there be a lot of tourists in September?

   ....

f   There's a shop on the corner. ....

g   There wasn't a lot of traffic. ....

h   Will there be a new project soon? ....

i   There wasn't time. ....

j   We/You need to earn more. ....

The subjunctive

> ## What is the subjunctive?
> The **subjunctive** is a verb form that is used in certain circumstances especially when expressing some sort of feeling or when there is doubt about whether something will happen or whether something is true. It is only used occasionally in modern English, for example, *If I were you, ...; So be it.; I wish you were here.*

Using the subjunctive

➤ Although you may not know it, you will already be familiar with many of the forms of the present subjunctive, as it is used when giving orders and instructions not to do something as well as in the **usted**, **ustedes** and **nosotros** forms of instructions to do something. For example, if you phone someone in Spain, they will probably answer with ¡**diga!** or ¡**dígame!**, an imperative form taken from the present subjunctive of **decir**.

  ⇨ *For more information on* **Imperatives**, *see page 124.*

➤ In Spanish, the subjunctive is used after certain verbs and conjunctions when two parts of a sentence have different subjects.

  Tengo miedo de que le ocurra algo.   I'm afraid <u>something</u> may (*subjunctive*)

                                             happen to him.

(The subject of the first part of the sentence is *I*; the subject of the second part of the sentence is *something*.).

➤ In English, in a sentence like *We want him/José to be happy*, we use an infinitive (*to be*) for the second verb even though *want* and *be happy* have different subjects (*we* and *him/José*).

➤ In Spanish you cannot do this. You have to use the <u>subjunctive</u> for the second verb.

  Queremos que él <u>sea</u> feliz.   We want him to be happy.
  Queremos que José <u>sea</u> feliz.   We want José to be happy.

➤ You <u>CAN</u> use an infinitive for the second verb in Spanish when the subject of both verbs is the same.

  Queremos ser felices.   We want to be happy.

Coming across the subjunctive

➤ The subjunctive has several tenses, the main ones being the <u>present subjunctive</u> and the <u>imperfect subjunctive</u>. The tense used for the subjunctive verb depends on the tense of the previous verb.

  ⇨ *For more information on* **Tenses with the subjunctive**, *see page 195.*

For further explanation of grammatical terms, please see pages viii-xii.

➤ In sentences containing two verbs with different subjects, you will find that the second verb is in the subjunctive when the first verb:

- expresses a wish

Quiero que <u>vengan</u>.	I want them to come.
Quiero que se <u>vaya</u>.	I want him/her to leave.
Deseamos que <u>tengan</u> éxito.	We want them to be successful.

- expresses an emotion

Siento mucho que no <u>puedas</u> venir.	I'm very sorry that you can't come.
Espero que <u>venga</u>.	I hope he comes.
Me sorprende que no <u>esté</u> aquí.	I'm surprised that he isn't here.
Me alegro de que te <u>gusten</u>.	I'm pleased that you like them.

➤ If the subject of both verbs is the same, an infinitive is used as the second verb instead of a subjunctive.

➤ Compare the following examples. In the examples on the left, both the verb expressing the wish or emotion and the second verb have the same subject, so the second verb is an <u>infinitive</u>. In the examples on the right, each verb has a different subject, so the second verb is in the <u>subjunctive</u>.

Infinitive construction	**Subjunctive construction**
Quiero <u>estudiar</u>.	**Quiero que José <u>estudie</u>.**
I want to study.	I want José to study.
Maite quiere <u>irse</u>.	**Maite quiere que me <u>vaya</u>.**
Maite wants to leave.	Maite wants me to leave.
Siento no <u>poder</u> venir.	**Siento que no <u>puedas</u> venir.**
I'm sorry I can't come.	I'm sorry that you can't come.
Me alegro de <u>poder</u> ayudar.	**Me alegro de que <u>puedas</u> ayudar.**
I'm pleased to be able to help.	I'm pleased you can help.

➤ You will also come across the verb + **que** + subjunctive construction (often with a personal object such as **me**, **te** and so on) when the first verb is one you use to ask or advise somebody to do something.

Solo te pido que <u>tengas</u> cuidado.	I'm only asking you to be careful.
Te aconsejo que no <u>llegues</u> tarde.	I'd advise you not to be late.

➤ You will also come across the subjunctive in the following cases:

- after verbs expressing doubt or uncertainty, and verbs saying what you think about something that are used with **no**

Dudo que <u>tenga</u> tiempo.	I doubt I'll have time.
No creo que <u>venga</u>.	I don't think she'll come.
No pienso que <u>esté</u> bien.	I don't think it's right.

- in impersonal constructions that show a need to do something

¿Hace falta que <u>vaya</u> Jaime?	Does Jaime need to go?
No es necesario que <u>vengas</u>.	You don't need to come.

- in impersonal constructions that do not express facts

Es posible que <u>tengan</u> razón.	They may be right.

⇨ *For more information on **Impersonal verbs**, see page 185.*

Grammar Extra!

Use the <u>indicative</u> (that is, any verb form that isn't subjunctive) after impersonal expressions that state facts provided they are <u>NOT</u> in the negative.

Es verdad que <u>es</u> interesante. It's true that it's interesting.
Es cierto que me <u>gusta</u> el café. It's true I like coffee.
Parece que se va a ir. It seems that he's going to go.

➤ The subjunctive is used after **que** to express wishes.
    ¡Que lo <u>pases</u> bien! Have a good time!
    ¡Que te <u>diviertas</u>! Have fun!

➤ The subjunctive is also used after certain conjunctions linking two parts of a sentence which each have different subjects.

- **antes de que** before
  ¿Quieres decirle algo antes de Do you want to say anything to him
    que se <u>vaya</u>? before he goes?

- **para que** so that
  Es para que te <u>acuerdes</u> de mí. It's so that you'll remember me.

- **sin que** without
  Salimos sin que nos <u>vieran</u>. We left without them seeing us.

⇨ *For more information on **Conjunctions**, see page 258.*

Tip

Use **para**, **sin** and **antes de** with the <u>infinitive</u> when the subject of both verbs is the <u>same</u>.

Fue en taxi para no <u>llegar</u> tarde. He went by taxi so that he wouldn't be late.
Pedro se ha ido sin <u>esperarnos</u>. Pedro's gone without waiting for us.
Cenamos antes de <u>ir</u> al teatro. We had dinner before we went to the theatre.

Forming the present subjunctive

➤ To form the present subjunctive of most verbs, take off the **-o** ending of the **yo** form of the <u>present simple</u>, and add a fixed set of endings.

➤ For **-ar** verbs, the endings are: **-e, -es, -e, -emos, -éis, -en**.

➤ For both **-er** and **-ir** verbs, the endings are: **-a, -as, -a, -amos, -áis, -an**.

For further explanation of grammatical terms, please see pages viii-xii.

➤ The following table shows the present subjunctive of three regular verbs: **hablar** (meaning *to speak*), **comer** (meaning *to eat*) and **vivir** (meaning *to live*).

Infinitive	(yo)	(tú)	(él) (ella) (usted)	(nosotros) (nosotras)	(vosotros) (vosotras)	(ellos) (ellas) (ustedes)
hablar to speak	hable	hables	hable	hablemos	habléis	hablen
comer to eat	coma	comas	coma	comamos	comáis	coman
vivir to live	viva	vivas	viva	vivamos	viváis	vivan

Quiero que comas algo.   I want you to eat something.
Me sorprende que no hable inglés.   I'm surprised he doesn't speak English.
No es verdad que trabajen aquí.   It isn't true that they work here.

➤ Some verbs have very irregular **yo** forms in the ordinary present tense and these irregular forms are reflected in the stem for the present subjunctive.

Infinitive	(yo)	(tú)	(él) (ella) (usted)	(nosotros) (nosotras)	(vosotros) (vosotras)	(ellos) (ellas) (ustedes)
decir to say	diga	digas	diga	digamos	digáis	digan
hacer to do/make	haga	hagas	haga	hagamos	hagáis	hagan
poner to put	ponga	pongas	ponga	pongamos	pongáis	pongan
salir to leave	salga	salgas	salga	salgamos	salgáis	salgan
tener to have	tenga	tengas	tenga	tengamos	tengáis	tengan
venir to come	venga	vengas	venga	vengamos	vengáis	vengan

Voy a limpiar la casa antes de   I'm going to clean the house before
  que vengan.   they come.

ⓘ Note that only the **vosotros** form has an accent.

> *Tip*
> The present subjunctive endings are the opposite of what you'd expect, as -**ar** verbs have endings starting with -**e**, and -**er** and -**ir** verbs have endings starting with -**a**.

Forming the present subjunctive of irregular verbs

➤ The following verbs have irregular subjunctive forms:

Infinitive	(yo)	(tú)	(él) (ella) (usted)	(nosotros) (nosotras)	(vosotros) (vosotras)	(ellos) (ellas) (ustedes)
dar to give	dé	des	dé	demos	deis	den
estar to be	esté	estés	esté	estemos	estéis	estén
haber to have	haya	hayas	haya	hayamos	hayáis	hayan
ir to go	vaya	vayas	vaya	vayamos	vayáis	vayan
saber to know	sepa	sepas	sepa	sepamos	sepáis	sepan
ser to be	sea	seas	sea	seamos	seáis	sean

No quiero que te <u>vayas</u>.	I don't want you to go.
Dudo que <u>esté</u> aquí.	I doubt if it's here.
No piensan que <u>sea</u> él.	They don't think it's him.
Es posible que <u>haya</u> problemas.	There may be problems.

➤ Verbs that change their stems (<u>radical-changing verbs</u>) in the ordinary present usually change them in the same way in the present subjunctive.

➪ *For more information on **radical-changing verbs**, see page 113.*

Infinitive	(yo)	(tú)	(él) (ella) (usted)	(nosotros) (nosotras)	(vosotros) (vosotras)	(ellos) (ellas) (ustedes)
pensar to think	<u>pien</u>se	<u>pien</u>ses	<u>pien</u>se	pensemos	penséis	<u>pien</u>sen
entender to understand	<u>entien</u>da	<u>entien</u>das	<u>entien</u>da	entendamos	entendáis	<u>entien</u>dan
poder to be able	<u>pue</u>da	<u>pue</u>das	<u>pue</u>da	podamos	podáis	<u>pue</u>dan
querer to want	<u>quie</u>ra	<u>quie</u>ras	<u>quie</u>ra	queramos	queráis	<u>quie</u>ran
volver to return	<u>vue</u>lva	<u>vue</u>lvas	<u>vue</u>lva	volvamos	volváis	<u>vue</u>lvan

No hace falta que <u>vuelvas</u>.	There's no need for you to come back.
Es para que lo <u>entiendas</u>.	It's so that you understand.
Me alegro de que <u>puedas</u> venir.	I'm pleased you can come.

➤ Sometimes the stem of the **nosotros** and **vosotros** forms isn't the same as it is in the ordinary present tense.

Infinitive	(yo)	(tú)	(él) (ella) (usted)	(nosotros) (nosotras)	(vosotros) (vosotras)	(ellos) (ellas) (ustedes)
dormir to sleep	duerma	duermas	duerma	<u>durmamos</u>	<u>durmáis</u>	duerman
morir to die	muera	mueras	muera	<u>muramos</u>	<u>muráis</u>	mueran
pedir to ask for	pida	pidas	pida	<u>pidamos</u>	<u>pidáis</u>	pidan
seguir to follow	siga	sigas	siga	<u>sigamos</u>	<u>sigáis</u>	sigan
sentir to feel	sienta	sientas	sienta	<u>sintamos</u>	<u>sintáis</u>	sientan

Queremos hacerlo antes de que nos <u>muramos</u>.	We want to do it before we die.
Vendré a veros cuando os <u>sintáis</u> mejor.	I'll come and see you when you feel better.

Tenses with the subjunctive

➤ If the verb in the first part of the sentence is in the <u>present</u>, <u>future</u> or <u>imperative</u>, the second verb will usually be in the <u>present subjunctive</u>.

Quiero (*present*) **que lo hagas** (*present subjunctive*). I want you to do it.
Iremos (*future*) **por aquí para que no nos vean** (*present subjunctive*). We'll go this way so that they won't see us.

➤ If the verb in the first part of the sentence is in the <u>conditional</u> or a <u>past tense</u>, the second verb will usually be in the <u>imperfect subjunctive</u>.

Me gustaría (*conditional*) **que llegaras** (*imperfect subjunctive*) **temprano.**
I'd like you to arrive early.
Les pedí (*preterite*) **que me esperaran** (*imperfect subjunctive*).
I asked them to wait for me.

Indicative or subjunctive?

➤ Many expressions are followed by the <u>indicative</u> (the ordinary form of the verb) when they state facts, and by the <u>subjunctive</u> when they refer to possible or intended future events and outcomes.

➤ Certain conjunctions relating to time such as **cuando** (meaning *when*), **hasta que** (meaning *until*), **en cuanto** (meaning *as soon as*) and **mientras** (meaning *while*) are used with the <u>indicative</u> when the action has happened or when talking about what happens regularly.

¿Qué dijo cuando te <u>vio</u>?	What did he say when he saw you?
Siempre lo compro cuando <u>voy</u> a España.	I always buy it when I go to Spain.
Me quedé allí hasta que <u>volvió</u> Antonio.	I stayed there until Antonio came back.

➤ The same conjunctions are followed by the subjunctive when talking about a vague future time.

¿Qué quieres hacer cuando <u>seas</u> mayor?	What do you want to do when you grow up? *(but you're not grown up yet)*
¿Por qué no te quedas aquí hasta que <u>vuelva</u> Antonio?	Why don't you stay here until Antonio comes back? *(but Antonio hasn't come back yet)*
Lo haré en cuanto <u>pueda</u> or **tan pronto como <u>pueda</u>.**	I'll do it as soon as I can. *(but I'm not able to yet)*

Grammar Extra!

aunque is used with the <u>indicative</u> (the ordinary verb forms) when it means *although* or *even though*. In this case, the second part of the sentence is stating a fact.

Me gusta el francés aunque <u>prefiero</u> el alemán.	I like French although I prefer German.
Seguí andando aunque me <u>dolía</u> la pierna.	I went on walking even though my leg hurt.

aunque is used with the <u>subjunctive</u> when it means *even if*. Here, the second part of the sentence is not yet a fact.

Te llamaré cuando vuelva aunque <u>sea</u> tarde.	I'll ring you when I get back, even if it's late.

Forming the imperfect subjunctive

➤ For all verbs, there are <u>two</u> imperfect subjunctive forms that are exactly the same in meaning.

➤ The stem for both imperfect subjunctive forms is the same: you take off the **-aron** or **-ieron** ending of the **ellos** form of the preterite and add a fixed set of endings to what is left.

⇨ *For more information on the* **Preterite**, *see page 149.*

➤ For **-ar** verbs, the endings are: **-ara, -aras, -ara, -áramos, -arais, -aran** or **-ase, -ases, -ase, -ásemos, -aseis, -asen**. The first form is more common.

➤ For **-er** and **-ir** verbs, the endings are: **-iera, -ieras, -iera, -iéramos, -ierais, -ieran** or **-iese, -ieses, -iese, -iésemos, -ieseis, -iesen**. The first form is more common.

➤ The following table shows the imperfect subjunctive of three regular verbs: **hablar** (meaning *to speak*), **comer** (meaning *to eat*) and **vivir** (meaning *to live*).

Infinitive	(yo)	(tú)	(él) (ella) (usted)	(nosotros) (nosotras)	(vosotros) (vosotras)	(ellos) (ellas) (ustedes)
hablar to speak	hablara hablase	hablaras hablases	hablara hablase	habláramos hablásemos	hablarais hablaseis	hablaran hablasen
comer to eat	comiera comiese	comieras comieses	comiera comiese	comiéramos comiésemos	comierais comieseis	comieran comiesen
vivir to live	viviera viviese	vivieras vivieses	viviera viviese	viviéramos viviésemos	vivierais vivieseis	vivieran viviesen

➤ Many verbs have irregular preterite forms which are reflected in the stem for the imperfect subjunctive. For example:

Infinitive	(yo)	(tú)	(él) (ella) (usted)	(nosotros) (nosotras)	(vosotros) (vosotras)	(ellos) (ellas) (ustedes)
dar to give	diera diese	dieras dieses	diera diese	diéramos diésemos	dierais dieseis	dieran diesen
estar to be	estuviera estuviese	estuvieras estuvieses	estuviera estuviese	estuviéramos estuviésemos	estuvierais estuvieseis	estuvieran estuviesen
hacer to do/make	hiciera hiciese	hicieras hicieses	hiciera hiciese	hiciéramos hiciésemos	hicierais hicieseis	hicieran hiciesen
poner to put	pusiera pusiese	pusieras pusieses	pusiera pusiese	pusiéramos pusiésemos	pusierais pusieseis	pusieran pusiesen
tener to have	tuviera tuviese	tuvieras tuvieses	tuviera tuviese	tuviéramos tuviésemos	tuvierais tuvieseis	tuvieran tuviesen
ser to be	fuera fuese	fueras fueses	fuera fuese	fuéramos fuésemos	fuerais fueseis	fueran fuesen
venir to come	viniera viniese	vinieras vinieses	viniera viniese	viniéramos viniésemos	vinierais vinieseis	vinieran viniesen

Forming the imperfect subjunctive of some irregular **-ir** verbs

➤ In some irregular **-ir** verbs – the ones that don't have an **i** in the **ellos** form of the preterite – **-era, -eras, -era, -éramos, -erais, -eran** *or* **-ese, -eses, -ese, -ésemos, -eseis, -esen** are added to the preterite stem instead of **-iera** and **-iese** and so on.

⇨ *For more information on the **Preterite**, see page 149.*

Infinitive	(yo)	(tú)	(él) (ella) (usted)	(nosotros) (nosotras)	(vosotros) (vosotras)	(ellos) (ellas) (ustedes)
decir to say	dijera dijese	dijeras dijeses	dijera dijese	dijéramos dijésemos	dijerais dijeseis	dijeran dijesen
ir to go	fuera fuese	fueras fueses	fuera fuese	fuéramos fuésemos	fuerais fueseis	fueran fuesen

i Note that the imperfect subjunctive forms of **ir** and **ser** are identical.

Teníamos miedo de que se <u>fuera</u>.	We were afraid he might leave.
No era verdad que <u>fueran</u> ellos.	It wasn't true that it was them.

Present indicative or imperfect subjunctive after si

➤ Like some other conjunctions, **si** (meaning *if*) is sometimes followed by the ordinary present tense (the <u>present indicative</u>) and sometimes by the <u>imperfect subjunctive</u>.

➤ **si** is followed by the <u>present indicative</u> when talking about likely possibilities.

Si <u>quieres</u>, te dejo el coche.	If you like, I'll lend you the car. *(and you may well want to borrow the car)*
Compraré un bolígrafo si <u>tienen</u>.	I'll buy a pen if they have any. *(and there may well be some pens)*

➤ **si** is followed by the <u>imperfect subjunctive</u> when talking about unlikely or impossible conditions.

Si <u>tuviera</u> más dinero, me lo compraría.	If I had more money, I'd buy it. *(but I haven't got more money)*
Si yo <u>fuera</u> tú, lo compraría.	If I were you, I'd buy it. *(but I'm not you)*

> *Tip*
> You probably need the imperfect subjunctive in Spanish after **si** if the English sentence has <u>would</u> in it.

> **KEY POINTS**
> ✔ After certain verbs you have to use a subjunctive in Spanish when there is a different subject in the two parts of the sentence.
> ✔ A subjunctive is also found after impersonal expressions, as well as after certain conjunctions.
> ✔ Structures with the subjunctive can often be avoided if the subject of both verbs is the same. An infinitive can often be used instead.
> ✔ The endings of the present subjunctive in regular **-ar** verbs are: **-e**, **-es**, **-e**, **-emos**, **-éis**, **-en**.
> ✔ The endings of the present subjunctive in regular **-er** and **-ir** verbs are: **-a**, **-as**, **-a**, **-amos**, **-áis**, **-an**.
> ✔ The endings of the imperfect subjunctive in regular **-ar** verbs are: **-ara**, **-aras**, **-ara**, **-áramos**, **-arais**, **-aran** or **-ase**, **-ases**, **-ase**, **-ásemos**, **-aseis**, **-asen**.
> ✔ The endings of the imperfect subjunctive in regular **-er** and **-ir** verbs are: **-iera**, **-ieras**, **-iera**, **-iéramos**, **-ierais**, **-ieran** or **-iese**, **-ieses**, **-iese**, **-iésemos**, **-ieseis**, **-iesen**.
> ✔ Some verbs have irregular subjunctive forms.

Test yourself

57 Complete the following with the correct form of the present subjunctive.

a   que yo .... (hablar)

b   que vosotros .... (decir)

c   que ellos .... (venir)

d   que él .... (vivir)

e   que tú .... (querer)

f   que ustedes .... (trabajar)

g   que ellas lo .... (hacer)

h   que nosotros .... (tener)

i   que el tren .... (salir)

j   que ellos .... (ponerse)

58 Match the infinitive and subjunctive forms.

a   saber   haya

b   ir   esté

c   haber   sepa

d   estar   fuese

e   ser   vaya

59 Match the verb to the subject.

a   nosotros   supieran

b   usted   me vaya

c   ellos   hablaras

d   tú   hayamos

e   yo   vaya

Test yourself

60 Complete the following sentences with the correct form of the subjunctive.

a   Quiero que José y Elena .... felices. **(ser)**

b   No creo que tus amigos .... hoy. **(venir)**

c   Prefiero que te .... **(irse)**

d   Siento que tu hermano no .... venir. **(poder)**

e   Me alegro de que te .... salido bien. **(haber)**

f   Espero que les .... el regalo. **(gustar)**

g   Quiero que tú se lo .... **(decir)**

h   Te pido que .... cuidado. **(tener)**

i   Espero que no .... tarde el tren. **(llegar)**

j   No creo que esa .... la razón. **(ser)**

PRACTICE PRACTICE PRACTICE PRACTICE PRACTICE PRACTICE

The Infinitive

> ## What is the infinitive?
> The **infinitive** is a form of the verb that hasn't had any endings added to it and doesn't relate to any particular tense. In English, the infinitive is usually shown with *to*, as in *to speak*, *to eat*, *to live*.

Using the infinitive

➤ In English, the infinitive is usually thought of as being made up of two words, for example, *to speak*. In Spanish, the infinitive consists of one word and is the verb form that ends in **-ar**, **-er** or **-ir**, for example, **hablar**, **comer**, **vivir**.

➤ When you look up a verb in the dictionary, you will find that information is usually listed under the infinitive form.

➤ In Spanish, the infinitive is often used in the following ways:

- after a preposition such as **antes de** (meaning *before*), **después de** (meaning *after*)

  Después de comer, fuimos a casa de Pepe.
  After eating, we went round to Pepe's.

  Salió sin hacer ruido.
  She went out without making a noise.

  Siempre veo la tele antes de acostarme.
  I always watch TV before going to bed.

  ⓘ Note that in English we always use the *-ing* form of the verb after a preposition, for example, *before going*. In Spanish you have to use the infinitive form after a preposition.

- in set phrases, particularly after adjectives or nouns

  Estoy encantada de poder ayudarte.
  I'm delighted to be able to help you.

  Está contento de vivir aquí.
  He's happy living here.

  Tengo ganas de salir.
  I feel like going out.

  No hace falta comprar leche.
  We/You don't need to buy any milk.

  Me dio mucha alegría verla.
  I was very pleased to see her.

  Me da miedo cruzar la carretera.
  I'm afraid of crossing the road.

- after another verb, sometimes as the object of it

  Debo llamar a casa.
  I must phone home.

  Prefiero esquiar.
  I prefer skiing.

  Me gusta escuchar música.
  I like listening to music.

  Nos encanta nadar.
  We love swimming.

  ¿Te apetece ir al cine?
  Do you fancy going to the cinema?

  ⓘ Note that, when it comes after another verb, the Spanish infinitive often corresponds to the *-ing* form in English.

- in instructions that are aimed at the general public – for example in cookery books or on signs

  Cocer a fuego lento.
  Cook on a low heat.

  Prohibido pisar el césped.
  Don't walk on the grass.

- as a noun, where in English we would use the -ing form of the verb
  Lo importante es <u>intentarlo</u>.   Trying is the important thing.

⚠ Note that, when the infinitive is the subject of another verb, it may have the article **el** before it, particularly if it starts the sentence.

  El viajar tanto me resulta cansado.   I find so much travelling tiring.

> *Tip*
> Be especially careful when translating the English -ing form. It is often translated by the infinitive in Spanish.

Linking two verbs together

➤ There are three ways that verbs can be linked together when the second verb is an infinitive:

- with no linking word in between
  ¿Quieres venir?   Do you want to come?
  Necesito hablar contigo.   I need to talk to you.

- with a preposition
  ir <u>a</u> hacer algo   to be going to do something
  aprender <u>a</u> hacer algo   to learn to do something
  dejar <u>de</u> hacer algo   to stop doing something
  Voy <u>a</u> comprarme un móvil.   I'm going to buy a mobile.
  Aprendimos <u>a</u> esquiar.   We learnt to ski.
  Quiere dejar <u>de</u> fumar.   He wants to stop smoking.

⚠ Note that you have to learn the preposition required for each verb.

- in set structures
  tener que hacer algo   to have to do something
  Tengo que salir.   I've got to go out.
  Tendrías que comer más.   You should eat more.
  Tuvo que devolver el dinero.   He had to pay back the money.

Verbs followed by the infinitive with no preposition

➤ Some Spanish verbs and groups of verbs can be followed by an infinitive with no preposition:

- **poder** (meaning *to be able to, can, may*), **saber** (meaning *to know how to, can*), **querer** (meaning *to want*) and **deber** (meaning *to have to, must*)
  No <u>puede venir</u>.   He can't come.
  <u>¿Sabes esquiar</u>?   Can you ski?
  <u>Quiere estudiar</u> medicina.   He wants to study medicine.
  <u>Debes hacerlo</u>.   You must do it.

- verbs like **gustar**, **encantar** and **apetecer**, where the infinitive is the subject of the verb
  <u>Me gusta estudiar</u>.   I like studying.
  <u>Nos encanta bailar</u>.   We love dancing.
  <u>¿Te apetece ir</u> al cine?   Do you fancy going to the cinema?

For further explanation of grammatical terms, please see pages viii-xii.

- verbs that relate to seeing or hearing, such as **ver** (meaning *to see*) and **oír** (meaning *to hear*)

  Nos <u>ha visto llegar</u>.   He saw us arrive.
  Te <u>he oído cantar</u>.   I heard you singing.

- the verbs **hacer** (meaning *to make*) and **dejar** (meaning *to let*)

  ¡No me <u>hagas reír</u>!   Don't make me laugh!
  Mis padres no me <u>dejan salir</u>   My parents don't let me go out at night.
    por la noche.

- the following common verbs

decidir	to decide
desear	to wish, want
esperar	to hope
evitar	to avoid
necesitar	to need
odiar	to hate
olvidar	to forget
pensar	to think
preferir	to prefer
recordar	to remember
sentir	to regret

  Han <u>decidido comprarse</u> una casa.   They've decided to buy a house.
  No <u>desea tener</u> más hijos.   She doesn't want to have any more children.
  <u>Espero poder</u> ir.   I hope to be able to go.
  <u>Evita gastar</u> demasiado dinero.   He avoids spending too much money.
  <u>Necesito salir</u> un momento.   I need to go out for a moment.
  <u>Olvidó dejar</u> su dirección.   She forgot to leave her address.
  <u>Pienso hacer</u> una paella.   I'm thinking of making a paella.
  <u>Siento molestarte</u>.   I'm sorry to bother you.

➤ Some of these verbs combine with infinitives to make set phrases with a special meaning:

- **querer decir**   to mean

  ¿Qué <u>quiere decir</u> eso?   What does that mean?

- **dejar caer**   to drop

  <u>Dejó caer</u> la bandeja.   She dropped the tray.

Verbs followed by the preposition a and the infinitive

➤ The following verbs are the most common ones that can be followed by **a** and the infinitive:

- verbs relating to movement such as **ir** (meaning *to go*) and **venir** (meaning *to come*)

  Se va <u>a</u> comprar un caballo.   He's going to buy a horse.
  Viene <u>a</u> vernos.   He's coming to see us.

- the following common verbs

aprender <u>a</u> hacer algo	to learn to do something
comenzar <u>a</u> hacer algo	to begin to do something
decidirse <u>a</u> hacer algo	to decide to do something
empezar <u>a</u> hacer algo	to begin to do something

llegar a hacer algo	to manage to do something
llegar a ser algo	to become something
probar a hacer algo	to try to do something
volver a hacer algo	to do something again

Me gustaría aprender a nadar.	I'd like to learn to swim.
No llegó a terminar la carrera.	He didn't manage to finish his degree course.
Llegó a ser primer ministro.	He became prime minister.
No vuelvas a hacerlo nunca más.	Don't ever do it again.

➤ The following verbs can be followed by **a** and a person's name or else by **a** and a noun or pronoun referring to a person, and then by another **a** and an infinitive.

ayudar a alguien a hacer algo	to help someone to do something
enseñar a alguien a hacer algo	to teach someone to do something
invitar a alguien a hacer algo	to invite someone to do something

¿Le podrías ayudar a Antonia a fregar los platos?	Could you help Antonia do the dishes?
Le enseñó a su hermano a nadar.	He taught his brother to swim.
Los he invitado a tomar unas copas en casa.	I've invited them over for drinks.

Verbs followed by the preposition de and the infinitive

➤ The following verbs are the most common ones that can be followed by **de** and the infinitive:

aburrirse de hacer algo	to get bored with doing something
acabar de hacer algo	to have just done something
acordarse de haber hecho/ de hacer algo	to remember having done/ doing something
alegrarse de hacer algo	to be glad to do something
dejar de hacer algo	to stop doing something
tener ganas de hacer algo	to want to do something
tratar de hacer algo	to try to do something

Me aburría de no poder salir de casa.	I was getting bored with not being able to leave the house.
Acabo de comprar un móvil.	I've just bought a mobile.
Acababan de llegar cuando...	They had just arrived when...
Me alegro de verte.	I'm glad to see you.
¿Quieres dejar de hablar?	Will you stop talking?
Tengo ganas de volver a España.	I want to go back to Spain.

Verbs followed by the preposition con and the infinitive

➤ The following verbs are the most common ones that can be followed by **con** and the infinitive:

amenazar con hacer algo	to threaten to do someting
soñar con hacer algo	to dream about doing something
Amenazó con denunciarlos.	He threatened to report them.
Sueño con vivir en España.	I dream about living in Spain.

For further explanation of grammatical terms, please see pages viii-xii.

Verbs followed by the preposition en and the infinitive

➤ The verb **quedar** is the most common one that can be followed by **en** and the infinitive:

quedar en hacer algo	to agree to do something
Habíamos quedado en encontrarnos a las ocho.	We had agreed to meet at eight.

KEY POINTS

✔ Infinitives are found after prepositions, set phrases and in instructions to the general public.

✔ They can also function as the subject or object of a verb, when the infinitive corresponds to the -ing form in English.

✔ Many Spanish verbs can be followed by another verb in the infinitive.

✔ The two verbs may be linked by nothing at all, or by **a**, **de** or another preposition.

✔ The construction in Spanish does not always match the English. It's best to learn these constructions when you learn a new verb.

Test yourself

61 Match the Spanish and English.

a	**dejar caer**	to think of doing
b	**esperar poder**	to drop
c	**querer decir**	to need to do
d	**pensar hacer**	to mean
e	**deber hacer**	to hope to be able to

62 Complete the following sentences with the prepositions a, de, or con.

a   Voy .... decírselo.

b   Aprendimos .... bailar.

c   Se aburrieron .... ver la tele.

d   Empezó .... llover.

e   Me alegro .... haberte conocido.

f   Acabamos .... llegar.

g   Soñaba .... ser famoso.

h   Deja .... llamarme.

i   Basta .... decirlo una vez.

j   Tengo ganas .... salir.

63 Create a sentence using the elements below. Don't forget to add the relevant preposition if it is required.

a   Voy/comprarme/coche ....

b   Decidió/comprarse/moto ....

c   Vamos/visitar/tu tía ....

d   Necesito/hablar/él ....

e   Tratamos/vivir/vida tranquila ....

f   Nos aburrimos/esperar ....

g   Quiero/aprender/hablar inglés ....

h   Esperamos/poder/ir ....

i   No vuelvas/llegar tarde. ....

j   Me gustaría/ir/Argentina ....

Prepositions after verbs

➤ In English, there are some phrases which are made up of verbs and prepositions, for example, *to accuse somebody of something*, *to look forward to something* and *to rely on something*.

➤ In Spanish there are also lots of set phrases made up of verbs and prepositions. Often the prepositions in Spanish are not the same as they are in English, so you will need to learn them. Listed below are phrases using verbs and some common Spanish prepositions.

⇨ *For more information on verbs used with a preposition and the infinitive, see page 203.*

Verbs followed by a

➤ **a** is often the equivalent of the English word *to* when it is used with an indirect object after verbs like **enviar** (meaning *to send*), **dar** (meaning *to give*) and **decir** (meaning *to say*).

dar algo a alguien	to give something to someone
decir algo a alguien	to say something to someone
enviar algo a alguien	to send something to someone
escribir algo a alguien	to write something to someone
mostrar algo a alguien	to show something to someone

⇨ *For more information on **Indirect objects**, see page 65.*

> *Tip*
> There is an important difference between Spanish and English with this type of verb. In English, you can say either *to give something to someone* or *to give someone something*.
>
> You can NEVER miss out **a** in Spanish in the way that you can sometimes miss out *to* in English.

➤ Here are some verbs taking **a** in Spanish that have a different construction in English.

asistir a algo	to attend something, to be at something
dirigirse a (un lugar)	to head for (a place)
dirigirse a alguien	to address somebody
jugar a algo	to play something (*sports/games*)
llegar a (un lugar)	to arrive at (a place)
oler a algo	to smell of something
parecerse a alguien/algo	to look like somebody/something
subir(se) a un autobús/un coche	to get on a bus/into a car
subir(se) a un árbol	to climb a tree
tener miedo a alguien	to be afraid of somebody
Este perfume huele a jazmín.	This perfume smells of jasmine.
¡De prisa, sube al coche!	Get into the car, quick!
Nunca tuvieron miedo a su padre.	They were never afraid of their father.

⇨ *For verbs such as gustar, encantar and faltar, see **Verbal idioms** on page 212.*

Verbs followed by de

➤ Here are some verbs taking **de** in Spanish that have a different construction in English:

acordarse **de** algo/alguien	to remember something/somebody
alegrarse **de** algo	to be glad about something
bajarse **de** un autobús/un coche	to get off a bus/out of a car
darse cuenta **de** algo	to realize something
depender **de** algo/alguien	to depend on something/somebody
despedirse **de** alguien	to say goodbye to somebody
preocuparse **de** algo/alguien	to worry about something/somebody
quejarse **de** algo	to complain about something
reírse **de** algo/alguien	to laugh at something/somebody
salir **de** (un cuarto/un edificio)	to leave (a room/a building)
tener ganas **de** algo	to want something
trabajar **de** (camarero/secretario)	to work as (a waiter/secretary)
tratarse **de** algo/alguien	to be a question of something/ to be about somebody

Nos acordamos muy bien **de** aquellas vacaciones.	We remember that holiday very well.
Se bajó **del** coche.	He got out of the car.
No depende **de** mí.	It doesn't depend on me.
Se preocupa mucho **de** su apariencia.	He worries a lot about his appearance.

Verbs followed by con

➤ Here are some verbs taking **con** in Spanish that have a different construction in English:

contar **con** alguien/algo	to rely on somebody/something
encontrarse **con** alguien	to meet somebody (*by chance*)
enfadarse **con** alguien	to get annoyed with somebody
hablar **con** alguien	to talk to somebody
soñar **con** alguien/algo	to dream about somebody/something

Cuento **contigo**.	I'm relying on you.
Me encontré **con** ella al entrar en el banco.	I met her as I was going into the bank.
¿Puedo hablar **con** usted un momento?	May I talk to you for a moment?

Verbs followed by en

➤ Here are some verbs taking **en** in Spanish that have a different construction in English:

entrar **en** (un edificio/un cuarto)	to enter, go into (a building/a room)
pensar **en** algo/alguien	to think about something/somebody
No quiero pensar **en** eso.	I don't want to think about that.

Verbs followed by <u>por</u>

➤ Here are some verbs taking **por** in Spanish that have a different construction in English:

interesarse <u>por</u> algo/alguien	to ask about something/somebody
preguntar <u>por</u> alguien	to ask for/about somebody
preocuparse <u>por</u> algo/alguien	to worry about something/somebody

Me interesaba mucho <u>por</u> la arqueología.	I was very interested in archaeology.
Se preocupa mucho <u>por</u> su apariencia.	He worries a lot about his appearance.

Verbs taking a direct object in Spanish but not in English

➤ In English there are a few verbs that are followed by *at*, *for* or *to* which, in Spanish, are not followed by any preposition other than the personal **a**.

⇨ *For more information on **Personal** a, see page 246.*

mirar algo/a alguien	to look at something/somebody
escuchar algo/a alguien	to listen to something/somebody
buscar algo/a alguien	to look for something/somebody
pedir algo	to ask for something
esperar algo/a alguien	to wait for something/somebody
pagar algo	to pay for something

Mira esta foto.	Look at this photo.
Me gusta escuchar música.	I like listening to music.
Estoy buscando las gafas.	I'm looking for my glasses.
Pidió una taza de té.	He asked for a cup of tea.
Estamos esperando el tren.	We're waiting for the train.
Ya he pagado el billete.	I've already paid for my ticket.
Estoy buscando a mi hermano.	I'm looking for my brother.

KEY POINTS

✔ The prepositions used with Spanish verbs are often very different from those used in English, so make sure you learn common expressions involving prepositions in Spanish.

✔ The most common prepositions used with verbs in Spanish are **a**, **de**, **con**, **en** and **por**.

✔ Some Spanish verbs are not followed by a preposition, but are used with a preposition in English.

Test yourself

64 Complete the following sentences with the correct form of a, or de.

   a   Jugamos .... tenis.

   b   Dale tu correo electrónico .... Pepa.

   c   Trabaja .... enfermera.

   d   Se parece .... su padre.

   e   No me di cuenta .... la hora.

   f   ¿Vamos .... tomar un café?

   g   ¿Tienes ganas .... ir al parque?

   h   Se quejaron .... la comida.

   i   Salieron .... edificio corriendo.

   j   No te rías .... mí.

65 Complete the following sentences with the prepositions con, en or por.

   a   Estoy muy enfadada .... ella.

   b   Me preocupo .... ellos.

   c   Siempre está pensando .... el trabajo.

   d   Me preguntó .... mis padres.

   e   Entró .... mi oficina sin llamar.

   f   Soñaba .... ser rico.

   g   Necesito hablar .... usted un momento.

   h   No podemos contar .... ellos.

   i   Se interesa mucho .... la historia.

   j   Me encontré .... tu hermana en el centro.

Test yourself

66 Translate the following sentences into Spanish.

a   I'm looking for a dictionary.

....

b   They were looking at the people on the beach.

....

c   He was looking at the sky.

....

d   He asked me for the address.

....

e   She paid for my ticket.

....

f   He likes watching television.

....

g   I'm waiting for my mother.

....

h   I've already paid for the coffees.

....

i   Look at this.

....

j   Help me look for my keys.

....

PRACTICE PRACTICE PRACTICE PRACTICE PRACTICE

Verbal Idioms

Present tense of gustar

➤ You will probably already have come across the phrase **me gusta...** meaning *I like...* .
Actually, **gustar** means literally *to please*, and if you remember this, you will be able to use **gustar** much more easily.

Me gusta el chocolate.	I like chocolate. (*literally: chocolate pleases me*)
Me gustan los animales.	I like animals. (*literally: animals please me*)
Nos gusta el español.	We like Spanish. (*literally: Spanish pleases us*)
Nos gustan los españoles.	We like Spanish people. (*literally: Spanish people please us*)

➤ Even though **chocolate**, **animales**, and so on, come after **gustar**, they are the subject of the verb (the person or thing performing the action) and therefore the endings of **gustar** change to agree with them.

➤ When the thing that you like is <u>singular</u>, you use **gusta** (*third person singular*), and when the thing that you like is <u>plural</u>, you use **gustan** (*third person plural*).

Le gusta Francia.	He/She likes France. (*literally: France pleases him/her*)
Le gustan los caramelos.	He/She likes sweets. (*literally: Sweets please him/her*)

ℹ️ Note that **me**, **te**, **le**, **nos**, **os** and **les**, which are used with **gustar**, are indirect object pronouns.

⇨ For more information on **Indirect object pronouns**, *see page 65.*

Other tenses of gustar

➤ You can use **gustar** in other tenses in Spanish.

Les gustó la fiesta.	They liked the party.
Les gustaron los fuegos artificiales.	They liked the fireworks.
Te va a gustar la película.	You'll like the film.
Te van a gustar las fotos.	You'll like the photos.
Les ha gustado mucho el museo.	They really liked the museum.
Les han gustado mucho los cuadros.	They really liked the paintings.

➤ You can also use **más** with **gustar** to say what you prefer.

A mí me gusta más el rojo.	I prefer the red one. (*literally: the red one pleases me more*)
A mí me gustan más los rojos.	I prefer the red ones. (*literally: the red ones please me more*)

Other verbs like gustar

➤ There are several other verbs which behave in the same way as **gustar**:

- encantar

Me encanta el flamenco.	I love flamenco.
Me encantan los animales.	I love animals.

- faltar

Le faltaba un botón.	He had a button missing.
Le faltaban tres dientes.	He had three teeth missing.

For further explanation of grammatical terms, please see pages viii-xii.

- quedar
  No les <u>queda</u> nada.   They have nothing left.
  Solo nos <u>quedan</u> dos kilómetros.   We've only got two kilometres left.

- doler
  Le <u>dolía</u> la cabeza.   His head hurt.
  Le <u>dolían</u> las muelas.   His teeth hurt.

- interesar
  Te <u>interesará</u> el libro.   The book will interest you.
  Te <u>interesarán</u> sus noticias.   His news will interest you.

- importar
  No me <u>importa</u> la lluvia.   The rain doesn't matter to me. *or* I don't mind the rain.

  Me <u>importan</u> mucho mis estudios.   My studies matter to me a lot.

- hacer falta
  Nos <u>hace</u> falta un ordenador.   We need a computer.
  Nos <u>hacen</u> falta libros.   We need books.

Grammar Extra!
All the examples given above are in the third persons singular and plural as these are by far the most common. However, it is also possible to use these verbs in other forms.

Creo que le <u>gustas</u>.   I think he likes you. (*literally: I think you please him*)

Verbal idioms used with another verb

➤ In English you can say *I like playing football, we love swimming* and so on, and in Spanish you can also use another verb with most of the verbs like **gustar**. However, the verb form you use for the second verb in Spanish is the <u>infinitive</u>.
  Le <u>gusta jugar</u> al fútbol.   He/She likes playing football.
  No me <u>gusta bailar</u>.   I don't like dancing.
  Nos <u>encanta estudiar</u>.   We love studying.
  No me <u>importa tener</u> que esperar.   I don't mind having to wait.

⇨ *For more information on the* **Infinitive**, *see page 201.*

KEY POINTS

✔ There are a number of common verbs in Spanish which are used in the opposite way to English, for example, **gustar**, **encantar**, **hacer falta**, and so on. With all these verbs, the object of the English verb is the subject of the Spanish verb.
✔ The endings of these verbs change according to whether the thing liked or needed and so on is singular or plural.
✔ All these verbs can be followed by another verb in the infinitive.

67 Cross out the subjects that the verb cannot refer to.

a   **le gusta**   España/el chocolate/los dulces/el fútbol/los ingleses

b   **me gustan**   las naranjas/el café/el cine/bailar/los zapatos de tacón

c   **¿te gustó**   la fiesta/la comida/las flores/las fotos/el regalo?

d   **te va a gustar**   mis amigos/la película/la universidad/el restaurante/sus ideas

e   **nos han gustado**   Francia/sus amigos/los museos/Londres/el viaje

f   **no me gusta**   la playa/el cine/las manzanas/los dulces

g   **les ha gustado**   la cena/el restaurante/las vacaciones/la fiesta

h   **¿te gustan**   las rosas/mi casa/las fotos/el chocolate/el azul?

i   **me gusta**   Londres/el italiano/los americanos/leer/los animales

j   **¿os gusta**   bailar/los chocolates/viajar/el pescado/los perros?

68 Match the two columns.

a   Me hace falta   el calor.

b   Les hacen falta   la cabeza.

c   Le duele   los perros.

d   No me importa   un ordenador.

e   Le encantan   unas vacaciones.

69 Complete the following sentences with the correct form of the present tense.

a   No me .... el calor. **(importar)**

b   Me .... mucho los dulces. **(gustar)**

c   Le .... la cabeza. **(doler)**

d   Me .... diez páginas por leer. **(quedar)**

e   Les .... la playa. **(encantar)**

f   Nos .... gente. **(faltar)**

g   No le .... las consecuencias. **(importar)**

h   Nos .... más sillas. **(hacer falta)**

i   Le .... aprender. **(interesar)**

j   ¿Os .... más el rojo o el verde? **(gustar)**

Negatives

no

➤ In English, we often make sentences negative by adding *don't*, *doesn't* or *didn't* before the verb. In Spanish you simply add **no** (meaning *not*) before the main verb.

Positive		Negative
Trabaja. He works.	→	**No** trabaja. He doesn't work.
Comen. They eat.	→	**No** comen. They don't eat.
Salió. She went out.	→	**No** salió. She didn't go out.
Lo he visto. I've seen it.	→	**No** lo he visto. I haven't seen it.
Sabe nadar. He can swim.	→	**No** sabe nadar. He can't swim.

> *Tip*
> NEVER translate *don't, doesn't, didn't* using **hacer.**

➤ Where there is a subject (the person doing the action) in the sentence, put **no** between the subject and the verb.

Juan <u>no</u> vive aquí.	Juan doesn't live here.
Mi hermana <u>no</u> lee mucho.	My sister doesn't read much.
Mis padres <u>no</u> han llamado.	My parents haven't called.
Él <u>no</u> lo comprenderá.	He won't understand.

ⓘ Note that the Spanish word **no** also means *no* in answer to a question.

➤ Where the subject is only shown by the verb ending, **no** goes before the verb.

<u>No</u> tenemos tiempo.	We haven't got time.
Todavía <u>no</u> ha llegado.	He hasn't arrived yet.
<u>No</u> hemos comido.	We haven't eaten.
<u>No</u> llevará mucho tiempo.	It won't take long.

➤ If there are any object pronouns (for example, **me, te, lo, los, le** and so on) before the verb, **no** goes BEFORE them.

<u>No</u> lo he visto.	I didn't see it.
<u>No</u> me gusta el fútbol.	I don't like football.

➤ In phrases consisting only of *not* and another word, such as *not now* or *not me*, the Spanish **no** usually goes AFTER the other word.

Ahora <u>no</u>.	Not now.
Yo <u>no</u>.	Not me.
Todavía <u>no</u>.	Not yet.

➤ Some phrases have a special construction in Spanish.

Espero que sí.   I hope so.   **Espero que no.**   I hope not.
Creo que sí.   I think so.   **Creo que no.**   I don't think so.

Other negative words

➤ In Spanish, you can form negatives using pairs and groups of words, as you can in English.

- **no … nunca**   never *or* not … ever
  No la veo **nunca**.   I never see her *or* I don't ever see her.

- **no … jamás**   never *or* not … ever
  No la veo **jamás**.   I never see her *or* I don't ever see her.

- **no … nada**   nothing *or* not … anything
  No ha dicho **nada**.   He has said nothing *or* He hasn't said anything.

- **no … nadie**   nobody *or* not … anybody
  No hablaron con **nadie**.   They spoke to nobody *or* They didn't speak to anybody.

- **no … tampoco**   not … either
  Yo **no** la vi. — Yo **tampoco**.   I didn't see her. — Neither did I *or* I didn't either *or* Nor did I.

  A él **no** le gusta el café y a mí **tampoco**.   He doesn't like coffee and neither do I.

- **no … ni … ni**   neither … nor
  No vinieron **ni** Carlos **ni** Ana.   Neither Carlos nor Ana came.

- **no … más**   no longer *or* not .. any more
  No te veré **más**.   I won't see you any more.

- **no … ningún/ninguna** + *noun*   no *or* not … any
  No tiene **ningún** interés en ir.   She has no interest in going.

➤ Most of these negative words can also be used without **no** provided they come before any verb.
Nunca *or* **Jamás** la veo.   I never see her.
Nadie vino.   No one came.
Ni Pedro **ni** Pablo fuman.   Neither Pedro nor Pablo smokes.
¿Quién te ha dicho eso? — **Nadie**.   Who told you that? — No one.
¿Qué has hecho? — **Nada**.   What have you done? — Nothing.

➤ Sometimes negative expressions combine with each other.
Nunca hacen **nada**.   They never do anything.
Nunca viene **nadie**.   No one ever comes.
No lo haré **nunca más**.   I'll never do it again.

Word order with negatives

➤ In English you can put words like *never* and *ever* between *have/has/had* and the past participle, for example, *We have never been to Argentina*. You should <u>NEVER</u> separate **he**, **has**, **ha**, **había** and so on from the past participle of the verb in Spanish.

<u>**Nunca**</u> **hemos estado en Argentina.**	We have never been to Argentina.
<u>**Nunca**</u> **había visto** <u>**nada**</u> **así.**	I had never seen anything like this.
<u>**Ninguno**</u> **de nosotros había esquiado** <u>**nunca**</u>.	None of us had ever skied.

⇨ *For more information on **Past participles**, see page 164.*

KEY POINTS

✔ The Spanish word **no** is equivalent to both *no* and *not* in English.

✔ You can make sentences negative by putting **no** before the verb (and before any object pronouns that are in front of the verb).

✔ Other negative words also exist, such as **nunca**, **nadie** and **nada.** Use them in combination with **no,** with the verb sandwiched in between. Most of them also work on their own provided they go <u>before</u> any verb.

✔ Never insert negative words, or anything else, between **he**, **has**, **ha**, **había** and so on and the past participle.

Test yourself

1 **Create a negative sentence in the present tense using the elements below.**

a Elena/vivir/Londres/no ....

b Mis padres/hablar inglés/no ....

c Jorge/tener tiempo/no ....

d Me/gustar/el chocolate/no ....

e Isabel/comer carne/no ....

f llevar/mucho tiempo/no ....

g Belén/querer/venir conmigo/no ....

h yo/gastar/mucho dinero/no ....

i Cristina/saber/conducir/no ....

j Mis padres/entender/a mí/no ....

2 **Circle the correct alternative.**

a Yo no lo vi   Yo tampoco./Yo también.

b No hablamos con   alguien/nadie.

c No he dicho   algo/nada.

d Nada para ellos   y para mí también/y para mí tampoco.

e A mi marido no le gusta el vino   y a mí también/y a mí tampoco.

f No tengo   alguno/ninguno.

g No vino   alguien/nadie.

h Nunca hacen   algo/nada.

i Nunca veo a   alguien/nadie.

j Él no quiere ir   y yo también/y yo tampoco.

PRACTICE PRACTICE PRACTICE PRACTICE PRACTICE

Test yourself

3 **Translate the following sentences into Spanish.**

a I don't want to go. ....

b He never comes with us. ....

c I don't have time. ....

d I've never seen them. ....

e I can't play the piano. ....

f I don't eat meat. ....

g They don't live here any more. ....

h I hope not. ....

i I don't think she knows. ....

j It doesn't take long. ....

Questions

Asking questions in Spanish

There are three main ways of asking questions in Spanish:

- by making your voice go up at the end of the sentence

- by changing normal word order

- by using a question word

Tip
Don't forget the opening question mark in Spanish. It goes at the beginning of the question or of the question part of the sentence.

¿No quieres tomar algo?	Wouldn't you like something to eat or drink?
Eres inglés, ¿verdad?	You're English, aren't you?

Asking a question by making your voice go up

➤ If you are expecting the answer *yes* or *no*, there is a very simple way of asking a question. You keep the word order exactly as it would be in a normal sentence but you turn it into a question by making your voice go up at the end.

¿Hablas español?	Do you speak Spanish?
¿Es profesor?	Is he a teacher?
¿Hay leche?	Is there any milk?
¿Te gusta la música?	Do you like music?

➤ When the subject (the person or thing doing the action) of the verb is a noun, pronoun or name it can be given before the verb, just as in an ordinary sentence. But you turn the statement into a question by making your voice go up at the end.

¿Tu hermana ha comprado pan?	Did your sister buy any bread?
¿Tú lo has hecho?	Did you do it?
¿Tu padre te ha visto?	Did your father see you?
¿El diccionario está aquí?	Is the dictionary here?

For further explanation of grammatical terms, please see pages viii-xii.

Asking a question by changing word order

➤ When the subject of the verb is specified, another even more common way of asking questions is to change the word order so that the verb comes <u>BEFORE</u> the subject instead of after it.

¿Lo has hecho tú?	Did you do it?
¿Te ha visto tu padre?	Did your father see you?
¿Está el diccionario aquí?	Is the dictionary here?

🅘 Note that the position of object pronouns is not affected.

⇨ *For more information on **Word order with object pronouns**, see pages 61, 66 and 70.*

Grammar Extra!
If the verb has an object, such as *any bread* in *Did your sister buy any bread?*, the subject comes <u>AFTER</u> the object, provided the object is short.

¿Ha compado <u>pan</u> tu hermana?	Did your sister buy any bread?
¿Vio <u>la película</u> tu novio?	Did your boyfriend see the film?

If the object is made up of several words, the subject goes <u>BEFORE</u> it.

Se han comprado tus padres <u>aquella casa de que me hablaste</u>?	Have your parents bought that house you told me about?

When there is an adverbial phrase (to the party, in Barcelona) after the verb, the subject can go <u>BEFORE OR AFTER</u> the adverbial phrase.

¿Viene <u>a la fiesta</u> Andrés? *or*	Is Andrés coming to the party?
¿Viene Andrés <u>a la fiesta</u>?	

Asking a question by using a question word

➤ Question words are words like *when, what, who, which, where* and *how* that are used to ask for information. In Spanish, <u>ALL</u> question words have an accent on them.

¿adónde?	where … to?
¿cómo?	how?
¿cuál/cuáles?	which?
¿cuándo?	when?
¿cuánto/cuánta?	how much?
¿cuántos/cuántas?	how many?
¿dónde?	where?
¿para qué?	what for?
¿por qué?	why?
¿qué?	what?, which?
¿quién?	who?

> *Típ*
> Be careful not to mix up **por qué** (meaning *why*) with **porque** (meaning *because*).

¿Cuándo se fue?	When did he go?
¿Qué te pasa?	What's the matter?
¿Qué chaqueta te vas a poner?	Which jacket are you going to wear?
¿Cuál de los dos quieres?	Which do you want?
¿Cuánto azúcar quieres?	How much sugar do you want?
¿Cuánto tiempo llevas esperando?	How long have you been waiting?

⇨ *For more information on question words, see* **Interrogative adjectives** *on page 45 and* **Interrogative pronouns** *on page 93.*

➤ When the question starts with a question word that isn't the subject of the verb, the noun or pronoun (if given) that is the subject of the verb goes <u>AFTER</u> it.

¿De qué color es <u>la moqueta</u>?	What colour's the carpet?
¿A qué hora comienza <u>el concierto</u>?	What time does the concert start?
¿Dónde están <u>tus pantalones</u>?	Where are your trousers?
¿Adónde iba <u>tu padre</u>?	Where was your father going?
¿Cómo están <u>tus padres</u>?	How are your parents?
¿Cuándo volverán <u>ustedes</u>?	When will you come back?

Which question word to use?

➤ **qué** or **cuál** or **cuáles** can be used to mean *which*:

- always use **qué** before a noun

¿<u>Qué chaqueta</u> te vas a poner?	<u>Which jacket</u> are you going to wear?

- otherwise use **cuál** (*singular*) or **cuáles** (*plural*)

¿Cuál quieres?	<u>Which (one)</u> do you want?
¿Cuáles quieres?	<u>Which (ones)</u> do you want?

➤ **quién** or **quiénes** can be used to mean *who*:

- use **quién** when asking about one person

¿Quién ganó?	<u>Who</u> won?

- use **quiénes** when asking about more than one person

¿Quiénes estaban?	<u>Who</u> was there?

ⓘ Note that you need to put the personal **a** before **quién** and **quiénes** when it acts as an object.

¿<u>A quién</u> viste?	<u>Who</u> did you see?

⇨ *For more information on* **Personal a**, *see page 246.*

➤ **de quién** or **de quiénes** can be used to mean *whose*:

- use **de quién** when there is likely to be one owner
  ¿De quién es este abrigo?   <u>Whose</u> coat is this?

- use **de quiénes** when there is likely to be more than one owner
  ¿De quiénes son estos abrigos?   <u>Whose</u> coats are these?

> 🛈 Note that the structure in Spanish is the equivalent of *Whose <u>is</u> this coat?/Whose <u>are</u> these coats?* Don't try putting **¿de quién?** or **¿de quiénes?** immediately before a noun.

➤ **qué**, **cómo**, **cuál** and **cuáles** can all be used to mean *what* although **qué** is the most common translation:

- use **cómo** not **qué** when asking someone to repeat something that you didn't hear properly
  ¿Cómo (has dicho)?   <u>What</u> (did you say)?

- use **¿cuál es …?** and **¿cuáles son …?** to mean *what is …?* and *what/are …?* when you aren't asking for a definition
  ¿Cuál es la capital de Francia?   <u>What's</u> the capital of France?
  ¿Cuál es su número de teléfono?   <u>What's</u> his telephone number?

- use **¿qué es …?** and **¿qué son …?** to mean *what is …?* and *what are …?* when you are asking for a definition
  ¿Qué son los genes?   <u>What are</u> genes?

- always use **qué** to mean *what* before another noun
  ¿Qué hora es?   <u>What time</u> is it?
  ¿Qué asignaturas estudias?   <u>What subjects</u> are you studying?

Tip

You can finish an English question (or sentence) with a preposition such as *about*, for example, *Who did you write to?*; *What are you talking about?* You can <u>NEVER</u> end a Spanish question or sentence with a preposition.

¿Con quién hablaste?   Who did you speak <u>to</u>?

Grammar Extra!

All the questions we have looked at so far have been straight questions, otherwise known as <u>direct questions</u>. However, sometimes instead of asking directly, for example, *Where is it?* or *Why did you do it?*, we ask the question in a more roundabout way, for example, *Can you tell me where it is?* or *Please tell me why you did it*. These are called indirect questions.

In indirect questions in English we say *where <u>it is</u>* instead of *where <u>is it</u>* and *why <u>you did it</u>* instead of *why <u>did you do it</u>*, but in Spanish you still put the subject <u>AFTER</u> the verb.

¿Sabes adónde <u>iba tu padre</u>?	Do you know where your father was going?
¿Puedes decirme para qué <u>sirven los diccionarios</u>?	Can you tell me what dictionaries are for?

The subject also goes <u>AFTER</u> the verb in Spanish when you report a question in indirect speech.

Quería saber adónde <u>iba mi padre</u>.	He wanted to know where my father was going.

[*i*] Note that you still put accents on question words in Spanish even when they are in indirect and reported questions or when they come after expressions of uncertainty:

No sé <u>qué</u> hacer.	I don't know what to do.
No sabemos <u>por qué</u> se fue.	We don't know why he left.

Negative questions

➤ When you want to make a negative question, put **no** before the verb in the same way that you do in statements (non-questions).

¿<u>No</u> vienes?	Aren't you coming?
¿<u>No</u> lo has visto?	Didn't you see it?

➤ You can also use **o no** at the end of a question in the same way that we can ask *or not* in English.

¿Vienes <u>o no</u>?	Are you coming <u>or not</u>?
¿Lo quieres <u>o no</u>?	Do you want it <u>or not</u>?

Short questions

➤ In English we sometimes check whether our facts and beliefs are correct by putting *isn't it?*, *don't they?*, *are they?* and so on at the end of a comment.
In Spanish, you can add **¿verdad?** in the same way.

Hace calor, ¿<u>verdad</u>?	It's hot, <u>isn't it</u>?
Te gusta, ¿<u>verdad</u>?	You like it, <u>don't you</u>?
No te olvidarás, ¿<u>verdad</u>?	You won't forget, <u>will you</u>?
No vino, ¿<u>verdad</u>?	He didn't come, <u>did he</u>?

For further explanation of grammatical terms, please see pages viii-xii.

➤ You can also use **¿no?**, especially after positive comments.

Hace calor, ¿no?	It's hot, <u>isn't it</u>?
Te gusta, ¿no?	You like it, <u>don't you</u>?

Answering questions

➤ To answer a question which requires a *yes* or *no* answer, just use **sí** or **no**.

¿Te gusta? — Sí/No.	Do you like it? — Yes, I do/No, I don't.
¿Está aquí? — Sí/No.	Is he here? — Yes he is/No, he isn't.
¿Tienes prisa? — Sí/No.	Are you in a hurry? — Yes, I am/No, I'm not.
No lo has hecho, ¿verdad? — Sí/No.	You haven't done it, have you? — Yes, I have/No, I haven't.

➤ You can also often answer **sí** or **no** followed by the verb in question. In negative answers this may mean that you say **no** twice.

Quieres acompañarme? — Sí, quiero.	Would you like to come with me? — Yes, I would.
¿Vas a ir a la fiesta? — No, no voy.	Are you going to the party? — No, I'm not.

KEY POINTS

✔ You ask a question in Spanish by making your voice go up at the end of the sentence, by changing normal word order, and by using question words.

✔ Question words always have an accent on them.

✔ To make a negative question, add **no** before the verb.

✔ You can add **¿verdad?** to check whether your facts or beliefs are correct.

Test yourself

1 **Complete the following sentences by adding a question word.**

    a ¿ .... vais?

    b ¿ .... estás?

    c ¿ .... empiezas a trabajar?

    d ¿ .... años tienes?

    e ¿ .... son los tuyos?

    f ¿ .... están mis llaves?

    g ¿ .... quieres hacer hoy?

    h ¿ .... te lo ha dicho?

    i ¿ .... no te gusta?

    j ¿ .... hermanos tienes?

2 **Make these statements into questions by changing the word order and adding question marks.**

    a Mi hermana se lo dijo.

    ....

    b Tu padre no viene.

    ....

    c Tus hijos vieron la película.

    ....

    d Lucía ha llegado.

    ....

    e Viven aquí.

    ....

    f Tino se ha comprado aquél coche que quería.

    ....

    g Luis viene al bar.

    ....

    h Javier conduce bien.

    ....

    i Julia quiere acompañarnos.

    ....

    j Sus tíos les regalaron el cuadro que querían.

    ....

Adverbs

What is an adverb?
An **adverb** is a word usually used with verbs, adjectives or other adverbs that gives more information about when, how, where, or in what circumstances something happens, or to what degree something is true, for example, *quickly, happily, now, extremely, very.*

How adverbs are used

➤ In general, adverbs are used together with verbs, adjectives and other adverbs, for example, *act quickly; smile cheerfully; rather ill; a lot happier; really slowly; very well.*

➤ Adverbs can also relate to the whole sentence. In this case they often tell you what the speaker is thinking or feeling.
    Fortunately, Jan had already left.

How adverbs are formed

The basic rules

➤ In English, adverbs that tell you how something happened are often formed by adding *-ly* to an adjective, for example, *sweet → sweetly.* In Spanish, you form this kind of adverb by adding **-mente** to the feminine singular form of the adjective.

Masculine adjective	Feminine adjective	Adverb	Meaning
lento	**lenta**	**lentamente**	slowly
normal	**normal**	**normalmente**	normally

Habla muy lentamente.	He speaks very slowly.
¡Hazlo inmediatamente!	Do it immediately!
Normalmente llego a las nueve.	I normally arrive at nine o'clock.

i Note that adverbs NEVER change their endings in Spanish to agree with anything.

Tip
You don't have to worry about adding or removing accents on the adjective when you add **-mente**; they stay as they are.

fácil easy   →   **fácilmente** easily

Grammar Extra!

When there are two or more adverbs joined by a conjunction such as **y** (meaning *and*) or **pero** (meaning *but*), leave out the **-mente** ending on all but the last adverb.

Lo hicieron <u>lenta</u> pero <u>eficazmente</u>.   They did it slowly but efficiently.

Use the form **recién** rather than **recientemente** (meaning *recently*) before a past participle (the form of the verb ending in **-ado** and **-ido** in regular verbs).

El comedor está <u>recién</u> pintado.   The dining room has just been painted.

⇨ For more information on *Past participles*, see page 164.

In Spanish, adverbs ending in **-mente** are not as common as adverbs ending in *-ly* in English. For this reason, you will come across other ways of expressing an adverb in Spanish, for example, **con** used with a noun or **de manera** used with an adjective.

Conduce <u>con cuidado</u>.   Drive carefully.
Todos estos cambios ocurren   All these changes happen naturally.
  <u>de manera natural</u>.

Irregular adverbs

➤ The adverb that comes from **bueno** (meaning *good*) is **bien** (meaning *well*). The adverb that comes from **malo** (meaning *bad*) is **mal** (meaning *badly*).
  Habla <u>bien</u> el español.   He speaks Spanish <u>well</u>.
  Está muy <u>mal</u> escrito.   It's very <u>badly</u> written.

➤ Additionally, there are some other adverbs in Spanish which are exactly the same as the related masculine singular adjective:

- **alto** (adjective: *high*, *loud*; adverb: *high*, *loudly*)
  El avión volaba <u>alto</u> sobre las montañas. The plane flew <u>high</u> over the mountains.
  Pepe habla muy <u>alto</u>.   Pepe talks very <u>loudly</u>.

- **bajo** (adjective: *low*, *quiet*; adverb: *low*, *quietly*)
  El avión volaba muy <u>bajo</u>.   The plane was flying very <u>low</u>.
  ¡Habla <u>bajo</u>!   Speak <u>quietly</u>.

- **barato** (adjective: *cheap*; adverb: *cheaply*)
  Aquí se come muy <u>barato</u>.   You can eat really <u>cheaply</u> here.

- **claro** (adjective: *clear*; adverb: *clearly*)
  Lo oí muy <u>claro</u>.   I heard it very <u>clearly</u>.

- **derecho** (adjective: *right*, *straight*; adverb: *straight*)
  Vino <u>derecho</u> hacia mí.   He came <u>straight</u> towards me.

- **fuerte** (adjective: *loud*, *hard*; adverb: *loudly*, *hard*)
  Habla muy <u>fuerte</u>.   He talks very <u>loudly</u>.
  No lo golpees tan <u>fuerte</u>.   Don't hit it so <u>hard</u>.

- rápido   (adjective: *fast, quick*; adverb: *fast, quickly*)
  Conduces demasiado <u>rápido</u>.   You drive too <u>fast</u>.
  Lo hice tan <u>rápido</u> como pude.   I did it as <u>quickly</u> as I could.

i Note that, when used as adverbs, these words do NOT agree with anything.

⇨ *For more information on words which can be both adjectives and adverbs, see page 239.*

Grammar Extra!

Sometimes an <u>adjective</u> is used in Spanish where in English we would use an <u>adverb</u>.

Esperaban <u>impacientes</u>.   They were waiting <u>impatiently</u>.
Vivieron muy <u>felices</u>.   They lived very <u>happily</u>.

i Note that these Spanish <u>adjectives</u> describe the person or thing being talked about and therefore <u>MUST</u> agree with them.

Often you could equally well use an adverb or an adverbial expression in Spanish.

Esperaban <u>impacientemente</u> *or*   They were waiting <u>impatiently</u>.
  con impaciencia.

> ## KEY POINTS
> ✔ To form adverbs that tell you how something happens, you can usually add **-mente** to the feminine singular adjective in Spanish.
> ✔ Adverbs don't agree with anything.
> ✔ Some Spanish adverbs are irregular, as in English.
> ✔ Some Spanish adverbs are identical in form to their corresponding adjectives; when used as adverbs, they never agree with anything.

Test yourself

1 Replace the English highlighted adverb with the Spanish equivalent.

a   Lo hago .... **(quickly)**

b   Lo hizo muy .... **(well)**

c   Aquí se come .... **(cheaply)**

d   Se ve muy .... **(clearly)**

e   Habla muy .... **(loudly)**

f   Dile que venga .... **(immediately)**

g   Se abre .... **(easily)**

h   Hazlo .... **(carefully)**

i   El coche venía .... **(straight)** hacia nosotros.

j   Viven .... **(happily and peacefully)**

2 Translate the following sentences into Spanish.

a   Call them immediately!

....

b   It can be easily done.

....

c   I can't see it very well.

....

d   He treats us very badly.

....

e   Don't speak so loudly.

....

f   He drives really fast.

....

g   Normally, I call her.

....

h   Write it clearly.

....

i   Do it carefully.

....

j   You speak English really well.

....

Test yourself

3 **Replace the highlighted adverb with an equivalent adverbial phrase.**

a   impacientemente ....

b   inteligentemente ....

c   rápidamente ....

d   naturalmente ....

e   eficazmente ....

f   cuidadosamente ....

g   alegremente ....

h   claramente ....

i   fuertemente ....

j   felizmente ....

Comparatives and superlatives of adverbs

Comparative adverbs

> **What is a comparative adverb?**
> A **comparative adverb** is one which, in English, has -er on the end of it or
> *more* or *less* in front of it, for example, *earlier, later, more/less often*.

➤ Adverbs can be used to make comparisons in Spanish, just as they can in English. The comparative of adverbs (*more often, more efficiently, faster*) is formed using the same phrases as for adjectives:

- **más ... (que)**   more ... (than)
  más rápido (que)   faster (than), more quickly (than)
  Corre más rápido que tú.   He runs faster than you do.

- **menos ... (que)**   less ... (than)
  menos rápido (que)   less fast (than), less quickly (than)
  Conduce menos rápido que tú.   He drives less fast than you do.

Superlative adverbs

> **What is a superlative adverb?**
> A **superlative adverb** is one which, in English, has -est on the end of it or
> *most* or *least* in front of it, for example, *soonest, most/least often*.

➤ The superlative of adverbs (*the most often, the most efficiently, the fastest*) is formed in the same way in Spanish as the comparative, using **más** and **menos**. In this case they mean *the most* and *the least*.

María es la que corre más rápido.	Maria is the one who runs (the) fastest.
la chica que sabe más	the girl who knows (the) most
la chica que sabe menos	the girl who knows (the) least
El que llegó menos tarde fue Miguel.	Miguel was the one who arrived least late.

🛈 Note that even though comparative and superlative adverbs are usually identical in Spanish, you can tell which one is meant by the rest of the sentence.

Irregular comparative and superlative adverbs

➤ Some common Spanish adverbs have irregular comparatives and superlatives.

Adverb	Meaning	Comparative	Meaning	Superlative	Meaning
bien	well	**mejor**	better	**mejor**	(the) best
mal	badly	**peor**	worse	**peor**	(the) worst
mucho	a lot	**más**	more	**más**	(the) most
poco	little	**menos**	less	**menos**	(the) least

For further explanation of grammatical terms, please see pages viii-xii.

La conozco <u>mejor</u> que tú.	I know her <u>better</u> than you do.
¿Quién lo hace <u>mejor</u>?	Who does it (the) <u>best</u>?
Ahora salgo <u>más/menos</u>.	I go out <u>more/less</u> these days.

> *Tip*
>
> When saying more than, less than or fewer than followed by a number, use **más** and **menos de** rather than **más** and **menos que**.
>
> **más/menos de veinte cajas**   more/fewer than twenty boxes

[i] Note that in phrases like *it's the least one can expect* or *it's the least I can do*, where the adverb is qualified by further information, in Spanish you have to put **lo** before the adverb.

Es <u>lo menos que</u> se puede esperar.   It's the least one can expect.

Other ways of making comparisons

➤ There are other ways of making comparisons in Spanish:

* tanto como   as much as
  No lee <u>tanto como</u> tú.   He doesn't read <u>as much as</u> you.

* tan ... como   as ... as
  Vine <u>tan</u> pronto <u>como</u> pude.   I came <u>as</u> fast <u>as</u> I could.

KEY POINTS

✔ **más** + adverb (+ **que**) = *more* + adverb + (*than*)
✔ **menos** + adverb (+ **que**) = *less* + adverb + (*than*)
✔ **más** + adverb = (*the*) *most* + adverb
✔ **menos** + adverb = (*the*) *least* + adverb
✔ There are a few irregular comparative and superlative adverbs.
✔ There are other ways of making comparisons in Spanish: **tanto como**, **tan ... como**.

Test yourself

4 Create a sentence using the elements below.

a   Conduce/rápido/tú/+ ....

b   Nadas/bien/tu hermano/+ ....

c   Llegué/tarde/él/- ....

d   Cocina/bien/yo/+ ....

e   Canta/mal/yo/+ ....

f   Gana/poco/ella/- ....

g   Pepe/trabaja/duro/Antonio/+ ....

h   Carmen/carre/rápido/su hermana/+ ....

i   Nos/acostamos/tarde/que vosotros/+ ....

j   Sabemos/poco/ellos/- ....

5 Complete the following with de or que.

a   Había menos .... veinte personas.

b   Lo hice mejor .... tú.

c   Gano menos .... él.

d   Hay más .... 150 invitados.

e   Les pagan menos .... 500€.

f   Me gusta éste más .... ese.

g   Invité a más .... 20 amigos.

h   Compré más .... 30 lápices.

i   Ahora salimos algo más .... antes.

j   Pagamos más .... ellos.

Test yourself

6 **Replace the highlighted adverb with the superlative form.**

a el chico que sabe **mucho**

....

b el producto que cuesta **poco**

....

c el que corre **muy rápido**

....

d el que se vende **muy barato**

....

e los niños que estudian **poco**

....

f los que lo hacen **mal**

....

g los que cantan **bien**

....

h los que se venden **bien**

....

i los empleados que ganan **poco**

....

j los que están **bien** escritos

....

PRACTICE PRACTICE PRACTICE PRACTICE PRACTICE

Common adverbs

One-word adverbs not ending in -mente

➤ There are some common adverbs that do not end in -mente, most of which give more information about when or where something happens or to what degree something is true.

- ahí   there
  ¡Ahí están!   There they are!

- ahora   now
  ¿Dónde vamos ahora?   Where are we going now?

- allá   there
  allá arriba   up there

- allí   there
  Allí está.   There it is.

- anoche   last night
  Anoche llovió.   It rained last night.

- anteanoche   the night before last
  Anteanoche nevó.   It snowed the night before last.

- anteayer   the day before yesterday
  Anteayer hubo tormenta.   There was a storm the day before yesterday.

- antes   before
  Esta película ya la he visto antes.   I've seen this film before.

- apenas   hardly
  Apenas podía levantarse.   He could hardly stand up.

- aquí   here
  Aquí está el informe.   Here's the report.

- arriba   above, upstairs
  **Visto desde arriba parece más
    pequeño.**   Seen from above it looks smaller.
  Arriba están los dormitorios.   The bedrooms are upstairs.

- atrás   behind
  Yo me quedé atrás.   I stayed behind.

- aun   even
  Aun sentado me duele la pierna.   Even when I'm sitting down, my leg hurts.

- aún   still, yet
  ¿Aún te duele?   Does it still hurt?

For further explanation of grammatical terms, please see pages viii-xii.

> *Tip*
> The following mnemonic (memory jogger) should help you remember
> when to use **aun** and when to use **aún**:
> <u>Even</u> **aun** doesn't have an accent.
> **aún** <u>still</u> has an accent.
> **aún** hasn't lost its accent <u>yet</u>.

- ayer   yesterday
  <u>Ayer</u> me compré un bolso.   I bought a handbag <u>yesterday</u>.

- casi   almost
  Son <u>casi</u> las cinco.   It's <u>almost</u> five o'clock.

- cerca   near
  El colegio está muy <u>cerca</u>.   The school is very <u>near</u>.

- claro   clearly
  Lo oí muy <u>claro</u>.   I heard it very <u>clearly</u>.

- debajo   underneath
  Miré <u>debajo</u>.   I looked <u>underneath</u>.

- dentro   inside
  ¿Qué hay <u>dentro</u>?   What's <u>inside</u>?

- despacio   slowly
  Conduce <u>despacio</u>.   Drive <u>slowly</u>.

- después   afterwards
  <u>Después</u> estábamos muy cansados.   We were very tired <u>afterwards</u>.

- detrás   behind
  Vienen <u>detrás</u>.   They're coming along <u>behind</u>.

- enfrente   opposite
  la casa de <u>enfrente</u>   the house <u>opposite</u>

- enseguida   straightaway
  La ambulancia llegó <u>enseguida</u>.   The ambulance arrived <u>straightaway</u>.

- entonces   then
  ¿Qué hiciste <u>entonces</u>?   What did you do <u>then</u>?

- hasta   even
  Estudia <u>hasta</u> cuando está de   He studies <u>even</u> when he's on holiday.
  vacaciones.

- hoy   today
  <u>Hoy</u> no tenemos clase.   We haven't any lessons <u>today</u>.

- jamás   never
  <u>Jamás</u> he visto nada parecido.   I've <u>never</u> seen anything like it.

- lejos   far
  ¿Está <u>lejos</u>?   Is it <u>far</u>?

- luego   then, later
  <u>Luego</u> fuimos al cine.   <u>Then</u> we went to the cinema.

- muy   very
  Estoy <u>muy</u> cansada.   I'm <u>very</u> tired.

- no   no, not
  <u>No</u>, no me gusta.   <u>No</u>. I don't like it.

- nunca   never
  No viene <u>nunca</u>.   He <u>never</u> comes.
  '¿Has estado alguna vez en   'Have you ever been to Argentina?' –
    Argentina?' — 'No, <u>nunca</u>.'   'No, <u>never</u>.'

- pronto   soon, early
  Llegarán <u>pronto</u>.   They'll be here <u>soon</u>.
  ¿Por qué has llegado tan <u>pronto</u>? Why have you arrived so <u>early</u>?

- quizás   perhaps
  <u>Quizás</u> está cansado.   <u>Perhaps</u> he's tired.

[i] Note that you use the present subjunctive after **quizás** if referring to the future.

<u>Quizás</u> venga mañana.   <u>Perhaps</u> he'll come tomorrow.

⇨ *For more information on the **Subjunctive**, see page 190.*

- sí   yes
  ¿Te apetece un café? — <u>Sí</u>, gracias.   Do you fancy a coffee? — <u>Yes</u>, please.

- siempre   always
  <u>Siempre</u> dicen lo mismo.   They <u>always</u> say the same thing.

- solo   only
  <u>Solo</u> cuesta tres euros.   It <u>only</u> costs three euros.

- también   also, too
  A mí <u>también</u> me gusta.   I like it <u>too</u>.

- tampoco   either, neither
  Yo <u>tampoco</u> lo compré.   I didn't buy it <u>either</u>.
  Yo no la vi. — Yo <u>tampoco</u>.   I didn't see her. — <u>Neither</u> did I.

- tan   as, so
  Vine <u>tan</u> pronto <u>como</u> pude.   I came as fast as I could.
  Habla <u>tan</u> deprisa <u>que</u> no la entiendo.   She speaks so fast that I can't understand her.

- tarde   late
  Se está haciendo tarde.   It's getting <u>late</u>.

- temprano   early
  Tengo que levantarme <u>temprano</u>.   I've got to get up <u>early</u>.

- todavía   still, yet, even
  <u>Todavía</u> tengo dos.   I've <u>still</u> got two.
  <u>Todavía</u> no han llegado.   They haven't arrived yet.
  mejor <u>todavía</u>   <u>even</u> better

- ya   already
  <u>Ya</u> lo he hecho.   I've <u>already</u> done it.

Words which are used both as adjectives and adverbs

➤ **bastante**, **demasiado**, **tanto**, **mucho** and **poco** can be used both as adjectives and as adverbs. When they are <u>adjectives</u>, their endings change in the feminine and plural to agree with what they describe. When they are <u>adverbs</u>, the endings don't change.

	Adjective use	**Adverb use**
bastante enough; quite a lot; quite	**Hay <u>bastantes</u> libros.** There are enough books.	**Ya has comido <u>bastante</u>.** You've had enough to eat. **Son <u>bastante</u> ricos.** They are quite rich.
demasiado too much (*plural*: too many); too	**<u>demasiada</u> mantequilla** too much butter **<u>demasiados</u> libros** too many books	**He comido <u>demasiado</u>.** I've eaten too much. **Llegamos <u>demasiado</u> tarde.** We arrived too late.
tanto as much (*plural*: as many); as often	**Ahora no bebo <u>tanta</u> leche.** I don't drink as much milk these days. **Tengo <u>tantas</u> cosas que hacer.** I've so many things to do.	**Se preocupa <u>tanto</u> que no puede dormir.** He worries so much that he can't sleep. **Ahora no la veo <u>tanto</u>.** I don't see her so often now.
mucho a lot (of), much (*plural*: many)	**Había mucha gente.** There were a lot of people. <u>**muchas**</u> **cosas** a lot of things	**¿Lees <u>mucho</u>?** Do you read a lot? **¿Está <u>mucho</u> más lejos?** Is it much further?
poco little, not much, (*plural*: few, not many); not very	**Hay <u>poca</u> leche.** There isn't much milk. **Tiene <u>pocos</u> amigos.** He hasn't got many friends.	**Habla muy <u>poco</u>.** He speaks very little. **Es <u>poco</u> sociable.** He's not very sociable.

Tip
Don't confuse **poco**, which means *little*, *not much* or *not very*, with **un poco**, which means *a little* or *a bit*.

Come <u>poco</u>.   He eats <u>little</u>.
¿Me das un <u>poco</u>?   Can I have <u>a bit</u>?

➤ **más** and **menos** can also be used both as adjectives and adverbs. However, they <u>NEVER</u> change their endings, even when used as adjectives.

	Adjective use	Adverb use
más more	**No tengo <u>más</u> dinero.** I haven't any more money. **<u>más</u> libros** more books	**Es <u>más</u> inteligente que yo.** He's more intelligent than I am. **Mi hermano trabaja <u>más</u> ahora.** My brother works more now.
menos less; fewer	**<u>menos</u> mantequilla** less butter **Había <u>menos</u> gente que ayer.** There were fewer people than yesterday.	**Estoy <u>menos</u> sorprendida** **que tú.** I'm less surprised than you are. **Trabaja <u>menos</u> que yo.** He doesn't work as hard as I do.

Adverbs made up of more than one word

➤ Just as in English, some Spanish adverbs are made up of two or more words instead of just one.

a veces	sometimes
a menudo	often
de vez en cuando	from time to time
todo el tiempo	all the time
hoy en día	nowadays
en seguida	immediately

> ### KEY POINTS
> ✔ There are a number of common adverbs in Spanish which do not end in -mente.
> ✔ **bastante**, **demasiado**, **tanto**, **mucho** and **poco** can be used both as adjectives and as adverbs. Their endings change in the feminine and plural when they are adjectives, but when they are adverbs their endings <u>do not</u> change.
> ✔ **más** and **menos** can be both adjectives and adverbs – their endings <u>never</u> change.
> ✔ A number of Spanish adverbs are made up of more than one word.

Test yourself

7 Create a sentence using the elements below.

a Soy/inteligente/él/+ ....

b Ramón/trabajar/su jefe/+ ....

c Esa cuenta/pagar/esta/- ....

d Óscar/leer/su hermano/+ ....

e Quedé/sorprendida/ella/+ ....

f Esta planta/crecer/esa/- ....

g Maruja/comer/su marido/- ....

h Daniel/conducir/rápido/yo/+ ....

i Pagaron/nosotros/- ....

j Su perro/ladrar/el nuestro/+ ....

8 Match the two columns.

a	**hoy en día**	all the time
b	**de vez en cuando**	often
c	**en seguida**	nowadays
d	**todo el tiempo**	from time to time
e	**a menudo**	immediately

9 Cross out the words which don't work.

a	**demasiado**	tarde/rápido/gente/dinero/comida
b	**demasiada**	tarde/rápido/gente/dinero/comida
c	**bastante**	gente/dinero/personas/tarde/ricos/libros/comida/rápido
d	**bastantes**	personas/gente/dinero/libros
e	**tanto**	gente/tonto/chocolate
f	**tantas**	cosas/veces/amigos/canciones
g	**mucho**	mejor/feliz/peor/rico
h	**muchas**	veces/cosas/gente/razones
i	**poco**	feliz/inteligente/gente/comida/dinero
j	**pocas**	amigas/gente/flores/razones

Position of adverbs

Adverbs with verbs

➤ In English, adverbs can come in various places in a sentence, at the beginning, in the middle or at the end.
>
> I'm <u>never</u> coming back.
> See you <u>soon</u>!
> <u>Suddenly</u>, the phone rang.
> I'd <u>really</u> like to come.

➤ In Spanish, the rules for the position of adverbs in a sentence are more fixed. The adverb can either go immediately <u>AFTER</u> the verb or <u>BEFORE</u> it for emphasis.

No conocemos <u>todavía</u> al nuevo médico.	We still haven't met the new doctor.
<u>Todavía</u> estoy esperando.	I'm still waiting.
<u>Siempre</u> le regalaban flores.	They always gave her flowers.

➤ When the adverb goes with a verb in the perfect tense or in the pluperfect, you can <u>NEVER</u> put the adverb between **haber** and the past participle.

Lo he hecho <u>ya</u>.	I've already done it.
No ha estado <u>nunca</u> en Italia.	She's never been to Italy.

⇨ *For more information on the **Perfect tense**, see page 164.*

Adverbs with adjectives and adverbs

➤ The adverb normally goes <u>BEFORE</u> any adjective or adverb it is used with.

un sombrero <u>muy</u> bonito	a very nice hat
hablar <u>demasiado</u> alto	to talk too loudly

KEY POINTS
- ✔ Adverbs follow the verb in most cases.
- ✔ Adverbs can go before verbs for emphasis.
- ✔ You can <u>never</u> separate **haber**, **he**, **ha** and so on from the following past participle (the **-ado/-ido** form of regular verbs).
- ✔ Adverbs generally come just before an adjective or another adverb.

Test yourself

10 Translate the following into Spanish.

   a   She talks too loudly.

      ....

   b   a very pretty girl

      ....

   c   I always do it.

      ....

   d   They've already done it.

      ....

   e   I've never been to America.

      ....

   f   We're still waiting.

      ....

   g   I haven't told him yet.

      ....

   h   I would never tell them.

      ....

   i   Let's go now!

      ....

   j   See you soon!

      ....

11 Replace the highlighted adverb with the Spanish equivalent.

   a   Conduce .... **(too)** rápido.

   b   una chica .... **(very)** rubia

   c   Come .... **(as much as)** yo.

   d   No se lo he dicho .... **(still)**

   e   Ven .... **(immediately)**

   f   Me gusta .... **(a lot)**

   g   No pienso volver .... **(never)**

   h   Iremos .... **(soon)**

   i   Lo he hecho .... **(already)**

   j   Canta .... **(very)** bien.

Prepositions

What is a preposition?

A **preposition** is a word such as *at*, *for*, *with*, *into* or *from*, which is usually followed by a noun, pronoun or, in English, a word ending in *-ing*. Prepositions show how people and things relate to the rest of the sentence, for example, *She's <u>at</u> home.*; *a tool <u>for</u> cutting grass*; *It's <u>from</u> David*.

Using prepositions

➤ Prepositions are used in front of nouns and pronouns (such as *people*, *the man*, *me*, *him* and so on), and show the relationship between the noun or pronoun and the rest of the sentence. Although prepositions can be used before verb forms ending in *-ing* in English, in Spanish, they're followed by the <u>infinitive</u> – the form of the verb ending in **-ar**, **-er**, or **-ir**.

Le enseñé el billete <u>a</u> la revisora.	I showed my ticket <u>to</u> the ticket inspector.
Ven <u>con</u> nosotros.	Come <u>with</u> us.
Sirve <u>para</u> limpiar zapatos.	It's <u>for</u> cleaning shoes.

⇨ *For more information on **Nouns, Pronouns** and **Infinitives**, see pages 1, 55 and 201.*

➤ Prepositions are also used after certain adjectives and verbs and link them to the rest of the sentence.

Estoy muy contento <u>con</u> tu trabajo.	I'm very happy <u>with</u> your work.
Estamos hartos <u>de</u> repetirlo.	We're fed up <u>with</u> repeating it.
¿Te gusta jugar <u>al</u> fútbol?	Do you like playing football?

➤ As in English, Spanish prepositions can be made up of several words instead of just one.

delante de	in front of
antes de	before

➤ In English, we can end a sentence with a preposition such as *for*, *with* or *into*, even though some people think this is not good grammar. You can <u>NEVER</u> end a Spanish sentence with a preposition.

<u>¿Para</u> qué es?	What's it <u>for</u>?
la chica <u>con</u> la que hablaste	the girl you spoke <u>to</u>

> ### Tip
> The choice of preposition in Spanish is not always what we might expect, coming from English. It is often difficult to give just one English equivalent for a particular Spanish preposition, since prepositions are used so differently in the two languages. This means that you need to learn how they are used and look up set phrases involving prepositions (such as *to be fond of somebody* or *dressed in white*) in a dictionary in order to find an equivalent expression in Spanish.

a, de, en, para and por

a

➤ a can mean *to* with places and destinations.

Voy a Madrid.	I'm going to Madrid.
Voy al cine.	I'm going to the cinema.

> **Tip**
> **de** is also used with **a** to mean *from ... to ...*
>
> | | |
> |---|---|
> | **de la mañana a la noche** | from morning to night |
> | **de 10 a 12** | from 10 to 12 |

➤ a can mean *to* with indirect objects.

Se lo dio a María.	He gave it to María.

➤ a can mean *to* after **ir** when talking about what someone is *going* to do.

Voy a verlo mañana.	I'm going to see him tomorrow.

➤ a can mean *at* with times.

a las cinco	at five o'clock
a las dos y cuarto	at quarter past two
a medianoche	at midnight

➤ a can me   with prices and rates.

s el kilo	(at) two euros a kilo
or hora	at 100 km per hour

ith ages.

at (the age of) 18

h places, but generally only after verbs suggesting movement.

ar a la estación.	I'll meet you at the station.
l aeropuerto	when he arrived at the airport

> to mean **at** when talking about a building, area, or village
> e is. Use **en** instead.
>
> | |
> |---|
> | He's at home. |

➤ a can mean *onto*.

    Se cayó al suelo.   He fell <u>onto</u> the floor.

➤ a can mean *into*.

    pegar una foto al álbum   to stick a photo <u>into</u> the album

➤ a is also used to talk about distance.

    a 8 km de aquí   (at a distance of) 8 km from here

➤ a is also used after certain adjectives and verbs.

    parecido a esto   similar to this

➤ a can mean *from* after certain verbs.

    Se lo compré a mi hermano.   I bought it <u>from</u> my brother.
    Les robaba dinero a sus compañeros   He was stealing money <u>from</u> his classmates.
     de clase.

    ⇨ *For more information on **Prepositions after verbs**, see page 207.*

➤ a is used in set phrases.

a final/finales/fines de mes	at the end of the month
a veces	at times
a menudo	often
a la puerta	at the door
a mano	by hand
a caballo	on horseback
a pie	on foot
a tiempo	on time
al sol	in the sun
a la sombra	in the shade

Grammar Extra!

a is often used to talk about the manner in which something is done.

a la inglesa	in the English manner
a paso lento	slowly
poco a poco	little by little

The Spanish equivalent of the English construction *on* with a verb ending in *-ing* is al followed by the <u>infinitive</u>.

al levantarse	on getting up
al abrir la puerta	on opening the door

Personal a

➤ When the direct object of a verb is a specific person or pet animal, a is placed immediately before it.

    Querían mucho a sus hijos.   They loved their children dearly.
    Cuido a mi hermana pequeña.   I look after my little sister.

For further explanation of grammatical terms, please see pages viii-xii.

[i] Note that personal **a** is <u>NOT</u> used after the verb **tener**.

Tienen dos hijos.   They have two children.

⇨ *For more information on **Direct objects**, see pages 61 and 66.*

de

> *Tip*
> When **de** is followed by **el**, the two words merge to become **del**.

➤ **de** can mean *from*.
    Soy <u>de</u> Londres.   I'm <u>from</u> London.
    un médico <u>de</u> Valencia   a doctor <u>from</u> Valencia

> *Tip*
> **de** is also used with **a** to mean *from ... to ...*
> **de la mañana a la noche**   from morning to night
> **de 10 a 12**   from 10 to 12

➤ **de** can mean *of*.
    el presidente <u>de</u> Francia   the president <u>of</u> France
    dos litros <u>de</u> leche   two litres <u>of</u> milk

➤ **de** shows who or what something belongs to.
    el sombrero <u>de</u> mi padre   my father's hat (*literally: the hat <u>of</u> my father*)
    la oficina <u>del</u> presidente   the president's office (*literally: the office <u>of</u> the president*)

➤ **de** can indicate what something is made of, what it contains or what it is used for.
    un vestido <u>de</u> seda   a silk dress
    una caja <u>de</u> cerillas   a box of matches
    una taza <u>de</u> té   a cup of tea *or* a teacup
    una silla <u>de</u> cocina   a kitchen chair
    un traje <u>de</u> baño   a swimming costume

➤ **de** is used in comparisons when a number is mentioned.
    Había más/menos <u>de</u> 100 personas.   There were more/fewer than 100 people.

[i] Note that you do <u>NOT</u> use **que** with **más** or **menos** when there is a number involved.

➤ **de** can mean *in* after superlatives (*the most..., the biggest, the least...*).
    la ciudad más/menos   the most/least polluted city in
    contaminada <u>del</u> mundo   the world

⇨ *For more information on **Superlative adjectives**, see page 35.*

➤ **de** is used after certain adjectives and verbs.

contento <u>de</u> ver	pleased to see
Es fácil/difícil <u>de</u> entender.	It's easy/difficult to understand.
Es capaz <u>de</u> olvidarlo.	He's quite capable of forgetting it.

⇨ *For more information on **Prepositions after verbs**, see page 207.*

Grammar Extra!

de is often used in descriptions.

la mujer <u>del</u> sombrero verde	the woman <u>in</u> the green hat
un chico <u>de</u> ojos azules	a boy <u>with</u> blue eyes

---

en

➤ **en** can mean *in* with places.

<u>en</u> el campo	<u>in</u> the country
<u>en</u> Londres	<u>in</u> London
<u>en</u> la cama	<u>in</u> bed
con un libro <u>en</u> la mano	with a book <u>in</u> his hand

➤ **en** can mean *at*.

<u>en</u> casa	<u>at</u> home
<u>en</u> el colegio	<u>at</u> school
<u>en</u> el aeropuerto	<u>at</u> the airport
<u>en</u> la parada de autobús	<u>at</u> the bus stop
<u>en</u> Navidad	<u>at</u> Christmas

➤ **en** can mean *in* with months, years and seasons and when saying how long something takes or took.

<u>en</u> marzo	<u>in</u> March
<u>en</u> 2005	<u>in</u> 2005
Nació <u>en</u> invierno.	He was born <u>in</u> winter.
Lo hice <u>en</u> dos días.	I did it <u>in</u> two days.

ⓘ Note the following time phrase which does not use *in* in English.

en este momento	<u>at</u> this moment

Tip

There are two ways of talking about a length of time in Spanish which translate the same in English, but have very different meanings.

Lo haré <u>dentro de</u> una semana.	I'll do it <u>in</u> a week.
Lo haré <u>en</u> una semana.	I'll do it <u>in</u> a week.

Though both can be translated in the same way, the first sentence means that you'll do it in a week's time; the second means that it will take you a week to do it.

For further explanation of grammatical terms, please see pages viii-xii.

➤ **en** can mean *in* with languages and in set phrases.

Está escrito en español.	It's written in Spanish.
en voz baja	in a low voice

➤ **en** can mean *on*.

sentado en una silla	sitting on a chair
en la planta baja	on the ground floor
Hay dos cuadros en la pared.	There are two pictures on the wall.

➤ **en** can mean *by* with most methods of transport.

en coche	by car
en avión	by plane
en tren	by train

➤ **en** can mean *into*.

No entremos en la casa.	Let's not go into the house.
Metió la mano en el bolso.	She put her hand into her handbag.

➤ **en** is also used after certain adjectives and verbs.

Es muy buena/mala en geografía.	She is very good/bad at geography.
Fueron los primeros/últimos/ únicos en llegar.	They were the first/last/only ones to arrive.

⇨ *For more information on* **Prepositions after verbs**, *see page 207.*

para

➤ **para** can mean *for* with a person, destination or purpose.

Para mí un zumo de naranja.	An orange juice for me.
Salen para Cádiz.	They are leaving for Cádiz.
¿Para qué lo quieres?	What do you want it for?

🛈 Note that you cannot end a sentence in Spanish with a preposition as you can in English.

➤ **para** can mean *for* with time.

Es para mañana.	It's for tomorrow.
una habitación para dos noches	a room for two nights

➤ **para** is also used with an infinitive with the meaning of (*in order*) *to*.

Lo hace para ganar dinero.	He does it to earn money.
Lo hice para ayudarte.	I did it to help you.

> *Tip*
> para mí can be used to mean *in my opinion*.
> **Para mí, es estupendo.**   In my opinion, it's great.

por

➤ por can mean *for* when it means *for the benefit of* or *because of*.

Lo hice por mis padres.	I did it <u>for</u> my parents.
Lo hago por ellos.	I'm doing it <u>for</u> them.
por la misma razón	<u>for</u> the same reason

➤ por can mean *for* when it means *in exchange for*.

¿Cuánto me darán por este libro?	How much will they give me <u>for</u> this book?
Te lo cambio por este.	I'll swap you it <u>for</u> this one.

➤ por can mean *by* in passive constructions.

descubierto por unos niños	discovered <u>by</u> some children
odiado por sus enemigos	hated <u>by</u> his enemies

⇨ *For more information on the* **Passive,** *see page* 175.

➤ por can mean *by* with means of transport when talking about freight.

por barco	<u>by</u> boat
por tren	<u>by</u> train
por avión	<u>by</u> airmail
por correo aéreo	<u>by</u> airmail

➤ por can mean *along*.

Vaya por ese camino.	Go <u>along</u> that path.

➤ por can mean *through*.

por el túnel	<u>through</u> the tunnel

➤ por can mean *around*.

pasear por el campo	to walk <u>around</u> the countryside

➤ por is used to talk vaguely about where something or someone is.

Tiene que estar por aquí.	It's got to be around here somewhere.
Lo busqué por todas partes.	I looked for him everywhere.

➤ por is used to talk about time.

por la mañana	<u>in</u> the morning
por la tarde	<u>in</u> the afternoon/evening
por la noche	<u>at</u> night

➤ por is used to talk about rates.

90 km por hora	90 km an hour
un cinco por ciento	five per cent
Ganaron por 3 a 0.	They won by 3 to 0.

➤ por is used in certain phrases which talk about the reason for something.

¿por qué?	why?, for what reason?
por todo eso	because of all that
por lo que he oído	judging by what I've heard

➤ por is used to talk about how something is done.

llamar por teléfono	to telephone
Lo oí por la radio.	I heard it on the radio.

For further explanation of grammatical terms, please see pages viii-xii.

Grammar Extra!

por is often combined with other Spanish prepositions and words, usually to show movement.

Saltó <u>por encima</u> de la mesa.	She jumped over the table.
Nadamos <u>por debajo del</u> puente.	We swam under the bridge.
Pasaron <u>por delante de</u> Correos.	They went past the post office.

KEY POINTS

✔ a, de, en, para and por are very frequently used prepositions which you will need to study carefully.

✔ Each of them has several possible meanings, which depend on the context they are used in.

Test yourself

1 Complete the following sentences with the relevant preposition.

a   Estamos muy contentos .... el regalo.

b   Se lo dije .... tus padres.

c   Vete .... ellos.

d   Estaba harta .... decírselo.

e   Le gusta jugar .... fútbol.

f   No vale .... nada.

g   Dáselo .... tu madre.

h   Enséñamelo .... mí.

i   Producen miel .... vender.

j   Ese coche es mío no .... mis padres.

2 Complete the following with the correct form of de, del, etc.

a   una taza .... café

b   un vaso .... plástico

c   la puerta .... coche

d   la oficina .... director

e   un vaso .... leche

f   el hotel más caro .... mundo

g   fácil .... abrir

h   el chico .... ojos verdes

i   un abogado .... Salamanca

j   la mujer .... vestido rosa

Test yourself

3 **Complete the following with por or para.**

a Son .... ti.

b Lo haré .... la tarde.

c Lo dejo .... mañana.

d No lo hagas .... mí.

e Es mejor ir .... aquí.

f Alquilaron un apartamento .... el mes de agosto.

g Me lo dio .... debajo de la mesa.

h .... mí, es un gran artista.

i Mañana salimos .... el pueblo.

j .... lo que se ve

4 **Match the two columns.**

a **debajo de**   since then

b **delante de**   downwards

c **contra**   under

d **desde entonces**   against

e **hacia abajo**   in front of

Some other common prepositions

➤ The following prepositions are also frequently used in Spanish.

- **antes de**   before
  antes de las 5   before 5 o'clock

ⓘ Note that, like many other prepositions, **antes de** is used before infinitives in Spanish where in English we'd usually use the *-ing* form of the verb.

Antes de abrir el paquete,   Before opening the packet, read
  lea las instrucciones.   the instructions.

- **bajo**   below, under
  un grado bajo cero   one degree below zero
  bajo la cama   under the bed

ⓘ Note that **debajo de** is more common than **bajo** when talking about the actual position of something.

debajo de la cama   under the bed

- **con**   with
  Vino con su amigo.   She came with her friend.

ⓘ Note that **con** can be used after certain adjectives as well as in a few very common phrases.

enfadado con ellos   angry with them
un café con leche   a white coffee
un té con limón   a (cup of) tea with a slice of lemon

- **contra**   against
  Estaba apoyado contra la pared.   He was leaning against the wall.
  El domingo jugamos contra el Málaga.   We play against Malaga on Sunday.

- **debajo de**   under
  debajo de la cama   under the bed

- **delante de**   in front of
  Iba delante de mí.   He was walking in front of me.

- **desde**   from, since
  Desde aquí se puede ver.   You can see it from here.
  Llamaron desde España.   They phoned from Spain.
  desde otro punto de vista   from a different point of view
  desde entonces   from then onwards
  desde la una hasta las siete   from one o'clock to seven
  desde la boda   since the wedding

Tip

Spanish uses the <u>present tense</u> with **desde** (meaning *since*) and the expressions **desde hace** and **hace ... que** (meaning *for*) to talk about actions that started in the past and are still going on.

Estoy aquí desde las diez. I've been here since ten o'clock.
Estoy aquí desde hace dos   I've been here for two hours.
  horas. *or* **Hace dos horas que**
  estoy aquí.

If you are saying how long something has <u>NOT</u> happened for, in European Spanish you can use the <u>perfect tense</u> with **desde** and **desde hace**.

No <u>ha trabajado</u> desde el   He hasn't worked since the
  accidente.   accident.
No <u>ha trabajado</u> desde hace   He hasn't worked for two months.
  dos meses.

⇨ For more information on the *Present tense* and the *Perfect tense*, see pages 103 and 164.

- **después de** after
  <u>después del</u> partido   <u>after</u> the match

ⁱ Note that, like many other prepositions, **después de** is used before infinitives in Spanish where in English we'd usually use the *-ing* form of the verb.

  <u>Después de ver</u> la televisión   <u>After watching</u> television I went to bed.
  me fui a la cama.

- **detrás de** behind
  Están <u>detrás de</u> la puerta.   They are behind the door.

- **durante** during, for
  <u>durante</u> la guerra   <u>during</u> the war
  Anduvieron <u>durante</u> 3 días.   They walked <u>for</u> 3 days.

- **entre** between, among
  <u>entre</u> 8 y 10   <u>between</u> 8 and 10
  Hablaban <u>entre</u> sí.   They were talking <u>among</u> themselves.

- **hacia** towards, around
  Van <u>hacia</u> ese edificio.   They're going <u>towards</u> that building.
  <u>hacia</u> las tres   at <u>around</u> three (o'clock)
  <u>hacia</u> finales de enero   <u>around</u> the end of January

---

Grammar Extra!
hacia can also combine with some adverbs to show movement in a particular direction.

hacia arriba	upwards
hacia abajo	downwards
hacia adelante	forwards
hacia atrás	backwards

- **hasta** until, as far as, to, up to
hasta la noche	<u>until</u> night
Fueron en coche <u>hasta</u> Sevilla.	They drove <u>as far as</u> Seville.
<u>desde</u> la una <u>hasta</u> las tres	<u>from</u> one o'clock <u>to</u> three
<u>Hasta</u> ahora no ha llamado nadie.	No one has called <u>up to</u> now.

[i] Note that there are some very common ways of saying goodbye using **hasta**.

¡<u>Hasta</u> luego!	See you!
¡<u>Hasta</u> mañana!	See you tomorrow!

- **sin** without
<u>sin</u> agua/dinero	<u>without</u> any water/money
<u>sin</u> mi marido	<u>without</u> my husband

> *Tip*
> Whereas in English we say *without a doubt*, *without a hat* and so on, in Spanish the indefinite article isn't given after **sin**.
>
> | | |
> |---|---|
> | **sin duda** | without a doubt |
> | **sin sombrero** | without a hat |

⇨ *For more information on **Articles**, see page 11.*

[i] Note that **sin** is used before infinitives in Spanish where in English we would use the *-ing* form of the verb.

Se fue <u>sin decir</u> nada.	He left <u>without saying</u> anything.

- **sobre** on, about
<u>sobre</u> la cama	<u>on</u> the bed
Ponlo <u>sobre</u> la mesa.	Put it <u>on</u> the table.
un libro <u>sobre</u> Shakespeare	a book <u>on</u> *or* <u>about</u> Shakespeare
Madrid tiene <u>sobre</u> 4 millones de habitantes.	Madrid has <u>about</u> 4 million inhabitants.
Vendré <u>sobre</u> las cuatro.	I'll come <u>about</u> four o'clock.

➤ Spanish prepositions can be made up of more than one word, for example, **antes de**, **detrás de**. Here are some more common prepositions made up of two or more words:

- **a causa de**   because of
  No salimos a causa de la lluvia.   We didn't go out <u>because of</u> the rain.

- **al lado de**   beside, next to
  al lado de la tele   <u>beside</u> the TV

- **cerca de**   near, close to
  Está cerca de la iglesia.   It's <u>near</u> the church.

- **encima de**   on, on top of
  Ponlo encima de la mesa.   Put it <u>on</u> the table.

- **por encima de**   above, over
  Saltó por encima de la mesa.   He jumped <u>over</u> the table.

- **en medio de**   in the middle of
  Está en medio de la plaza.   It's <u>in the middle of</u> the square.

- **junto a**   by
  Está junto al cine.   It's <u>by</u> the cinema.

- **junto con**   together with
  Fue detenido junto con su hijo.   He was arrested <u>together with</u> his son.

- **lejos de**   far from
  No está lejos de aquí.   It isn't <u>far from</u> here.

Conjunctions

What is a conjunction?

A **conjunction** is a word such as *and*, *but*, *or*, *so*, *if* and *because*, that links two words or phrases of a similar type, or two parts of a sentence, for example,
Diane <u>and</u> I have been friends for years.; *I left <u>because</u> I was bored*.

y, o, pero, porque, que and si

➤ **y**, **o**, **pero**, **porque**, **que** and **si** are the most common conjunctions that you need to know in Spanish:

- **y** and
  el coche y la casa   the car <u>and</u> the house

🔲 Note that you use **e** instead of **y** before words beginning with **i** or **hi** (but not **hie**).

  Diana e Isabel   Diana <u>and</u> Isabel
  madre e hija   mother <u>and</u> daughter
  BUT
  árboles y hierba   trees <u>and</u> grass

- **o** or
  patatas fritas o arroz   chips or rice

🔲 Note that you use **u** instead of **o** before words beginning with **o** or **ho**.

  diez u once   ten <u>or</u> eleven
  minutos u horas   minutes <u>or</u> hours

🔲 Note that you use **ó** instead of **o** between numerals to avoid confusion with zero.

  37 ó 38   37 or 38

➪ *For more information on* **Numbers,** *see page 272.*

- **pero** but
  Me gustaría ir, <u>pero</u> estoy muy   I'd like to go, <u>but</u> I am very tired.
  cansado.

🔲 Note that you use **sino** in direct contrasts after a negative.

  No es escocesa, <u>sino</u> irlandesa.   She's not Scottish <u>but</u> Irish.

- **porque** because
  Ha llamado <u>porque</u> necesita un libro.   He called <u>because</u> he needs a book.

🔲 Note that you don't use **porque** at the beginning of a sentence; you should use **como** instead.

For further explanation of grammatical terms, please see pages viii–xii.

Como está lloviendo no podemos salir.   Because or As it's raining, we can't go out.

> **Tip**
> Be careful not to mix up **porque** (meaning because) and **por qué** (meaning why).

- que that
  Dice que me quiere.   He says that he loves me.
  Dicen que te han visto.   They say that they've seen you.
  Sabe que estamos aquí.   He knows that we are here.

⇨ *For more information on* **que** *followed by the subjunctive and* **que** (meaning *than*) *in comparisons, see pages 192 and 35.*

> **Tip**
> In English we can say both *He says he loves me* and *He says that he loves me*, or *She knows you're here* and *She knows that you're here*. You can <u>NEVER</u> leave out **que** in Spanish in the way that you can leave out *that* in English.

- si if, whether
  Si no estudias, no aprobarás.   If you don't study, you won't pass.
  ¿Sabes si nos han pagado ya?   Do you know if or whether we've been paid yet?
  Avisadme si no podéis venir.   Let me know if you can't come.

⇨ *For information on* **si** *followed by the subjunctive, see page 198.*

> **Tip**
> There is no accent on **si** when it means *if*. Be careful not to confuse **si** (meaning *if*) with **sí** (meaning *yes* or *himself/herself/yourself/ themselves/ yourselves*).

Some other common conjunctions

➤ Here are some other common Spanish conjunctions:

- como as
  Como es domingo, puedes   As it's Sunday, you can stay in bed.
  quedarte en la cama.

- cuando when
  Cuando entré estaba leyendo.   She was reading when I came in.

⇨ *For information on* **cuando** *followed by the subjunctive, see page 195.*

- pues then, well
  Tengo sueño. — ¡Pues, vete a la cama!   I'm tired. —Then go to bed!
  Pues, no lo sabía.   Well, I didn't know.
  Pues, como te iba contando ...   Well, as I was saying ...

- mientras   while (*referring to time*)
  Lava tú <u>mientras</u> yo seco.   You wash <u>while</u> I dry.
  Él leía <u>mientras</u> yo cocinaba.   He would read <u>while</u> I cooked.

⇨ *For information on* **mientras** *followed by the subjunctive, see page 195.*

- mientras que   whereas
  Isabel es muy dinámica   Isabel is very dynamic <u>whereas</u>
  <u>**mientras que**</u> **Ana es más tranquila.**   Ana is more laid-back.

- aunque   although, even though
  Me gusta el francés, <u>aunque</u>   I like French <u>although</u> I prefer German.
  prefiero el alemán.
  Seguí andando <u>aunque</u> me   I went on walking <u>even though</u> my
  dolía mucho la pierna.   leg hurt a lot.

Grammar Extra!
aunque is also used to mean even if. In this case, it is followed by the subjunctive.

⇨ For more information on the ***Subjunctive***, see page 190.

Split conjunctions

In English, we have conjunctions which are made up of two parts (*both ... and, neither ... nor*). Spanish also has conjunctions which have more than one part, the commonest of which are probably **ni ... ni** (meaning *neither ... nor*) and **o ... o** (meaning *either ... or*):

- ni ... ni   neither ... nor
  Ni Carlos ni Sofía vinieron. *or*   <u>Neither</u> Carlos <u>nor</u> Sofía came.
  No vinieron ni Carlos ni Sofía.

⒤ Note that if you're putting **ni ... ni** after the verb you must put **no** before the verb.

  No tengo <u>ni</u> hermanos <u>ni</u> hermanas.   I have <u>neither</u> brothers <u>nor</u> sisters.

- o ... o   either ... or
  Puedes tomar <u>o</u> helado <u>o</u> yogur.   You can have <u>either</u> ice cream <u>or</u> yoghurt.

KEY POINTS

✔ **y, o, pero, porque, que** and **si** are the most common conjunctions that you need to know in Spanish.
✔ Use **e** rather than **y** before words beginning with **i** or **hi** (but not with **hie**).
✔ Use **u** rather than **o** before words beginning with **o** or **ho**.
✔ **que** very often means *that*. *That* is often missed out in English, but **que** can never be left out in Spanish.
✔ Some conjunctions such as **ni ... ni** and **o ... o** consist of two parts.

Test yourself

1 **Complete the following phrases with y or e as appropriate.**

    a   los brazos .... las piernas

    b   madre .... hijos

    c   una madre .... sus hijos

    d   Jorge .... Iván

    e   vamos .... venimos

    f   geografía .... historia

    g   nieve .... hielo

    h   pan .... aceite

    i   chicos .... chicas

    j   chinos .... indios

2 **Complete the following phrases with o or u as appropriate.**

    a   carne .... pescado

    b   en coche .... bicicleta

    c   plata .... hojalata

    d   patatas fritas .... arroz

    e   Francia .... Holanda

    f   Barcelona .... Madrid

    g   formato impreso .... electrónico

    h   Jesús .... Mario

    i   Sandra .... Olga

    j   este .... oeste

Test yourself

3 **Complete the following sentences with** pero, porque, como, **or** sino **as appropriate.**

a   No voy .... no me apetece.

b   Los invitamos .... no quieren venir.

c   No ha sido Susana .... su hermana.

d   No fuimos .... llovía.

e   .... no vinieron, sobró comida.

f   No son de cerdo .... de ternera.

g   Puede comprarlo .... no quiere.

h   .... no estudió, no aprobó.

i   No la llamé .... estaba cansada.

j   Hacemos la lotería .... nunca ganamos.

4 **Match the two columns.**

a   **aunque**   well, then

b   **como**   while

c   **mientras**   whereas

d   **pues**   as

e   **mientras que**   although

Spelling

Sounds that are spelled differently depending on the letter that follows

➤ Certain sounds are spelled differently in Spanish depending on what letter follows them. For example, the hard [k] sound heard in the English word *car* is usually spelled:

- **c** before **a**, **o** and **u**

- **qu** before **e** and **i**

➤ This means that the Spanish word for *singer* is spelled **cantante** (pronounced [*kan-tan-tay*]); the word for *coast* is spelled **costa** (pronounced [*ko-sta*]); and the word for *cure* is spelled **cura** (pronounced [*koo-ra*]).

➤ However, the Spanish word for cheese is spelled **queso** (pronounced [*kay-so*]) and the word for *chemistry* is spelled **química** (pronounced [*kee-mee-ka*]).

  🛈 Note that although the letter **k** is not much used in Spanish, it is found in words relating to *kilos*, *kilometres* and *kilograms*; for example **un kilo** (meaning *a kilo*); **un kilogramo** (meaning *a kilogram*); **un kilómetro** (meaning *a kilometre*).

➤ Similarly, the [g] sound heard in the English word *gone* is spelled:

- **g** before **a**, **o** and **u**

- **gu** before **e** and **i**

➤ This means that the Spanish word for *cat* is spelled **gato** (pronounced [*ga-toh*]); the word for *goal* is spelled **gol** (pronounced [*gol*]); and the word for *worm* is spelled **gusano** (pronounced [*goo-sa-no*]).

➤ However, the Spanish word for *war* is spelled **guerra** (pronounced [*gair-ra*]) and the word for *guitar* is spelled **guitarra** (pronounced [*ghee-tar-ra*]).

Letters that are pronounced differently depending on what follows

➤ Certain letters are pronounced differently depending on what follows them. As we have seen, when **c** comes before **a**, **o** or **u**, it is pronounced like a [k]. When it comes before **e** or **i**, in European Spanish it is pronounced like the [th] in the English word *pith* and in Latin American Spanish it is pronounced like the [s] in *sing*.

➤ This means that **casa** (meaning *house*) is pronounced [*ka-sa*], but **centro** (meaning *centre*) is pronounced [*then-tro*] in European Spanish and [*sen-tro*] in Latin American Spanish. Similarly, **cita** (meaning *date*) is pronounced [*thee-ta*] in European Spanish and [*see-ta*] in Latin American Spanish.

➤ In the same way, when **g** comes before **a**, **o** or **u**, it is pronounced like the [*g*] in *gone*. When it comes before **e** or **i**, however, it is pronounced like the [*ch*] in *loch*, as it is pronounced in Scotland.

➤ This means that **gas** (meaning *gas*) is pronounced [*gas*] but **gente** (meaning *people*) is pronounced [*chen-tay*]. Similarly, **gimnasio** (meaning *gym*) is pronounced [*cheem-na-see-o*].

Spelling changes that are needed in verbs to reflect the pronunciation

➤ Because **c** sounds like [*k*] before **a**, **o** and **u**, and like [*th*] or [*s*] before **e** and **i**, you sometimes have to alter the spelling of a verb when adding a particular ending to ensure the word reads as it is pronounced:

- In verbs ending in **-car** (which is pronounced [*kar*]), you have to change the **c** to **qu** before endings starting with an **e** to keep the hard [*k*] pronunciation. So the **yo** form of the preterite tense of **sacar** (meaning *to take out*) is spelled **saqué**. This spelling change affects the preterite and the present subjunctive of verbs ending in **-car**.

- In verbs ending in **-cer** and **-cir** (which are pronounced [*ther*] and [*thir*] or [*ser*] and [*sir*]), you have to change the **c** to **z** before endings starting with **a** or **o** to keep the soft [*th/s*] pronunciation. So while the **yo** form of the preterite tense of **hacer** is spelled **hice**, the **él/ella/usted** form is spelled **hizo**. This spelling change affects the ordinary present tense as well as the present subjunctive of verbs ending in **-cer** or **-cir**.

➤ Because **g** sounds like the [*g*] of *gone* before **a**, **o** and **u**, and like the [*ch*] of *loch* before **e** and **i**, you also sometimes have to alter the spelling of a verb when adding a particular ending to ensure the verb still reads as it is pronounced:

- In verbs ending in **-gar** (which is pronounced [*gar*]), you have to change the **g** to **gu** before endings starting with an **e** or an **i** to keep the hard [*g*] pronunciation. So the **yo** form of the preterite tense of **pagar** (meaning *to pay*) is spelled **pagué**. This spelling change affects the preterite and the present subjunctive of verbs ending in **-gar**.

- In verbs ending in **-ger** and **-gir** (which are pronounced [*cher*] and [*chir*]), you have to change the **g** to **j** before endings starting with **a** or **o** to keep the soft [*ch*] pronunciation. So while the **él/ella/usted** form of the present tense of **coger** (meaning *to take* or *to catch*) is spelled **coge**, the **yo** form is spelled **cojo**. This spelling change affects the ordinary present tense as well as the present subjunctive of verbs ending in **-ger** or **-gir**.

➤ Because **gui** sounds like [*ghee*] in verbs ending in **-guir**, but **gua** and **guo** sound like [*gwa*] and [*gwo*], you have to drop the **u** before **a** and **o** in verbs ending in **-guir**. So while the **él/ella/usted** form of the present tense of **seguir** (meaning *to follow*) is spelled **sigue**, the **yo** form is spelled **sigo**. This spelling change affects the ordinary present tense as well as the present subjunctive of verbs ending in **-guir**.

➤ Finally, although **z** is always pronounced [*th*] in European Spanish and [*s*] in Latin American Spanish, in verbs ending in **-zar** the **z** spelling is changed to **c** before **e**. So, while the **él/ella/usted** form of the preterite tense of **cruzar** is spelled **cruzó**, the **yo** form is spelled **crucé**. This spelling change affects the preterite and the present subjunctive of verbs ending in **-zar**.

For further explanation of grammatical terms, please see pages viii-xii.

Spelling changes that are needed when making nouns and adjectives plural

➤ In the same way that you have to make some spelling changes when modifying the endings of certain verbs, you sometimes have to change the spelling of nouns and adjectives when making them plural.

➤ This affects nouns and adjectives ending in -z. When adding the -es ending of the plural, you have to change the z to c.

una vez once, one time	→	**dos veces** twice, two times
una luz a light	→	**unas luces** some lights
capaz capable (*singular*)	→	**capaces** capable (*plural*)

➤ The following table shows the usual spelling of the various sounds discussed above:

Usual spelling

	before a	before o	before u	before e	before i
[k] sound (as in *cap*)	ca: casa house	co: cosa thing	cu: cubo bucket	que: queso cheese	qui: química chemistry
[g] sound (as in *gap*)	ga: gato cat	go: gordo fat	gu: gusto taste	gue: guerra war	gui: guitarra guitar
[th] sound (as in *pith*) (pronounced [s] in Latin America)	za: zapato shoe	zo: zorro fox	zu: zumo juice	ce: cero zero	ci: cinta ribbon
[ch] sound (as in *loch*)	ja: jardín garden	jo: joven young	ju: jugar to play	ge: gente people	gi: gigante giant

i Note that because j is still pronounced [ch] even when it comes before e or i, there are quite a number of words that contain je or ji; for example,

el jefe/la jefa	the boss
el jerez	sherry
el jersey	jersey
el jinete	jockey
la jirafa	giraffe
el ejemplo	the example
dije/dijiste	I said/you said
dejé	I left

Similarly, because z is also pronounced [th] or [s] even when it comes before i or e, there are one or two exceptions to the spelling rules described above; for example, **el zigzag** (meaning *zigzag*) and **la zeta** (the name of the letter z in Spanish).

Stress

Which syllable to stress

➤ Most words can be broken up into <u>syllables</u>. These are the different sounds that words are broken up into. They are shown in this section by | and the stressed syllable is underlined.

➤ There are some very simple rules to help you remember which part of the word to stress in Spanish, and when to write an accent.

➤ Words <u>DON'T</u> have a written acute accent if they follow the normal stress rules for Spanish. If they do not follow the normal stress rules, they <u>DO</u> need an accent.

> *Tip*
> The accent that shows stress is always an acute accent in Spanish (´).
> To remember which way an acute accents slopes try thinking of this saying:
> *It's low on the left, with the height on the right.*

<u>Words ending in a vowel or -n or -s</u>

➤ Words ending in a vowel (*a, e, i, o* or *u*) or **-n** or **-s** are normally stressed on the *last syllable but one*. If this is the case, they do <u>NOT</u> have any written accents.

<u>**ca**</u>**|sa**	house	<u>**ca**</u>**|sas**	houses
pa|<u>**la**</u>**|bra**	word	**pa|**<u>**la**</u>**|bras**	words
<u>**tar**</u>**|de**	afternoon	<u>**tar**</u>**|des**	afternoons
<u>**ha**</u>**|bla**	he/she speaks	<u>**ha**</u>**|blan**	they speak
<u>**co**</u>**|rre**	he/she runs	<u>**co**</u>**|rren**	they run

➤ Whenever words ending in a vowel or **-n** or **-s** are <u>NOT</u> stressed on the last syllable but one, they have a written accent on the vowel that is stressed.

<u>**úl**</u>**|ti|mo**	last
<u>**jó**</u>**|ve|nes**	young people
<u>**crí**</u>**|me|nes**	crimes

<u>Words ending in a consonant other than -n or -s</u>

➤ Words ending in a consonant (a letter that isn't a vowel) other than **-n** or **-s** are normally stressed on the <u>last syllable</u>. If this is the case, they do <u>NOT</u> have an accent.

re|<u>**loj**</u>	clock, watch
ver|<u>**dad**</u>	truth
trac|<u>**tor**</u>	tractor

➤ Whenever words ending in a consonant other than **-n** or **-s** are <u>NOT</u> stressed on the last syllable, they have an accent.

ca|<u>**rác**</u>**|ter**	character
di|<u>**fí**</u>**|cil**	difficult
<u>**fá**</u>**|cil**	easy

For further explanation of grammatical terms, please see pages viii-xii.

Accents on feminine and plural forms

➤ The same syllable is stressed in the plural form of adjectives and nouns as in the singular. To show this, you need to:

- add an accent in the plural in the case of unaccented nouns and adjectives of more than one syllable ending in **-n**

or|den	order	**ór|de|nes**	orders
e|xa|men	exam	**e|xá|me|nes**	exams
BUT: **tren**	train	**tre|nes**	trains

i Note that in the case of one-syllable words ending in **-n** or **-s**, such as **tren** above, no accent is needed in the plural, since the stress falls naturally on the last syllable but one thanks to the plural **-es** ending.

- drop the accent in the plural form of nouns and adjectives ending in **-n** or **-s** which have an accent on the last syllable in the singular

au|to|bús	bus	**au|to|bu|ses**	buses
re|vo|lu|ción	revolution	**re|vo|lu|cio|nes**	revolutions

➤ The feminine forms of nouns or adjectives whose masculine form ends in an accented vowel followed by **-n** or **-s** do <u>NOT</u> have an accent.

un francés	a Frenchman
una francesa	a French woman

Tip

Just because a word has a written accent in the singular does not necessarily mean it has one in the plural, and vice versa.

jo\|ven
*Ends in **n**, so rule is to stress last syllable but one; follows rule, so no accent needed in singular*

jó\|ve\|nes
*Ends in **s**, so rule is to stress last syllable but one; breaks rule, so accent is needed in plural to keep stress on **jo-***

lec\|ción
*Ends in **n**, so rule is to stress last syllable but one; breaks rule, so accent is needed in singular*

lec\|cio\|nes
*Ends in **s**, so rule is to stress last syllable but one; follows rule, so no accent needed in plural to keep stress on **-cio-***

Which vowel to stress in vowel combinations

➤ The vowels **i** and **u** are considered to be <u>weak</u>. The vowels **a, e** and **o** are considered to be <u>strong</u>.

➤ When a weak vowel (**i** or **u**) combines with a strong one (**a, e** or **o**), they form <u>ONE</u> sound that is part of the <u>SAME</u> syllable. Technically speaking, this is called a <u>diphthong</u>. The strong vowel is emphasized more.

bai|le	dance
cie|rra	he/she/it closes
boi|na	beret
pei|ne	comb
cau|sa	cause

> *Tip*
> To remember which are the weak vowels, try thinking of this saying: *U and I*
> *are weaklings and always lose out to other vowels!*

➤ When **i** is combined with **u** or **u** with **i** (the two weak vowels), they also form <u>ONE</u> sound within the <u>SAME</u> syllable; there is more emphasis on the second vowel.

ci**u**dad	city, town
fu**i**	I went

➤ When you combine two strong vowels (**a**, **e** or **o**), they form <u>TWO</u> separate sounds and are part of <u>DIFFERENT</u> syllables.

ca|er	to fall
ca|os	chaos
fe|o	ugly

Adding accents to some verb forms

➤ When object pronouns are added to the end of certain verb forms, an accent is often required to show that the syllable stressed in the verb form does not change. These verb forms are:

- the <u>gerund</u> whenever one or more pronouns are added

compr**a**ndo	buying
compr**á**ndo(se)lo	buying it (for him/her/them)

- the <u>infinitive</u>, when followed by two pronouns

vend**e**r	to sell
vend**é**rselas	to sell them to him/her/them

- <u>imperative</u> forms

compra	buy
cómpralo	buy it
hagan	do
háganselo	do it for him/her/them
BUT:	
comprad	buy
compradlo	buy it

⇨ *For more information on **Gerunds**, **Infinitives** and the **Imperative**, see pages 180, 201 and 124.*

Accents on adjectives and adverbs

➤ Adjectives ending in -**ísimo** always have an accent on -**ísimo**. This means that any other accents are dropped.

caro expensive	→	**carísimo** very expensive	
difícil difficult	→	**dificilísimo** very difficult	

➤ Accents on adjectives are <u>NOT</u> affected when you add -**mente** to turn them into adverbs.

fácil easy	→	**fácilmente** easily	

For further explanation of grammatical terms, please see pages viii-xii.

The acute accent used to show meaning

➤ The acute accent is often used to distinguish between the written forms of some words which are pronounced the same but have a different meaning or function.

Without an accent		With an accent	
mi	my	mí	me
tu	your	tú	you
te	you	té	tea
si	if	sí	yes; himself
el	the	él	he
de	of	dé	give
solo	alone; by oneself; only	sólo	only
mas	but	más	more

Han robado <u>mi</u> coche.	They've stolen my car.
A <u>mí</u> no me vio.	He didn't see me.
¿Te gusta <u>tu</u> trabajo?	Do you like your job?
<u>Tú</u>, ¿qué opinas?	What do you think?
...<u>si</u> no viene	...if he doesn't come
<u>Sí</u> que lo sabe.	Yes, he does know.
<u>El</u> puerto está cerca.	The harbour's nearby.
<u>Él</u> lo hará.	He'll do it.

ⓘ Note that nowadays the accent is only used on **sólo** in the sense of only where the sentence might otherwise be ambiguous.

Me bebí una cerveza <u>sólo</u>.	I only had one beer.
Me bebí una cerveza <u>solo</u>.	I had a beer on my own.

➤ The acute accent is sometimes used on the demonstrative pronouns (**éste/ésta**, **aquél/aquélla**, **ése/ésa** and so on) to distinguish them from the demonstrative adjectives (**este/esta**, **aquel/aquella**, **ese/esa** and so on).

Me gusta <u>esta</u> casa. (= *adjective*)	I like this house.
Me quedo con <u>ésta</u>. (= *pronoun*)	I'll take this one.
¿Ves <u>aquellos</u> edificios? (= *adjective*)	Can you see those buildings?
<u>Aquéllos</u> son más bonitos. (= *pronoun*)	Those are prettier.

ⓘ Note that no accent is given on the neuter pronouns **esto, eso** and **aquello** since there is no adjective form with which they might be confused.

⇨ *For more information on* **Demonstrative adjectives** *and* **Demonstrative pronouns**, *see pages 41 and 95.*

➤ An accent is needed on question words in direct and indirect questions as well as after expressions of uncertainty.

¿Cómo estás?	How are you?
Dime cómo estás.	Tell me how you are.
Me preguntó cómo estaba.	He asked me how I was.
¿Con quién viajaste?	Who did you travel with?
¿Dónde encontraste eso?	Where did you find that?
No sé dónde está.	I don't know where it is.

➭ *For more information on* **Questions**, *see page 220.*

➤ An accent is also needed on exclamation words.

¡Qué asco!	How revolting!
¡Qué horror!	How awful!
¡Qué raro!	How strange!
¡Cuánta gente!	What a lot of people!

KEY POINTS

✔ When deciding whether or not to write an accent on a word, think about how it sounds and what letter it ends in, as there are certain rules to say when an accent should be used.

✔ The vowels **i** and **u** are considered to be weak. The vowels **a**, **e** and **o** are considered to be strong. They can combine in a number of ways.

✔ Accents are added to written forms of words which are pronounced the same but have a different meaning, for example, **mi/mí**, **tu/tú** and so on.

✔ Accents are also sometimes added to most demonstrative pronouns so that they are not confused with demonstrative adjectives.

✔ Adjectives ending in **-ísimo** always have an accent on **-ísimo**, but no accent is added when adverbs are formed by adding **-mente** to adjectives.

✔ Question words used in direct and indirect questions as well as exclamation words always have an acute accent.

Test yourself

1 **Rewrite the highlighted words with an accent form where required.**

a   Dámelo a **mi**. ....

b   Lo hizo él **solo**. ....

c   Eso se cambia **facilmente**. ....

d   ¿**Por que** dices eso? ....

e   ¿**Cuantos** quieres? ....

f   No sé **cuando** volverán. ....

g   ¿Quieres venir a **mi** casa? ....

h   ¿**Como** lo has hecho? ....

i   Quiero **aquellos**. ....

j   Este regalo es para **ti**. ....

2 **Cross out the incorrect alternatives.**

a   **un regalo para**   mí/mi/ti/él/vosotros/el

b   **¿Qué quieres tomar?**   Un te/Un té/Un café solo/Un café sólo

c   **prefiero**   ésta mesa/esta mesa/tú mesa/tu mesa

d   **dáselo a**   el/ése/él/ella/aquel

e   **¿Quién lo hará?**   yo/mí/él/ella/tu/tú

f   **¿Cuál es tu casa?**   aquella/ésta/esa/esta

g   **Hazlo con**   él/esto/ese/eso/ellos/éste

h   **Me gusta**   esta camisa/éste edificio/ese parque/ése chico/eso

i   **Eso es de**   mi hermana/mí madre/tu hijo/tú padre

j   **Se lo dijeron a**   mis tíos/mí tía/tu madre/tú padre

3 **Replace the highlighted words with the correct accented form.**

a   **daselo** ....   f   **haganlo** ....

b   **diceselo** ....   g   **facilmente** ....

c   **facilisimo** ....   h   **haria** ....

d   **vendiendolo**   i   **frances** ....

e   **compradmelo** ....   j   **jovenes** ....

Numbers

1	uno (un, una)
2	dos
3	tres
4	cuatro
5	cinco
6	seis
7	siete
8	ocho
9	nueve
10	diez
11	once
12	doce
13	trece
14	catorce
15	quince
16	dieciséis
17	diecisiete
18	dieciocho
19	diecinueve
20	veinte
21	veintiuno (veintiún, veintiuna)
22	veintidós
23	veintitrés
24	veinticuatro
25	veinticinco
26	veintiséis
27	veintisiete
28	veintiocho
29	veintinueve
30	treinta

EJEMPLOS	EXAMPLES
Vive en el número diez.	He lives at number ten.
en la página diecinueve	on page nineteen
un diez por ciento	10%
un cien por cien(to)	100%

<u>uno, un or una?</u>

➤ Use **uno** when counting, unless referring to something or someone feminine.

➤ Use **un** before a masculine noun and **una** before a feminine noun even when the nouns are plural.

<u>un</u> **hombre**	one man
<u>una</u> **mujer**	one woman
treinta y <u>un</u> **días**	thirty-one days
treinta y <u>una</u> **noches**	thirty-one nights
veinti<u>ún</u> años	twenty-one years
veinti<u>una</u> chicas	twenty-one girls

For further explanation of grammatical terms, please see pages viii-xii.

cien or ciento?

➤ Use **cien** before both masculine and feminine nouns as well as before **mil** (meaning *thousand*) and **millones** (meaning *million* in the plural):

cien libros	one hundred books
cien mil hombres	one hundred thousand men
cien millones	one hundred million

➤ Use **ciento** before other numbers.

ciento un perros	one hundred and one dogs
ciento una ovejas	one hundred and one sheep
ciento cincuenta	one hundred and fifty

> ⓘ Note that you don't translate the *and* in 101, 220 and so on.

➤ Make **doscientos/doscientas, trescientos/trescientas, quinientos/quinientas** and so on agree with the noun in question.

doscientas veinte libras	two hundred and twenty pounds
quinientos alumnos	five hundred students

> ⓘ Note that **setecientos** and **setecientas** have no i after the first s. Similarly, **novecientos** and **novecientas** have an o rather than the **ue** you might expect.

Full stop or comma?

➤ Use a full stop, not a comma, to separate thousands and millions in figures.

700.000 (setecientos mil)	700,000 (seven hundred thousand)
5.000.000 (cinco millones)	5,000,000 (five million)

➤ Use a comma instead of a decimal point to show decimals in Spanish.

0,5 (cero coma cinco)	0.5 (nought point five)
3,4 (tres coma cuatro)	3.4 (three point four)

1st	**primero (1°), primer (1er), primera (1a)**
2nd	**segundo (2°), segunda (2a)**
3rd	**tercero (3°), tercer (3er), tercera (3a)**
4th	**cuarto (4°), cuarta (4a)**
5th	**quinto (5°), quinta (5a)**
6th	**sexto (6°), sexta (6a)**
7th	**séptimo (7°), séptima (7a)**
8th	**octavo (8°), octava (8a)**
9th	**noveno (9°), novena (9a)**
10th	**décimo (10°), décima (10a)**
100th	**centésimo (100°), centésima (100a)**
101st	**centésimo primero (101°), centésima primera (101a)**
1000th	**milésimo (1000°), milésima (1000a)**

EJEMPLOS	EXAMPLES
Vive en el quinto (piso).	He lives on the fifth floor.
Llegó tercero.	He came in third.

> *Típ*
> Shorten **primero** (meaning *first*) to **primer**, and **tercero** (meaning *third*) to
> **tercer** before a *masculine singular noun*.
>
> su <u>primer</u> cumpleaños   his first birthday
> el <u>tercer</u> premio   the third prize

[i] Note that when you are writing these numbers in figures, don't write *1st*, *2nd*, *3rd* as in
English. Use **1°**, **1ª**, **1er**, **2°**, **2ª** and **3°**, **3ª**, **3er** as required by the noun.

la 2ª lección   the 2nd lesson
el 3er premio   the 3rd prize

primero, segundo, tercero or uno, dos, tres?

➤ Apart from **primero** (meaning *first*) up to **décimo** (meaning *tenth*), as well as **centésimo**
(meaning *one hundredth*) and **milésimo** (meaning *one thousandth*), the ordinal numbers tend
not to be used very much in Spanish. Cardinal numbers (ordinary numbers) are used instead.

    Carlos <u>tercero</u>   Carlos the third
    Alfonso <u>trece</u>   Alfonso the thirteenth

⇨ *For numbers used in dates, see page 275.*

La hora	The time
¿Qué hora es?	What time is it?
Es la una menos veinte.	It's twenty to one.
Es la una menos cuarto.	It's (a) quarter to one.
Es la una.	It's one o'clock.
Es la una y diez.	It's ten past one.
Es la una y cuarto.	It's (a) quarter past one.
Es la una y media.	It's half past one.
Son las dos menos veinticinco.	It's twenty-five to two.
Son las dos menos cuarto.	It's (a) quarter to two.
Son las dos.	It's two o'clock.
Son las dos y diez.	It's ten past two.
Son las dos y cuarto.	It's (a) quarter past two.
Son las dos y media.	It's half past two.
Son las tres.	It's three o'clock.

> *Típ*
> Use **son las** for all times not involving **una** (meaning *one*).

¿A qué hora?	At what time?
a medianoche	at midnight
a mediodía	at midday
a la una (del mediodía)	at one o'clock (in the afternoon)
a las ocho (de la tarde)	at eight o'clock (in the evening)
a las 9:25 *or* a las nueve (y) veinticinco	at nine twenty-five
a las 16:50 *or* a las dieciséis (y) cincuenta	at 16:50 *or* sixteen fifty

For further explanation of grammatical terms, please see pages viii-xii.

☑ Note that in Spanish, as in English, you can also tell the time using the figures you see on a digital clock or watch or on a 24-hour timetable.

La fecha	The date
Los días de la semana	**The days of the week**
lunes	Monday
martes	Tuesday
miércoles	Wednesday
jueves	Thursday
viernes	Friday
sábado	Saturday
domingo	Sunday

¿Cuándo?	When?
el lunes	on Monday
los lunes	on Mondays
todos los lunes	every Monday
el martes pasado	last Tuesday
el viernes que viene	next Friday
el sábado que viene no, el otro	a week on Saturday
dentro de tres sábados	two weeks on Saturday

☑ Note that days of the week DON'T have a capital letter in Spanish.

Los meses	Months of the year
enero	January
febrero	February
marzo	March
abril	April
mayo	May
junio	June
julio	July
agosto	August
septiembre	September
octubre	October
noviembre	November
diciembre	December

¿Cuándo?	When?
en febrero	in February
el 1 *or* uno *or* 1° *or* primero de diciembre	on December 1st *or* first December
en 1998 (mil novecientos noventa y ocho)	in 1998 (nineteen ninety-eight)
el 15 de diciembre de 2003	on 15th December, 2003
el año dos mil	(the year) two thousand
dos mil cinco	two thousand and five

¿Qué día es hoy?	What day is it today?
Es...	It's...
lunes 26 de febrero	Monday, 26th February
domingo 1 de octubre	Sunday, 1st October
lunes veintiséis de febrero	Monday, the twenty-sixth of February
domingo uno de octubre	Sunday, the first of October

ⓘ Note that months of the year <u>DON'T</u> have a capital letter in Spanish.

> *Tip*
> Although in English we use *first*, *second*, *third* and so on in dates, in Spanish you use the equivalent of *one*, *two*, *three* and so on.
>
> **el dos de mayo**   the second of May

Frases útiles

Spanish	English
¿Cuándo?	**When?**
hoy	today
esta mañana	this morning
esta tarde	this afternoon
esta noche	this evening
¿Con qué frecuencia?	**How often?**
todos los días	every day
cada dos días	every other day
una vez por semana	once a week
dos veces por semana	twice a week
una vez al mes	once a month
¿Cuándo pasó?	**When did it happen?**
por la mañana	in the morning
por la noche	in the evening
ayer	yesterday
ayer por la mañana	yesterday morning
ayer por la tarde	yesterday afternoon/evening
ayer por la noche	yesterday evening/last night
anoche	last night
anteayer	the day before yesterday
hace una semana	a week ago
hace quince días	two weeks ago
la semana pasada	last week
el año pasado	last year
¿Cuándo va a pasar?	**When is it going to happen?**
mañana	tomorrow
mañana por la mañana	tomorrow morning
mañana por la tarde	tomorrow afternoon/evening
mañana por la noche	tomorrow evening/night
pasado mañana	the day after tomorrow
dentro de dos días	in two days' time
dentro de una semana	in a week's time
dentro de quince días	in two weeks' time
el mes que viene	next month
el año que viene	next year

Useful phrases

Solutions

Nouns

1.
   a. la reina
   b. la inglesa
   c. la empleada
   d. la princesa
   e. la hermana
   f. la dentista
   g. la profesora
   h. la estudiante
   i. la actriz
   j. la mujer

2.
   a. la amiga
   b. la reina
   c. la profesora
   d. la estudiante
   e. una inglesa
   f. la madre
   g. la princesa
   h. mujer
   i. camarera
   j. una empleada

3.
   a. La capital **de España es Madrid.**
   b. El cura **dice misa.**
   c. La guía **incluye un glosario.**
   d. El guía **lleva los turistas por la ciudad.**
   e. El capital **extranjero ayuda mucho en este país.**

4.
   a. los libros
   b. unas canciones
   c. unas tostadas
   d. unas noticias
   e. las luces
   f. los exámenes
   g. unos hombres-lobo
   h. unos jerseys
   i. los lunes
   j. unos muebles

5.
   a. televisión/mano
   b. profesor/lunes
   c. madre/inglesa/moto
   d. coche/planeta/padre
   e. televisiones/manos
   f. profesores/lunes
   g. madres/inglesas/motos
   h. coches/planetas/padres
   i. televisión/mano
   j. profesor/lunes

6.
   a. un
   b. una
   c. un
   d. un
   e. una
   f. un
   g. una
   h. un
   i. un
   j. un/una

Articles

1.
   a. mano/revista/cabeza/cárcel
   b. desayuno/hambre/lunes/verde/fútbol/jardín
   c. manos/ciudades/mesas/zapatillas
   d. deberes/dulces/colores/chocolates/animales/autobuses/ratones
   e. mano/revista/cabeza/cárcel
   f. desayunos/lunes/jardín
   g. manos/ciudades/mesas/zapatillas
   h. deberes/dulces/colores/animales/autobuses
   i. manos/revistas/cabezas/cárceles
   j. desayunos/jardines/ratones/pijamas

2.
   a. el
   b. la
   c. el
   d. la
   e. El
   f. El
   g. las
   h. Los
   i. las
   j. las

3.
   a. Me gustan los animales.
   b. No me gusta la carne.
   c. Me gusta el rojo.
   d. Tiene los ojos azules.
   e. Lávate la cara.
   f. El desayuno es entre las 7 y las 9.
   g. Trabajo los martes y los jueves.
   h. Es el hijo del médico/de la médica.
   i. El sábado fuimos al cine.
   j. Son 5 euros el kilo.

4.
   a. una
   b. un
   c. un
   d. un
   e. unos
   f. un
   g. un
   h. unas
   i. un
   j. unas

5.
   a. un
   b. -
   c. -
   d. una
   e. una
   f. un
   g. unas
   h. unas
   i. -
   j. -

6.
   a. Mi madre **es doctora.**
   b. Su padre **es un actor famoso.**
   c. Mis padres **viven en un piso.**
   d. Tenemos **un coche rojo.**
   e. Jaime **no tiene coche.**

7.
   a. Soy actor/actriz.
   b. Mi madre es médica/doctora.
   c. Es una buena enfermera.
   d. Quiero leer otro libro.

Solutions

Articles *cont.*

e No tienen jardín.
f Mi hermano es estudiante.
g Es un artista famoso.
h Tenemos vecinos australianos.
i Tiene un novio americano.
j No tengo novio.

8 a por lo menos = **at least**
   b a lo mejor = **maybe**
   c lo que dice tu hermana = **what your sister says**
   d lo buenos que son = **how good they are**
   e lo de tu hermana = **that business with your sister**

9 a lo
   b Lo que
   c Lo
   d lo
   e lo que
   f lo
   g lo que
   h lo que
   i Lo de
   j lo que

10 a Por lo general **cenamos temprano.**
    b A lo mejor **no vienen.**
    c Lo de tu primo **me sorprende mucho.**
    d Lo que más me gusta **es ir de tiendas.**
    e Lo que pasa **es que no quiere venir.**

11 a That's the most important thing.
    b The important thing is to be happy.
    c The good thing is that it's cheap.
    d Maybe they'll come tomorrow.
    e I generally eat at two.
    f The only thing is that it's very expensive.
    g At least eat something.
    h At least 20 people are coming.
    i What I like best is going to the cinema.
    j I'm very surprised about Isabel/that business with Isabel.

Adjectives

1 a un abrigo caro
   b una idea tonta
   c unas chicas altas
   d una chaqueta azul
   e mi hermana pequeña
   f mi hermana mayor
   g una señora inglesa
   h la cocina española
   i unas camisas blancas
   j unas mujeres muy charlatanas

2 a encantador
   b encantadores
   c nuevo
   d —
   e fáciles
   f pequeño
   g —
   h americanas
   i bonita/grande
   j nuevas

3 a buen
   b grande
   c gran
   d mal
   e tercer

f ningún
g ningún
h ninguna
i ninguna
j Cualquier

4 a Hace **mal tiempo.**
   b Hace una semana **de gran calor.**
   c Ven **a cualquier hora.**
   d Es una **gran pena.**
   e Está **de buen humor.**

5 a Es mi antiguo jefe. = **He's my old boss.**
   b La capilla es muy antigua. = **The chapel is really old.**
   c ¡Pobre de ti! = **Poor you!**
   d Es un país muy pobre. = **It's a very poor country.**
   e Me lo dijo ella misma. = **She told me herself.**

6 a azul/verde
   b blanca/grasos
   c gris/blancas/amarillas
   d mala/horrorosa/fría
   e mala/barata

f tonto
g llenas
h viejas/pequeñas
i precioso
j viejas/nueva

7 a españolas
   b ingleses
   c frío
   d pobres
   e negros
   f fría
   g difíciles
   h altos
   i crueles
   j siguientes

8 a una chaqueta **azul marino**
   b la hora **exacta**
   c un examen **difícil**
   d las costumbres **inglesas**
   e los hombres **españoles**

9 a Juan es más alto que mi hermano.
   b Mi padre es más viejo que el tuyo.

Solutions

Adjectives *cont.*

c Belén es más alta que tú.
d Este hotel es más barato que ese.
e Pedro es menos trabajador que Pepe.
f Lucía es más guapa que su hermana.
g Nuestro jardín es más pequeño que el vuestro.
h La película es menos interesante que el libro.
i La verde es más bonita que la azul.
j Mi tía es menos nerviosa que mi madre.

10 a tan
b tanto
c tan
d tanta
e tan
f tan
g tanta
h tanta
i tan
j tanta

11 a facilísimo
b delgadísima
c riquísimo
d viejísimo
e carísimos
f feísimo
g dificilísimos
h bonitísimo
i muchísima
j buenísima

12 a el hombre más alto
b los coches más caros
c los hoteles más baratos
d los empleados menos trabajadores
e los jardines más pequeños
f las escuelas más grandes
g la hija menor
h el hijo mayor
i el día peor
j el mejor de todos

13 a revista/serpiente/agua/ciudad

b año/sistema
c zapatillas/habitaciones/televisiones
d exámenes/cursos
e tienda/habitación
f profesor/sistema
g —
h ordenadores/trenes
i calle/mesa
j lápiz/restaurantes

14 a Esta
b Este
c Este
d Estos
e Ese
f aquellas
g estos/esos
h aquel
i ese
j esas

15 a Este jardín es precioso.
b No me gusta ese color.
c Este hospital es grande.
d Vivo en aquella casa de allí.
e Estos pantalones son muy caros.
f Esa película es malísima.
g Quiero comprar ese libro.
h ¿Quieres estas rosas o aquellas flores de allí?
i Quiero esta camisa y esos zapatos.
j ¿Te gustan esos colores?

16 a ¡Cuánto tiempo lleva! = **It takes such a long time!**
b ¿Cuánto tiempo lleva? = **How long does it take?**
c ¿Qué tiempo hace? = **What's the weather like?**
d ¡Qué tiempo tan bueno hace! = **It's lovely weather!**
e ¿Cuánto gana? = **How much does he earn?**

17 a mis
b su
c Mis
d vuestras

e nuestros
f tu
g tus
h Nuestros
i su
j mis

18 a mis
b mi
c tu
d tus
e sus
f nuestro
g vuestros
h vuestras
i nuestra
j sus

19 a pocas
b mismas
c muchas
d muchas
e poca
f mucha
g algunas
h todos
i mismas
j todas

20 a ¿Quieres otra tostada?
b Tengo que comprar otro libro.
c Tengo muchos amigos.
d Algún día queremos ir a Australia.
e Empezamos el mismo día.
f Nos vemos todos los días.
g ¿Quieres otro café?
h ¿Quieres agua?
i ¿Tenemos pan?
j ¿Necesitamos leche?

21 a Londres/el día
b nube
c paciencia
d flores
e casas/familias
f las familias/las noches
g gente/días
h hoteles
i día/color
j coche/hotel

Solutions

Pronouns

1
  a mi/ti
  b nosotros/ti
  c yo
  d ustedes/vosotros/mí
  e ti/mi
  f ti
  g mí/tu
  h mi/yo/tu
  i mi
  j ti

2
  a Tengo un coche nuevo.
  b ¿Tienes hermanos?
  c ¿Cuántos años tienes?
  d Tenemos un perro.
  e Tienen dos gatos.
  f Tiene el pelo rubio.
  g Somos nosotros.
  h No sabe nadar.
  i Habla inglés.
  j Comen mucho.

3
  a Necesito hablar con ellos.
  b Quiero casarme con él.
  c Nos vamos de vacaciones con ellas.
  d Puedes venir con nosotros.
  e Es tan tonto como él.
  f Es más listo que ella.
  g Anda siempre con ellos.
  h Siempre veranean en casa de ellos.
  i Gasta más que él.
  j Es un regalo para nosotros.

4
  a mi madre = **ella**
  b Samuel y yo = **nosotros**
  c el hermano de Pablo = **él**
  d mis primos = **ellos**
  e para ti y tus padres = **vosotros**

5
  a ¿Dónde la compras?
  b ¿Quién te la hace?
  c La comimos toda.
  d No las comas todas.
  e Nunca los veo.
  f Acompáñalos.
  g Ayúdala.
  h La veo todos los días.
  i No las tires.
  j Cómpralo.

6
  a No sé dónde viven. = **No lo sé.**
  b Estamos arreglando la casa. = **La estamos arreglando.**
  c Vamos a visitar a los abuelos. = **Los vamos a visitar.**
  d Cuéntame el asunto. = **Cuéntamelo.**
  e Compremos estas fresas. = **Comprémoslas.**

7
  a la
  b los
  c te
  d me
  e te
  f lo
  g nos
  h la
  i los
  j la

8
  a ¿Ves ese pájaro? — Sí, lo veo.
  b ¿Te gusta el fútbol? — No, lo odio.
  c ¿Lo oyes?
  d Llueve. — Ya lo sé.
  e Enrique y María están en el jardín. — Sí, los veo.
  f ¿Quieres este plátano? — No, no lo quiero.
  g Mi primo vive allí. Puedes visitarlo.
  h ¡Ayúdame!
  i Me gusta ese bolso. — ¡Cómpralo!
  j No encuentro las llaves. ¿Las ves?

9
  a Juan les envía un correo.
  b ¿Por qué no le escribes una postal?
  c Envíales este paquete.
  d Pablo le da un consejo.
  e Carlos le dice adiós.
  f Les dedico este poema.
  g No le prestes la bici.
  h Dale un beso.
  i Diles la verdad.
  j Hazle una foto.

10
  a Dime la verdad.
  b Tráeme una silla.
  c Respóndele ahora mismo.
  d ¿Por qué no le haces una tortilla?
  e Dale una manzana.
  f Dales las llaves.
  g Siempre lo trae con ella.
  h Les envío dinero todas las semanas.
  i Le leo una página todas las noches.
  j ¿Te da algún consejo?

11
  a ¿Me traes un vaso?
  b ¿Me traes un vaso de leche?
  c ¿Nos traes la cuenta?
  d ¿Les traes unas sillas?
  e ¿Me das eso?
  f ¿Le das la pelota?
  g ¿Me das un beso?
  h ¿Nos ayudas con esto?
  i ¿Los llamas esta tarde?
  j ¿Me llamas mañana?

12
  a Maruja me lo explicó.
  b Ana os los dará mañana.
  c ¿Tu hermano te la presta?
  d No se lo quiero pedir./No quiero pedírselo.
  e Mañana se lo doy.
  f Enséñamelos.
  g No me lo quiere dejar./No quiere dejármelo.
  h Nunca se la dice.
  i ¿Cuándo se lo damos?
  j ¿Cuándo se lo vas a decir?/¿Cuándo vas a decírselo?

13
  a Me los dio mi hermana.
  b ¿Me lo/la compras?
  c Préstaselo./Préstasela.
  d Envíaselo por correo electrónico.
  e Enséñamelo./Enséñamela.
  f Dánoslo./Dánosla.
  g Se lo/la presta a todos.
  h Todos me lo piden.
  i ¿Por qué no se lo pides?
  j Nos lo prometieron.

14
  a I will give it to him. = **Se lo doy yo.**
  b Show me them. = **Enséñamelos.**
  c Don't tell him that. = **No se lo digas.**
  d Don't buy it for her. = **No se lo compres.**
  e She sends me them every week. = **Me los manda todas las semanas.**

15
  a la
  b los
  c nos
  d os
  e los

Pronouns *cont.*

f la
g los
h las
i les
j os

16 a tú/mí
b me/tú/yo
c tú/sí
d tú/mí/sí
e tú/sí
f consigo/con tú/con ti
g contigo
h con ellos
i mí/ti
j ti

17 a Los invitamos.
b ¿Por qué no lo llevas contigo?
c ¿Cuándo la llamaron?
d Vamos a esperarlos al aeropuerto./Los vamos a esperar al aeropuerto.
e Quiero llevarla conmigo.
f Quiero acompañarla al teatro.
g ¿Te apetece acompañarlos al cine?
h No la conozco.
i Los llamo todas las noches.
j ¿Quién los lleva?

18 a Lo llevaré **conmigo.**
b Se lo lleva **consigo.**
c Los llevan **con ellos.**
d Queremos llevarlos **con nosotros.**
e Llévatelo **contigo.**

19 a el de
b las de
c el de
d las de
e los de
f la de
g la de
h las de
i la de
j el de

20 a el suyo
b la suya
c la nuestra
d el suyo
e la vuestra
f los suyos
g la suya

h el suyo
i del suyo
j las suyas

21 a Estos lápices son tuyos.
b Esas botas son mías.
c Estos asientos aquí son vuestros.
d Esas bicicletas allí son nuestras.
e Estos libros ¿son tuyos o los míos?
f Esa casa de allí es nuestra.
g Me gusta tu casa más que la suya.
h ¿Estos son nuestros asientos o los vuestros?
i ¿Este es mi periódico o el tuyo?
j He visto mi bolsa pero no la tuya.

22 a Ninguno **de ellos vino a la fiesta.**
b Todos **están estropeados.**
c ¿Había mucha gente? **Poca.**
d Todo **va bien.**
e ¿Cuántas tienes? **Muchas.**

23 a a
b a
c Me lo dijo alguien.
d a
e a
f No sé si alguien vendrá
g Pues no me lo había dicho nadie.
h a
i a
j Creo que alguien debería decírselo.

24 a a alguien
b nada
c A alguien
d alguien
e a alguien
f alguien
g alguien
h a alguien
i a alguien
j algo

25 a No viene nadie./Nadie viene.
b No quiero nada.
c ¿Quieres algo?

d No invitamos a nadie.
e ¿Quién lo sabe? — Nadie.
f ¿Qué compras? — Nada.
g No tengo ninguno.
h ¿Quieres alguno de estos?
i A mí nadie me dice nada.
j Cualquiera puede hacerlo.

26 a que
b las que/quienes
c [de]l que/de quien
d los que/quienes
e que
f la que
g [a]l que
h lo que
i [a]l que
j el que/el cual

27 a a quien
b quien
c quien
d quienes
e quien
f quienes
g quienes
h quienes
i quien
j quien

28 a la mujer que vive aquí
b el coche que quiero comprar
c el viaje del que siempre habla
d el restaurante al que siempre vamos
e Tiene novio, lo que es una gran sorpresa.
f Mi primo, cuya mujer es inglesa, viene mañana.
g ¿Cómo se llama el hombre con el que/con quien trabaja?
h las mujeres con las que/con quienes trabaja
i la compañía, cuyos empleados casi todos tienen menos de 30 años
j el cantante con el que/con quien se casó

29 a Cuánto
b quién
c Cuánta
d Cuál
e Cuáles
f quiénes

Solutions

Pronouns *cont.*

g quién
h Cuántos
i Cuántos
j quién

30 a Cuántos
b Cuáles
c quiénes
d quién
e cuántos

f Cuáles
g quién
h cuál
i Cuánto
j Cuántos

31 a ¿Cuáles prefieres?
b ¿Quién te lo dijo?
c ¿Quiénes son esas mujeres de allí?

d ¿A quién le vas a vender el coche?
e ¿A quién invitas?
f ¿De quién es esa casa?
g ¿Cuántos compras?
h ¿Prefieres este o aquel?
i Este bolígrafo escribe mejor que ese.
j ¿Qué es eso?

Verbs

1 a hablan
b viven
c llamo
d llama
e come
f trabajan
g queremos
h estudia
i hacen
j vamos

2 a Cenamos fuera a menudo.
b Le dais demasiado dinero.
c Manuel la adora.
d Siempre le regalan un viaje.
e Ahora juegan mejor.
f Se lo pregunto a Ana mañana.
g Su amiga viene a jugar hoy.
h Sus padres trabajan en el hospital.
i Queremos descansar un poco.
j Mañana se lo cuento a la profesora.

3 a Se llama Ben.
b ¿Cómo te llamas?
c Vivimos en Londres.
d Trabaja en una oficina.
e Tengo frío.
f Hace calor.
g Cenamos a las ocho.
h Hablan español.
i Viven juntos.
j Te quiero.

4 a Los niños **juegan en el patio.**
b Pepe **trabaja en Madrid.**
c No **hablo inglés.**
d Cenamos **todos juntos.**
e ¿Dónde **estudias?**

5 a compro
b Terminamos
c Das
d Tomo
e termina
f invitan
g Estudio
h trabajan
i hablan
j cenan

6 a ¿Cómo te llamas?
b ¿Hablas inglés?
c Trabaja mucho.
d Siempre cocina él.
e ¿Me compras este libro?
f Todos los días dan un paseo.
g Siempre compramos el pan aquí.
h Hablan con los abuelos todos los domingos.
i Se llama Paz.
j Fuma demasiado.

7 a Comemos a la una.
b José y Silvia venden la casa.
c Nos gusta ver la televisión por las noches.
d Juan crece mucho.
e Luego te veo.

8 a hace
b crece
c coméis
d vende
e lee
f leemos
g lees
h traen
i trae
j vende

9 a Laura me debe dinero.
b ¿A qué hora comen ustedes?
c Eso depende de vosotros.
d ¿Metes esto en tu maleta?
e Siempre la veo en el parque.
f Comen a las dos todos los días.
g Óscar come muy poco.
h Siempre te metes en mis asuntos.
i Esa tienda vende ropa.
j ¿No temes al profesor?

10 a vivimos
b vive
c viven
d vivís
e vivo
f parte
g recibimos
h permite
i permiten
j recibe

Verbs *cont.*

11 a Viven en Escocia.
b Mi hermana vive sola.
c Mi madre insiste.
d Eso no se permite.
e Recibo un cheque todos los meses.
f ¿Dónde viven tus amigos?
g Siempre imprime las invitaciones.
h Viven cerca de nosotros.
i Siempre me interrumpe.
j Recibimos muchas cartas.

12 a Antonio y yo vivimos aquí.
b ¿Dónde viven tus amigos?
c No se permite fumar.
d Los profesores no nos permiten móviles en clase.
e Siempre reciben muchos regalos.
f Nunca interrumpimos a la profesora.
g ¿Cuándo recibís la paga?
h ¿Por qué me interrumpes?
i Mis padres insisten.
j Vivo sola.

13 a es
b somos
c está
d estoy
e es
f son
g está
h estamos
i está
j Son

14 a está
b son
c es
d está
e está
f son
g está
h son
i es
j es

15 a Estoy aburrido. = **I'm bored.**
b Es muy aburrida. = **She's very boring.**
c Tu padre es muy joven. = **Your father's very young.**
d Tu padre está muy joven. = **Your father looks very young.**

16 a Estoy cansado/cansada.
b Está aburrida.
c La película es aburrida.
d Están de vacaciones.
e Mis padres están de viaje.
f La yoga está de moda.
g Este examen es fácil.
h El programa es muy interesante.
i Esto es para ti.
j ¿Cómo estáis?

17 a Está estudiando
b Estamos cenando
c Está viviendo
d Está escribiendo
e Estoy trabajando
f Están hablando
g Estamos viendo
h estás leyendo
i Estoy estudiando
j Están comprando

18 a Están trabajando mucho. = **They're working a lot.**
b Los están vendiendo baratos. = **They're selling them cheap.**
c Están haciéndose muy ricos. = **They're getting very rich.**
d Está leyendo un libro. = **He's reading a book.**
e Se están riendo de mí. = **They're laughing at me.**

19 a estoy comiendo
b estamos comprando
c Está hablando
d están viendo
e está haciendo
f estamos pintando
g están tomando
h está descansando
i está tomando el sol
j estoy bebiendo

20 a ¿Qué estás cocinando? **Estoy haciendo una tortilla.**
b ¿Qué queréis cenar? **Pescado con ensalada.**
c ¿Dónde está tu madre? **Está haciendo la compra.**

e Está muy rica. = **It's delicious.**

d ¿Qué estáis haciendo? **Estamos lavando el coche.**
e ¿Por qué está cantando? **Porque está contenta.**

21 a ¡No me hables!
b ¡Dame eso!
c ¡Dímelo ahora mismo!
d ¡No se lo envíes a ellos!
e ¡Dámelos!
f Esperémoslos aquí.
g ¡No lo toques!
h ¡No digas eso!
i Terminemos/Vamos a terminar este ejercicio.
j ¡Pon eso ahí!

22 a Trabaja más rápido.
b Comed en silencio.
c Compremos este coche.
d ¡Calla la boca!
e ¡No tardéis!
f Vamos al centro.
g ¡Esperadme ahí!
h ¡No hables tan alto!
i ¡Habla más bajito!
j ¡No hagáis tanto ruido.

23 a ¡Mira esto!
b ¡Escuchadme, por favor!
c ¡Dale un poco a tu hermana!
d ¡Cuéntamelo!
e ¡Espérame!
f ¡Cómpramelo!
g ¡Ayudadlos!
h ¡Termina los deberes antes de cenar!
i ¡Dime lo que te pasa!
j ¡Permíteme!

24 a Vete
b Déjame
c Come
d Comedlo
e Despiértame
f Dejadle
g Háblale
h Llámala
i Atrévete
j Esperémoslos

25 a ¿Quieres ducharte ahora?
b Tenemos que irnos ya.
c Está arreglándose para salir.
d Está afeitándose.

Solutions

Verbs cont.

  e Están llamándonos.
  f Quiero irme.
  g ¿Queréis sentaros?
  h Están lavándose las manos.
  i Vamos a acostarnos pronto.
  j No quiero reírme de ellos.

26 a No te levantes.
  b No te vayas.
  c No te quedes ahí.
  d No se sienten ahí.
  e No te mires al espejo.
  f No os relajéis del todo.
  g No nos vayamos mañana.
  h No te vistas de azul.
  i No te pongas el abrigo.
  j No me esperes.

27 a ¿Cómo te llamas?
  b ¿Cómo se llama tu hermano?
  c Se quieren mucho.
  d No nos conocemos.
  e Ya no se escriben.
  f No se permiten los móviles en la escuela.
  g ¿A qué hora te acuestas?
  h Solo tiene 12 años pero ya se afeita.
  i Me levanto muy temprano.
  j Lávate las manos antes de comer.

28 a Voy a hablar
  b Vamos a cenar
  c Van a ver
  d Vas a querer
  e Vais a ir
  f Van a comprar
  g Va a estudiar
  h van a querer
  i Vamos a hacer
  j Vas a trabajar

29 a hablaré
  b acompañaremos
  c Se irán
  d se casarán
  e compraré
  f hablarán
  g vendrá
  h abrirán
  i harán
  j saldrán

30 a Lo haré mañana.
  b Laura podrá ayudarte.
  c Tendrás que tener cuidado.
  d Llegaré a las nueve.
  e Mañana voy a levantarme temprano. *or* Mañana me voy a levantar temprano.
  f Tendrá tiempo de leer durante las vacaciones.
  g Mañana va a hacer calor.
  h ¿Cuándo volverán tus padres?
  i ¿Crees que irás a la playa mañana?
  j ¿Estaréis en Londres el domingo?

31 a gustaría
  b importaría
  c ayudarían
  d diría
  e deberías
  f podríamos
  g vendrían
  h acompañaríamos
  i Debería
  j haría

32 a gustaría
  b debería
  c podría
  d gustaría
  e encantaría
  f Sería
  g permitiríais
  h sabría
  i importaría
  j me atrevería

33 a Yo se lo diría.
  b Le dije que yo lo haría.
  c ¿Cómo lo harías tú?
  d ¿Te gustaría venir conmigo?
  e Debería decírselo.
  f Les dije que comeríamos juntos.
  g ¿Cuánto pagarías por ese coche?
  h Los niños lo pasarían bien aquí.
  i Deberías sacar algunas fotos.
  j Me gustaría comprártelo pero no puedo.

34 a duró
  b compramos
  c comprasteis
  d comieron
  e cerró
  f bailó
  g habló
  h naciste
  i comenté
  j vivieron

35 a Me **levanté temprano.**
  b Tino se **levantó a las once.**
  c Nos **levantamos a las ocho.**
  d ¿A qué hora te **levantaste?**
  e ¿A qué hora os **levantasteis hoy?**

36 a Condujiste
  b dijeron
  c estuvimos
  d di
  e anduvimos
  f estuvisteis
  g hiciste
  h fue
  i supieron
  j quisiste

37 a Me dio su número de teléfono.
  b Perdí el pasaporte en España.
  c Ganaron 2-1.
  d Ayer nos quedamos en casa.
  e Anoche salimos.
  f El sábado me compré un vestido nuevo.
  g Pidió helado de postre.
  h Tuvimos un accidente.
  i Ana compró un móvil nuevo.
  j El precio de la gasolina subió ayer.

38 a Llamaba
  b tomaban
  c llamaba
  d Venían
  e estábamos
  f cenaba
  g jugabais
  h hablábamos
  i vivíais
  j comíamos

Verbs cont.

39 a Cuando éramos jóvenes, nuestra madre no trabajaba.
b Hacía mucho frío.
c Todos estaban muy cansados.
d Estaban viendo/Veían una película.
e Éramos siete para cenar.
f Era más guapa que su hermana.
g Dijeron que iban al cine.
h Nos veíamos bastante a menudo.
i Hacía mucho tiempo que no nos veíamos./No, nos veíamos desde hacía mucho tiempo.
j Vino mucha gente a la fiesta.

40 a Hacía mucho tiempo **que no venían a vernos.**
b Cuando éramos jóvenes **nos gustaba ir a las fiestas.**
c Me levantaba temprano **para ducharme.**
d Leía un libro **para quedar a dormir.**
e Cuando venían a visitarnos **siempre les ofrecíamos algo de picar.**

41 a He terminado
b Has estado
c Hemos vendido
d Se han ido
e Has visto
f Hemos comido
g Han abierto
h ha hecho
i he puesto
j ha roto

42 a vendido
b visto
c vivido
d abierto
e dicho
f cubierto
g hecho
h puesto
i vuelto
j visto

43 a No la he visto.
b Ya lo he hecho.
c ¿Lo han hecho ya?

d Hemos llegado.
e ¿Quién ha roto la silla?
f ¿Habéis olvidado los libros todos?
g He abierto la ventana.
h ¿Quién te ha dicho eso?
i ¿Has/Habéis hecho los deberes?
j No los he visto desde hace mucho tiempo.

44 a ¿Cuándo **habéis vuelto?**
b ¿Quién te lo **ha dicho?**
c ¿Cómo lo **han hecho?**
d ¿Cuántos **han muerto?**
e ¿Dónde lo **habéis puesto?**

45 a Había terminado
b Habías estado
c Se habían ido
d habías visto
e habíamos comido
f Habían abierto
g había hecho
h había oído
i había puesto
j había roto

46 a Hacía mucho tiempo que no los habíamos visto./No los habíamos visto desde hacía mucho tiempo.
b Habían vivido en Inglaterra antes.
c Ya había decidido decírselo.
d ¿Ya se lo habías dicho?
e Jamás había trabajado allí.
f ¿Ya os habíais duchado por la mañana?
g Nunca habían estado en Escocia.
h Todavía no había ido a ver esa película.
i Ya habíamos decidido vender la casa.
j Ya había hecho el examen.

47 a Juan ya me había dicho lo del trabajo.
b Mi madre había frito el pescado demasiado.
c ¿Por qué no habíais hecho los deberes?
d ¿Dónde los habías visto?
e ¿Sabías quién había roto el espejo?
f Ya nos habíamos lavado las manos.

g No lo había visto desde el verano pasado.
h No habíamos oído lo que dijo.
i ¿Cuándo habíais vuelto de vacaciones?
j No sabía dónde había puesto las llaves.

48 a La carta fue escrita por Ramón.
b La tarta fue hecha por Manuel.
c El coche fue conducido por su primo.
d La tienda fue destrozada por dos chicos.
e Todos fueron afectados por la noticia.
f Los juguetes fueron hechos en China.
g La novela fue escrita por Jane Austen.
h La película fue dirigida por Almódovar.
i Los cuadros fueron pintados por mi tío.
j La casa fue alquilada por unos turistas alemanes.

49 a se construyó
b Se fabrican
c Se anunció
d se envió
e se compró
f se celebrará
g se explicará
h se compró
i Se escribió
j se tiró

50 a Este vino se produce en España.
b La película se rodó en Barcelona.
c Su padre le compró un coche.
d Se gasta mucho dinero en la lotería.
e (Se) han construido demasiados pisos en la zona.
f Se vendieron muchos coches el mes pasado.
g Tienen paella todos los domingos.
h El profesor de matemáticas le puso deberes.

Solutions

Verbs *cont.*

i Mary la invitó.
j Mi tío lo pintó.

51 a estudiando
b comiendo
c viviendo
d durmiendo
e leyendo
f pidiendo
g riendo
h creyendo
i yendo
j oyendo

52 a trabajando
b comiendo
c haciendo
d mirando
e hablando
f leyendo
g viendo
h viviendo
i esperando
j corriendo

53 a Me gusta nadar.
b Estaban sentados.
c Estaban jugando al tenis.
d El reírse es bueno para la salud.
e Prohibido fumar.
f Me encanta leer.
g Se está vistiendo./Está vistiéndose.
h Estaban diciendo la verdad.
i Estoy comprando un piso.
j Montar en bici es buen ejercicio.

54 a Hace frío.
b Hacía mucho calor.
c Mañana va a hacer sol.
d Hizo un tiempo muy bueno.
e Llueve./Está lloviendo.
f Va a nevar.
g Hacía mucho viento.
h ¿Qué tiempo hace?
i Mañana hará sol.
j Va a llover.

55 a Es posible que **vengan.**
b No vale la pena **decírselo.**
c Parece que **vendrán.**
d Se dice que **son muy ricos.**
e Se trata de **unos mil euros.**

56 a Hay una escuela en el pueblo.
b No hay un parque cerca de aquí.
c Había mucha gente en la fiesta.
d Hubo una reunión ayer.
e ¿Habrá muchos turistas en septiembre?
f Hay una tienda en la esquina.
g No había mucho tráfico.
h ¿Habrá un proyecto nuevo pronto?
i No hubo tiempo.
j Hay que ganar más.

57 a hable
b digáis
c vengan
d viva
e quieras
f trabajen
g hagan
h tengamos
i salga
j se pongan

58 a saber = **sepa**
b ir = **vaya**
c haber = **haya**
d estar = **esté**
e ser = **fuese**

59 a nosotros = **hayamos**
b usted = **vaya**
c ellos = **supieran**
d tú = **hablaras**
e yo = **me vaya**

60 a sean
b vengan
c vayas
d pueda
e haya
f guste
g digas
h tengas
i llegue
j sea

61 a dejar caer = **to drop**
b esperar poder = **to hope to be able to**
c querer decir = **to mean**
d pensar hacer = **to think of doing**

e deber hacer = **to need to do**

62 a a
b a
c de
d a
e de
f de
g con
h de
i con
j de

63 a Voy a comprarme un coche.
b Decidió comprarse una moto.
c Vamos a visitar a tu tía.
d Necesito hablar con él.
e Tratamos de vivir una vida tranquila.
f Nos aburrimos de esperar.
g Quiero aprender a hablar inglés.
h Esperamos poder ir.
i No vuelvas a llegar tarde.
j Me gustaría ir a Argentina.

64 a al
b a
c de
d a
e de
f a
g de
h de
i del
j de

65 a con
b por
c en
d por
e en
f con
g con
h con
i por
j con

66 a Busco un diccionario.
b Miraban a la gente en la playa.
c Miraba el cielo.
d Me pidió la dirección.
e Me pagó el billete.

Verbs *cont.*

f Le gusta ver la televisión.
g Estoy esperando a mi madre.
h Ya he pagado los cafés.
i Mira esto.
j Ayúdame a buscar las llaves.

67 a los dulces/los ingleses
b el café/el cine/bailar
c las flores/las fotos
d mis amigos/sus ideas
e Francia/Londres/el viaje

f las manzanas/los dulces
g las vacaciones
h mi casa/el chocolate/el azul
i los americanos/los animales
j los chocolates/los perros

68 a Me hace falta **un ordenador.**
b Les hacen falta **unas vacaciones.**
c Le duele **la cabeza.**

d No me importa **el calor.**
e Le encantan **los perros.**

69 a importa
b gustan
c duele
d quedan
e encanta
f falta
g importan
h hacen falta
i interesa
j gusta

Negatives

1 a Elena no vive en Londres.
b Mis padres no hablan inglés.
c Jorge no tiene tiempo.
d No me gusta el chocolate.
e Isabel no come carne.
f No lleva mucho tiempo.
g Belén no quiere venir conmigo.
h No gasto mucho dinero.
i Cristina no sabe conducir.
j Mis padres no me entienden.

2 a Yo tampoco.
b nadie
c nada
d y para mí tampoco
e y a mí tampoco
f ninguno
g nadie
h nada
i nadie
j tampoco

3 a No quiero ir.
b Nunca viene con nosotros.
c No tengo tiempo.
d Nunca/jamás los he visto./No los he visto nunca/jamás.
e No sé tocar el piano.
f No como carne.
g Ya no viven aquí.
h Espero que no.
i Creo que no lo sabe.
j No lleva mucho tiempo.

Questions

1 a Adónde
b Cómo
c cuándo
d Cuántos
e Cuáles
f Dónde
g Qué
h Quién
i Por qué
j Cuántos

2 a ¿Se lo dijo mi hermana?
b ¿No viene tu padre?
c ¿Vieron la película tus hijos?
d ¿Ha llegado Lucía?
e ¿Aquí viven?
f ¿Se ha comprado Tino aquél coche que quería?
g ¿Viene al bar Luis?/¿Viene Luis al bar?

h ¿Conduce bien Javier?
i ¿Nos quiere acompañar Julia?/¿Quiere acompañarnos Julia?
j ¿Les regalaron sus tíos el cuadro que querían?

Solutions

Adverbs

1
a rápidamente
b bien
c barato
d claro
e alto
f inmediatamente
g fácilmente
h con cuidado
i derecho
j feliz y tranquilamente

2
a ¡Llámalos inmediatamente!
b Se hace fácilmente.
c No lo veo muy bien.
d Nos trata muy mal.
e No hables tan alto.
f Conduce muy rápido.
g Normalmente la llamo yo.
h Escríbelo claramente./claro.
i Hazlo con cuidado.
j Hablas muy bien el inglés.

3
a con impaciencia
b de forma/manera inteligente
c con rapidez
d de forma/manera natural
e de forma/manera eficaz
f con cuidado
g con alegría
h con claridad *or* de forma/manera clara
i con fuerza
j con felicidad

4
a Conduce más rápido que tú.
b Nadas mejor que tu hermano.
c Llegué menos tarde que él.
d Cocina mejor que yo.
e Canta peor que yo.
f Gana menos que ella.
g Pepe trabaja más duro que Antonio.
h Carmen corre más rapido que su hermana.

i Nos acostamos más tarde que vosotros.
j Sabemos menos que ellos.

5
a de
b que
c que
d de
e de
f que
g de
h de
i que
j que

6
a más
b menos
c más rápido
d más barato
e menos
f peor
g mejor
h mejor
i menos
j mejor

7
a Soy más inteligente que él.
b Ramón trabaja más que su jefe.
c Esa cuenta paga menos que esta.
d Óscar lee más que su hermano.
e Quedé más sorprendida que ella.
f Esta planta crece menos que esa.
g Maruja come menos que su marido.
h Daniel conduce más rápido que yo.
i Pagaron menos que nosotros.
j Su perro ladra más que el nuestro.

8
a hoy en día = **nowadays**
b de vez en cuando = **from time to time**
c en seguida = **immediately**
d todo el tiempo = **all the time**
e a menudo = **often**

9
a gente/comida
b tarde/rápido/dinero
c personas/libros
d gente/dinero
e gente/tonto
f amigos
g feliz/rico
h gente
i gente/comida
j gente

10
a Habla demasiado alto.
b una chica muy guapa
c Siempre lo hago yo.
d Ya lo han hecho./Lo han hecho ya.
e Nunca he estado en Estados Unidos./No he estado nunca en Estados Unidos.
f Todavía estamos esperando.
g Todavía no se lo he dicho./No se lo he dicho todavía.
h Nunca/Jamás se lo diría.
i ¡Vamos ya!
j ¡Hasta pronto!

11
a demasiado
b muy
c tanto como
d todavía
e inmediatamente
f mucho
g nunca/jamás
h pronto
i ya
j muy

Solutions

Prepositions

1 a con
   b a
   c con
   d de
   e al
   f para
   g a
   h a
   i para
   j de

2 a de
   b de

   c del
   d del
   e de
   f del
   g de
   h de los
   i de
   j del

3 a para
   b por
   c para
   d por

   e por
   f para
   g por
   h para
   i para
   j por

4 a debajo de = **under**
   b delante de = **in front of**
   c contra = **against**
   d desde entonces = **since then**
   e hacia abajo = **downwards**

Conjunctions

1 a y
   b e
   c y
   d e
   e y
   f e
   g y
   h y
   i y
   j e

2 a o
   b o
   c u

   d o
   e u
   f o
   g o
   h o
   i u
   j u

3 a porque
   b pero
   c sino
   d porque
   e Como
   f sino

   g pero
   h Como
   i porque
   j pero

4 a aunque = **although**
   b como = **as**
   c mientras = **while**
   d pues = **well, then**
   e mientras que = **whereas**

Stress

1 a mí
   b solo
   c fácilmente
   d Por qué
   e Cuántos
   f cuándo
   g mi
   h Cómo
   i aquellos/aquéllos
   j ti

2 a mi/el
   b un te/un café sólo
   c ésta mesa/tu mesa
   d el
   e mí/tu
   f aquella/esa/esta
   g ese
   h éste edificio/ése chico
   i mi hermana
   j mis tíos

3 a dáselo
   b díceselo
   c facilísimo
   d vendiéndolo
   e comprádmelo
   f háganlo
   g fácilmente
   h haría
   i francés
   j jóvenes

Index

VERB TABLES

Introduction

This section is designed to help you find all the verb forms you need in Spanish.

From pages 2-6 you will find a list of 59 regular and irregular verbs with a summary of their main forms, followed on pages 7-13 by some very common regular and irregular verbs shown in full, with example phrases.

Spanish verb forms

INFINITIVE	PRESENT	PERFECT	PRETERITE	FUTURE	PRESENT SUBJUNCTIVE
1 **actuar**	yo actúo tú actúas él/ella/usted actúa nosotros/as actuamos vosotros/as actuáis ellos/ellas/ustedes actúan	he actuado	actué	actuaré	actúe
2 **adquirir** -ir verb with a spelling change	yo adquiero tú adquieres él/ella/usted adquiere nosotros/as adquirimos vosotros/as adquirís ellos/ellas/ustedes adquieren	he adquirido	adquirí	adquiriré	adquiera adquiramos adquiráis
3 **almorzar** -ar verb with a spelling change	yo almuerzo tú almuerzas él/ella/usted almuerza nosotros/as almorzamos vosotros/as almorzáis ellos/ellas/ustedes almuerzan	he almorzado	almorcé almorzaste	almorzaré	almuerce almorcemos almorcéis
4 **andar** -ar verb with a spelling change	yo ando tú andas él/ella/usted anda nosotros/as andamos vosotros/as andáis ellos/ellas/ustedes andan	he andado	anduve anduviste anduvo anduvimos anduvisteis anduvieron	andaré	ande
5 **caer** -er verb with a spelling change	yo caigo tú caes él/ella/usted cae nosotros/as caemos vosotros/as caéis ellos/ellas/ustedes caen	he caído	caí caíste cayó caímos caísteis cayeron	caeré	caiga
6 **cocer** -er verb with a spelling change	yo cuezo tú cueces él/ella/usted cuece nosotros/as cocemos vosotros/as cocéis ellos/ellas/ustedes cuecen	he cocido	cocí	coceré	cueza cozamos cozáis
7 **coger** -er verb with a spelling change	yo cojo tú coges él/ella/usted coge nosotros/as cogemos vosotros/as cogéis ellos/ellas/ustedes cogen	he cogido	cogí	cogeré	coja
8 **comer**	see full verb table page 8				
9 **conducir** -ir verb with a spelling change	yo conduzco tú conduces él/ella/usted conduce nosotros/as conducimos vosotros/as conducís ellos/ellas/ustedes conducen	he conducido	conduje condujiste condujo condujimos condujisteis condujeron	conduciré	conduzca
10 **construir** -ir verb with a spelling change	yo construyo tú construyes él/ella/usted construye nosotros/as construimos vosotros/as construís ellos/ellas/ustedes construyen	he construido	construí construyó construyeron	construiré	construya
11 **contar** -ar verb with a spelling change	yo cuento tú cuentas él/ella/usted cuenta nosotros/as contamos vosotros/as contáis ellos/ellas/ustedes cuentan	he contado	conté	contaré	cuente contemos contéis

	INFINITIVE	PRESENT	PERFECT	PRETERITE	FUTURE	PRESENT SUBJUNCTIVE
12	**crecer** similar to **cocer** [6]	yo crezco tú creces	he crecido	crecí	creceré	crezca
13	**cruzar** -**ar** verb with a spelling change	yo cruzo tú cruzas él/ella/usted cruza nosotros/as cruzamos vosotros/as cruzasteis ellos/ellas/ustedes cruzan	he cruzado	crucé	cruzaré	cruce crucemos crucéis
14	**dar**	yo doy tú das él/ella/usted da nosotros/as damos vosotros/as dais ellos/ellas/ustedes dan	he dado	di diste dio dimos disteis dieron	daré	dé des dé demos deis den
15	**decir**	yo digo tú dices él/ella/usted dice nosotros/as decimos vosotros/as decís ellos/ellas/ustedes dicen	he dicho	dije dijiste dijo dijimos dijisteis dijeron	diré	diga
16	**dirigir** -**ir** verb with a spelling change	yo dirijo tú diriges él/ella/usted dirige nosotros/as dirigimos vosotros/as dirigís ellos/ellas/ustedes dirigen	he dirigido	dirigí	dirigiré	dirija
17	**dormir** -**ir** verb with a spelling change	yo duermo tú duermes él/ella/usted duerme nosotros/as dormimos vosotros/as dormís ellos/ellas/ustedes duermen	he dormido	dormí durmió durmieron	dormiré	duerma durmamos durmáis
18	**elegir** similar to **dirigir** [16]	yo elijo	he elegido	elegí	elegiré	elija
19	**empezar** similar to **almorzar** [3]	yo empiezo tú empiezas él/ella/usted empieza nosotros/as empezamos vosotros/as empezáis ellos/ellas/ustedes empiezan	he empezado	empecé empezaste empezó empezamos empezasteis empezaron	empezaré	empiece empecemos empecéis
20	**entender** -**er** verb with a spelling change	yo entiendo tú entiendes él/ella/usted entiende nosotros/as entendemos vosotros/as entendéis ellos/ellas/ustedes entienden	he entendido	entendí	entenderé	entienda entendamos entendáis
21	**enviar** similar to **actuar** [1]	yo envío tú envías	he enviado	envié	enviaré	envíe
22	**estar**	see full verb table page 10				
23	**freír** -**ir** verb with a spelling change	yo frío tú fríes él/ella/usted fríe nosotros/as freímos vosotros/as freís ellos/ellas/ustedes fríen	he frito	freí freíste frió freímos freísteis frieron	freiré	fría
24	**haber**	yo he tú has él/ella/usted ha nosotros/as hemos vosotros/as habéis ellos/ellas/ustedes han	he habido	hube hubiste hubo hubimos hubisteis hubieron	habré	haya

	INFINITIVE	PRESENT	PERFECT	PRETERITE	FUTURE	PRESENT SUBJUNCTIVE
25	**hablar**	see full verb table page 7				
26	**hacer**	yo hago tú haces él/ella/usted hace nosotros/as hacemos vosotros/as hacéis ellos/ellas/ustedes hacen	he hecho	hice hiciste hizo hicimos hicisteis hicieron	haré	haga
27	**ir**	see full verb table page 11				
28	**jugar** -ar verb with a spelling change	yo juego tú juegas él/ella/usted juega nosotros/as jugamos vosotros/as jugáis ellos/ellas/ustedes juegan	he jugado	jugué jugaste	jugaré	juegue juguemos juguéis
29	**lavarse**	yo me lavo tu te lavas él/ella/usted se lava nosotros/as nos lavamos vosotros/as os laváis ellos/ellas/ustedes se lavan	me ha lavado	me lavé	me lavaré	me lave
30	**leer** -er verb with a spelling change	yo leo tú lees él/ella/usted lee nosotros/as leemos vosotros/as leéis ellos/ellas/ustedes leen	he leído	leí leíste leyó leímos leísteis leyeron	leeré	lea
31	**llover** impersonal verb	llueve	ha llovido	llovió	lloverá	llueva
32	**morir** -ir verb with a spelling change	yo muero tú mueres él/ella/usted muere nosotros/as morimos vosotros/as morís ellos/ellas/ustedes mueren	he muerto	morí murió murieron	moriré	muera muramos muráis
33	**mover** -er verb with a spelling change	yo muevo tú mueves él/ella/usted mueve nosotros/as movemos vosotros/as movéis ellos/ellas/ustedes mueven	he movido	moví	moveré	mueva movamos mováis
34	**negar** -ar verb with a spelling change	yo niego tú niegas él/ella/usted niega nosotros/as negamos vosotros/as negáis ellos/ellas/ustedes niegan	he negado	negué negaste	negaré	niegue neguemos neguéis
35	**oír** -ir verb with a spelling change	yo oigo tú oyes él/ella/usted oye nosotros/as oímos vosotros/as oís ellos/ellas/ustedes oyen	he oído	oí oíste oyó oímos oísteis oyeron	oiré	oiga
36	**oler** -er verb with a spelling change	yo huelo tú hueles él/ella/usted huele nosotros/as olemos vosotros/as oléis ellos/ellas/ustedes huelan	he olido	olí	oleré	huela olamos oláis

INFINITIVE	PRESENT	PERFECT	PRETERITE	FUTURE	PRESENT SUBJUNCTIVE
37 pagar -ar verb with a spelling change	yo pago tú pagas él/ella/usted paga nosotros/as pagamos vosotros/as pagáis ellos/ellas/ustedes pagan	he pagado	pagué pagaste	pagaré	pague
38 pedir -ir verb with a spelling change	yo pido tú pides él/ella/usted pide nosotros/as pedimos vosotros/as pedís ellos/ellas/ustedes piden	he pedido	pedí pidió pidieron	pediré	pida
39 pensar -ar verb with a spelling change	yo pienso tú piensas él/ella/usted piensa nosotros/as pensamos vosotros/as pensáis ellos/ellas/ustedes piensan	he pensado	pensé	pensaré	piense pensemos penséis
40 poder -er verb with a spelling change	yo puedo tú puedes él/ella/usted puede nosotros/as podemos vosotros/as podéis ellos/ellas/ustedes pueden	he podido	pude pudiste pudo pudimos pudisteis pudieron	podré	pueda podamos podáis
41 poner	yo pongo tú pones él/ella/usted pone nosotros/as ponemos vosotros/as ponéis ellos/ellas/ustedes ponen	he puesto	puse pusiste puso pusimos pusisteis pusieron	pondré	ponga pongas pongamos pongáis
42 prohibir similar to **adquirir** [2]	yo prohíbo tú prohíbes él/ella/usted prohíbe ellos/ellas/ustedes prohíben	he prohibido	prohibí	prohibiré	prohíba
43 querer	yo quiero tú quieres él/ella/usted quiere nosotros/as queremos vosotros/as queréis ellos/ellas/ustedes quieren	he querido	quise quisiste quiso quisimos quisisteis quisieron	querré	quiera
44 reír similar to **freír** [23], except for the perfect tense	yo río tú ríes él/ella/usted ríe nosotros/as reímos vosotros/as reís ellos/ellas/ustedes ríen	he reído	reí reíste rió reímos reísteis rieron	reiré	ría
45 reñir -ir verb with a spelling change	yo riño tú riñes él/ella/usted riñe nosotros/as reñimos vosotros/as reñís ellos/ellas/ustedes riñen	he reñido	reñí reñiste riñó reñimos reñisteis riñeron	reñiré	riña
46 reunir -ir verb with a spelling change	yo reúno tú reúnes él/ella/usted reúne nosotros/as reunimos vosotros/as reunís ellos/ellas/ustedes reúnen	he reunido	reuní	reuniré	reúna
47 saber	yo sé tú sabes él/ella/usted sabe nosotros/as sabemos vosotros/as sabéis ellos/ellas/ustedes saben	he sabido	supe supiste supo supimos supisteis supieron	sabré	sepa

INFINITIVE	PRESENT	PERFECT	PRETERITE	FUTURE	PRESENT SUBJUNCTIVE
48 sacar -**ar** verb with a spelling change	yo saco tú sacas él/ella/usted saca nosotros/as sacamos vosotros/as sacáis ellos/ellas/ustedes sacan	he sacado	saqué sacaste	sacaré	saque
49 salir similar to **decir** [15] except for the perfect and future tenses	yo salgo	he salido	salí	saldré	salga
50 seguir -**ir** verb with a spelling change	yo sigo tú sigues él/ella/usted sigue nosotros/as seguimos vosotros/as seguís ellos/ellas/ustedes siguen	he seguido	seguí siguió siguieron	seguiré	siga
51 sentir -**ir** verb with a spelling change	yo siento tú sientes él/ella/usted siente nosotros/as sentimos vosotros/as sentís ellos/ellas/ustedes sienten	he sentido	sentí sintió sintieron	sentiré	sienta sintamos sintáis
52 ser	see full verb table page 12				
53 tener	see full verb table page 13				
54 traer -**er** verb with a spelling change	yo traigo tú traes él/ella/usted trae nosotros/as traemos vosotros/as traéis ellos/ellas/ustedes traen	he traído	traje trajiste trajo trajimos trajisteis trajeron	traeré	traiga traigas traiga traigamos traigáis traigan
55 valer -**er** verb with a spelling change	yo valgo tú vales él/ella/usted vale nosotros/as valemos vosotros/as valéis ellos/ellas/ustedes valen	he valido	valí	valdré	valga
56 venir	yo vengo tú vienes él/ella/usted viene nosotros/as venimos vosotros/as venís ellos/ellas/ustedes vienen	he venido	vine viniste vino vinimos vinisteis vinieron	vendré	venga
57 ver similar to **comer** [8] except for the perfect tense	yo veo tú ves él/ella/usted ve nosotros/as vemos vosotros/as veis ellos/ellas/ustedes ven	he visto	vi viste vio vimos visteis vieron	veré	vea
58 vivir	see full verb table page 9				
59 volver -**er** verb with a spelling change	yo vuelvo tú vuelves él/ella/usted vuelve nosotros/as volvemos vosotros/as volvéis ellos/ellas/ustedes vuelven	he vuelto	volví	volveré	vuelva volvamos volváis

hablar (to speak, to talk)

PRESENT

yo	**hablo**
tú	**hablas**
él/ella/usted	**habla**
nosotros/as	**hablamos**
vosotros/as	**habláis**
ellos/ellas/ustedes	**hablan**

PRESENT SUBJUNCTIVE

yo	**hable**
tú	**hables**
él/ella/usted	**hable**
nosotros/as	**hablemos**
vosotros/as	**habléis**
ellos/ellas/ustedes	**hablen**

PRETERITE

yo	**hablé**
tú	**hablaste**
él/ella/usted	**habló**
nosotros/as	**hablamos**
vosotros/as	**hablasteis**
ellos/ellas/ustedes	**hablaron**

IMPERFECT

yo	**hablaba**
tú	**hablabas**
él/ella/usted	**hablaba**
nosotros/as	**hablábamos**
vosotros/as	**hablabais**
ellos/ellas/ustedes	**hablaban**

FUTURE

yo	**hablaré**
tú	**hablarás**
él/ella/usted	**hablará**
nosotros/as	**hablaremos**
vosotros/as	**hablaréis**
ellos/ellas/ustedes	**hablarán**

CONDITIONAL

yo	**hablaría**
tú	**hablarías**
él/ella/usted	**hablaría**
nosotros/as	**hablaríamos**
vosotros/as	**hablaríais**
ellos/ellas/ustedes	**hablarían**

IMPERATIVE

habla / hablad

PAST PARTICIPLE

hablado

GERUND

hablando

EXAMPLE PHRASES

Hoy **he hablado** con mi hermana. I've spoken to my sister today.
No **hables** tan alto. Don't talk so loud.
No **se hablan**. They don't talk to each other.

Remember that subject pronouns are not used very often in Spanish.

comer (to eat)

PRESENT

yo	**como**
tú	**comes**
él/ella/usted	**come**
nosotros/as	**comemos**
vosotros/as	**coméis**
ellos/ellas/ustedes	**comen**

PRESENT SUBJUNCTIVE

yo	**coma**
tú	**comas**
él/ella/usted	**coma**
nosotros/as	**comamos**
vosotros/as	**comáis**
ellos/ellas/ustedes	**coman**

PRETERITE

yo	**comí**
tú	**comiste**
él/ella/usted	**comió**
nosotros/as	**comimos**
vosotros/as	**comisteis**
ellos/ellas/ustedes	**comieron**

IMPERFECT

yo	**comía**
tú	**comías**
él/ella/usted	**comía**
nosotros/as	**comíamos**
vosotros/as	**comíais**
ellos/ellas/ustedes	**comían**

FUTURE

yo	**comeré**
tú	**comerás**
él/ella/usted	**comerá**
nosotros/as	**comeremos**
vosotros/as	**comeréis**
ellos/ellas/ustedes	**comerán**

CONDITIONAL

yo	**comería**
tú	**comerías**
él/ella/usted	**comería**
nosotros/as	**comeríamos**
vosotros/as	**comeríais**
ellos/ellas/ustedes	**comerían**

IMPERATIVE

come / comed

PAST PARTICIPLE

comido

GERUND

comiendo

EXAMPLE PHRASES

No **come** carne. He doesn't eat meat.
No **comas** tan deprisa. Don't eat so fast.
Se lo ha comido todo. He's eaten it all.

Remember that subject pronouns are not used very often in Spanish.

vivir (to live)

PRESENT

yo	**vivo**
tú	**vives**
él/ella/usted	**vive**
nosotros/as	**vivimos**
vosotros/as	**vivís**
ellos/ellas/ustedes	**viven**

PRESENT SUBJUNCTIVE

yo	**viva**
tú	**vivas**
él/ella/usted	**viva**
nosotros/as	**vivamos**
vosotros/as	**viváis**
ellos/ellas/ustedes	**vivan**

PRETERITE

yo	**viví**
tú	**viviste**
él/ella/usted	**vivió**
nosotros/as	**vivimos**
vosotros/as	**vivisteis**
ellos/ellas/ustedes	**vivieron**

IMPERFECT

yo	**vivía**
tú	**vivías**
él/ella/usted	**vivía**
nosotros/as	**vivíamos**
vosotros/as	**vivíais**
ellos/ellas/ustedes	**vivían**

FUTURE

yo	**viviré**
tú	**vivirás**
él/ella/usted	**vivirá**
nosotros/as	**viviremos**
vosotros/as	**viviréis**
ellos/ellas/ustedes	**vivirán**

CONDITIONAL

yo	**viviría**
tú	**vivirías**
él/ella/usted	**viviría**
nosotros/as	**viviríamos**
vosotros/as	**viviríais**
ellos/ellas/ustedes	**vivirían**

IMPERATIVE

vive / vivid

PAST PARTICIPLE

vivido

GERUND

viviendo

EXAMPLE PHRASES

Vivo en Valencia. I live in Valencia.
Vivieron juntos dos años. They lived together for two years.
Hemos vivido momentos difíciles. We've had some difficult times.

Remember that subject pronouns are not used very often in Spanish.

estar (to be)

PRESENT

yo	**estoy**
tú	**estás**
él/ella/usted	**está**
nosotros/as	**estamos**
vosotros/as	**estáis**
ellos/ellas/ustedes	**están**

PRESENT SUBJUNCTIVE

yo	**esté**
tú	**estés**
él/ella/usted	**esté**
nosotros/as	**estemos**
vosotros/as	**estéis**
ellos/ellas/ustedes	**estén**

PRETERITE

yo	**estuve**
tú	**estuviste**
él/ella/usted	**estuvo**
nosotros/as	**estuvimos**
vosotros/as	**estuvisteis**
ellos/ellas/ustedes	**estuvieron**

IMPERFECT

yo	**estaba**
tú	**estabas**
él/ella/usted	**estaba**
nosotros/as	**estábamos**
vosotros/as	**estabais**
ellos/ellas/ustedes	**estaban**

FUTURE

yo	**estaré**
tú	**estarás**
él/ella/usted	**estará**
nosotros/as	**estaremos**
vosotros/as	**estaréis**
ellos/ellas/ustedes	**estarán**

CONDITIONAL

yo	**estaría**
tú	**estarías**
él/ella/usted	**estaría**
nosotros/as	**estaríamos**
vosotros/as	**estaríais**
ellos/ellas/ustedes	**estarían**

IMPERATIVE

está / estad

PAST PARTICIPLE

estado

GERUND

estando

EXAMPLE PHRASES

Estoy cansado. I'm tired.
Estuvimos en casa de mis padres. We went to my parents'.
¿A qué hora **estarás** en casa? What time will you be home?

Remember that subject pronouns are not used very often in Spanish.

ir (to go)

PRESENT		PRESENT SUBJUNCTIVE	
yo	**voy**	yo	**vaya**
tú	**vas**	tú	**vayas**
él/ella/usted	**va**	él/ella/usted	**vaya**
nosotros/as	**vamos**	nosotros/as	**vayamos**
vosotros/as	**vais**	vosotros/as	**vayáis**
ellos/ellas/ustedes	**van**	ellos/ellas/ustedes	**vayan**

PRETERITE		IMPERFECT	
yo	**fui**	yo	**iba**
tú	**fuiste**	tú	**ibas**
él/ella/usted	**fue**	él/ella/usted	**iba**
nosotros/as	**fuimos**	nosotros/as	**íbamos**
vosotros/as	**fuisteis**	vosotros/as	**ibais**
ellos/ellas/ustedes	**fueron**	ellos/ellas/ustedes	**iban**

FUTURE		CONDITIONAL	
yo	**iré**	yo	**iría**
tú	**irás**	tú	**irías**
él/ella/usted	**irá**	él/ella/usted	**iría**
nosotros/as	**iremos**	nosotros/as	**iríamos**
vosotros/as	**iréis**	vosotros/as	**iríais**
ellos/ellas/ustedes	**irán**	ellos/ellas/ustedes	**irían**

IMPERATIVE	PAST PARTICIPLE
ve / id	**ido**

GERUND

yendo

EXAMPLE PHRASES

¿**Vamos** a comer al campo? Shall we have a picnic in the country?
El domingo **iré** a Edimburgo. I'll go to Edinburgh on Sunday.
Yo no **voy** con ellos. I'm not going with them.

Remember that subject pronouns are not used very often in Spanish.

ser (to be)

	PRESENT		PRESENT SUBJUNCTIVE
yo	**soy**	yo	**sea**
tú	**eres**	tú	**seas**
él/ella/usted	**es**	él/ella/usted	**sea**
nosotros/as	**somos**	nosotros/as	**seamos**
vosotros/as	**sois**	vosotros/as	**seáis**
ellos/ellas/ustedes	**son**	ellos/ellas/ustedes	**sean**

	PRETERITE		IMPERFECT
yo	**fui**	yo	**era**
tú	**fuiste**	tú	**eras**
él/ella/usted	**fue**	él/ella/usted	**era**
nosotros/as	**fuimos**	nosotros/as	**éramos**
vosotros/as	**fuisteis**	vosotros/as	**erais**
ellos/ellas/ustedes	**fueron**	ellos/ellas/ustedes	**eran**

	FUTURE		CONDITIONAL
yo	**seré**	yo	**sería**
tú	**serás**	tú	**serías**
él/ella/usted	**será**	él/ella/usted	**sería**
nosotros/as	**seremos**	nosotros/as	**seríamos**
vosotros/as	**seréis**	vosotros/as	**seríais**
ellos/ellas/ustedes	**serán**	ellos/ellas/ustedes	**serían**

IMPERATIVE	PAST PARTICIPLE
sé / sed	sido

GERUND

siendo

EXAMPLE PHRASES

Soy español. I'm Spanish.
¿**Fuiste** tú el que llamó? Was it you who phoned?
Era de noche. It was dark.

Remember that subject pronouns are not used very often in Spanish.

tener (to have)

	PRESENT			PRESENT SUBJUNCTIVE
yo	**tengo**		yo	**tenga**
tú	**tienes**		tú	**tengas**
él/ella/usted	**tiene**		él/ella/usted	**tenga**
nosotros/as	**tenemos**		nosotros/as	**tengamos**
vosotros/as	**tenéis**		vosotros/as	**tengáis**
ellos/ellas/ustedes	**tienen**		ellos/ellas/ustedes	**tengan**

	PRETERITE			IMPERFECT
yo	**tuve**		yo	**tenía**
tú	**tuviste**		tú	**tenías**
él/ella/usted	**tuvo**		él/ella/usted	**tenía**
nosotros/as	**tuvimos**		nosotros/as	**teníamos**
vosotros/as	**tuvisteis**		vosotros/as	**teníais**
ellos/ellas/ustedes	**tuvieron**		ellos/ellas/ustedes	**tenían**

	FUTURE			CONDITIONAL
yo	**tendré**		yo	**tendría**
tú	**tendrás**		tú	**tendrías**
él/ella/usted	**tendrá**		él/ella/usted	**tendría**
nosotros/as	**tendremos**		nosotros/as	**tendríamos**
vosotros/as	**tendréis**		vosotros/as	**tendríais**
ellos/ellas/ustedes	**tendrán**		ellos/ellas/ustedes	**tendrían**

IMPERATIVE

ten / tened

PAST PARTICIPLE

tenido

GERUND

teniendo

EXAMPLE PHRASES

Tengo sed. I'm thirsty.
No **tenía** suficiente dinero. She didn't have enough money.
Tuvimos que irnos. We had to leave.

Remember that subject pronouns are not used very often in Spanish.